Learning Resource Centre

Park Road, Uxbridge, Middlesex, UB8 1NQ

Renewals: **01895 853344**

Please return this item to the LRC on or before the
last date stamped below:

ISBN 978-0-9932311-3-1

Published by *RAR Medical Services Limited*
www.uniadmissions.co.uk
info@uniadmissions.co.uk
Tel: 0203 375 6294

The Ultimate Oxbridge Interview Guide

Dr. Rohan Agarwal

Edited by
Dr. Ranjna Garg

UniAdmissions

THE BASICS

What is an Oxbridge Interview?

An interview is a personal 20-30 minute session with one or two members of academic staff from Oxford or Cambridge. The interviewers will ask questions and **guide the applicant to an answer**. The answers usually require a large degree of creative and critical thought, as well as a good attitude and a sound foundation of subject-specific knowledge.

Why is there an Interview?

Most of the applicants to Oxbridge will have outstanding grades, predicted exam results, sample course work and personal statements. Interviews are used to help **determine which applicants are best-suited** for Oxbridge. During the interview each applicant has a unique chance to demonstrate their creativity and critical thinking abilities- skills that Oxford and Cambridge consider vital for successful students.

Who gets an Interview?

At Cambridge any applicant who might have a chance at being accepted to study will be called for interview. This corresponds to approximately **90%** of applicants. At Oxford a slightly smaller **40-80%** of applicants are interviewed (applicants are shortlisted based on their admissions test results and UCAS form). No one is offered a place to study without attending an interview.

Who are the interviewers?

The interviews are conducted by a senior member of staff for the subject you've applied to; usually this person is the **Director of Studies** for that subject. There may also be a second interviewer who takes notes on the applicant or also asks questions. Interviewers describe this experience as just as nerve-wracking for them as for the applicants, as they are responsible for choosing the right students for Oxford and Cambridge.

When is the Interview?

Interviews are held in the **beginning of December**, and some applicants may be invited back in January for a second round of interviews at another college. There are usually multiple interviews on the same day, either for different subjects or at different colleges. You will normally be given 2 weeks notice before your interview- so you should hear back by late November, but it is useful to **begin preparing for the interview before you're officially invited**.

Where is the Interview?

The interviews are held in Oxford and Cambridge **at the college you applied to**. Oxford applicants may have additional interviews at another college than the one applied to. Cambridge applicants may get 'pooled' – be required to have another set of interviews in January at a different college. If you are travelling from far away, most Oxbridge colleges will provide you free accommodation and food for the duration of your stay if you wish to arrive the night before your interview.

Very rarely, interviews can be held via Skype at an exam centre- this normally only applies to international students or for UK students in extreme circumstances.

How should I use this book?

The best way to gain the most from this book is to let it guide your independent learning.

1. Read through the **General Interview** section.
2. Read the **Subject Interview** chapter for your subject.
3. Read other **Relevant Chapters** corresponding to your subject.

Your Subject	Also read chapters on:
Biology	Psychology, Chemistry, Maths
Medicine	Psychology, Chemistry
Psychology	Biology, Maths
Chemistry	Biology, Physics, Material Sciences, Maths
Physics	Chemistry, Engineering, Material Sciences, Maths
Engineering	Chemistry, Physics, Material Sciences, Maths
Material Sciences	Chemistry, Physics, Engineering, Maths
Economics	PPE & HSPS, Maths
English	History
Earth Sciences	Biology, Chemistry, Physics
History	HSPS, English
PPE	Economics, Maths
HSPS	History, Psychology
Classics	Modern Languages
Modern Languages	Classics

Finally, work your way through the past interview questions – remember, you are not expected to know the answers to them, and they have been included here so that you can start to appreciate the style of questions that you may get asked. **It is not a test of what you know – but what you can do with what you already know.**

Oxbridge Tutorials & Supervisions

Hopefully by this point you're familiar with the unique Oxbridge teaching system. Students on the same course will have lectures and practicals together. These are supplemented by college-based tutorials/supervisions. A tutorial/supervision is an **individual or small group session** with an academic to **discuss ideas, ask questions and receive feedback** on your assignments. During the tutorial/supervision, you will be pushed to think critically about the material from the course in novel and innovative ways. To get the most out of Oxbridge, you need to be able to work in this setting, and take criticism with a positive and constructive attitude.

The **interviews are made to be model tutorials/supervisions**, with an academic questioning an applicant and seeing if they can learn, problem-solve, demonstrate motivation for their subject. It is by considering this ultimate goal of the interview that you can start to understand how to present and prepare yourself for the Oxbridge interview process.

What Are Interviewers Looking for?

There are several qualities an interviewer is looking for the applicant to demonstrate during the interview. While an applicant may think the most 'obvious' thing interviewers are looking for is excellent factual knowledge, this is already displayed through exam results. Whilst having an excellent depth of knowledge may help you perform better during an interview- **you're unlikely to be chosen based solely on your knowledge**. The main thing an interviewer is looking for is for the applicant to demonstrate critical thought, excellent problem-solving skills and intellectual flexibility, as well as **motivation for the subject and suitability for small group teaching**. It is also important for them to see that the applicant is willing to persevere with a challenging problem even if the answer is not immediately apparent.

How to Communicate Answers

The most important thing to do when communicating your answers is to **think out loud**. This will allow the interviewer to understand your thought processes. They will then be able to help you out if you get stuck. You should never give up on a question to show that you won't be perturbed at the first sign of hardship as a student, and to stay positive and **demonstrate your engagement with the material**. Interviewers enjoy teaching and working with students who are as enthusiastic about their subject as they are.

Try to **keep the flow of conversation going** between you and your interviewer so that you can engage with each other throughout the entire interview. The best way to do this is to just keep talking about what you are thinking. It is okay to take a moment when confronted with a difficult question or plan your approach, but ensure you let the interviewer know this by saying '*I'm going to think about this for a moment*'. Don't take too long- if you are finding the problems difficult, the **interviewers will guide and prompt you** to keep you moving forward. They can only do this if they realise that you're stuck!

The questions that you'll be asked are designed to be difficult, so don't panic up when you don't immediately know the answer. Tell the interviewer what you do know, offer some ideas, talk about ways you've worked through a similar problem that might apply here. If you've never heard anything like the question asked before, say that to the interviewer, '*I've never seen anything like this before*' or '*We haven't covered this yet at school*', but don't use that as an excuse to quit. This is **your chance to show that you are eager to engage with new ideas**, so finish with '*But let's see if I can figure it out!*' or '*But I'm keen to try something new!*'. There are many times at Oxbridge when students are in this situation during tutorials/supervisors and you need to show that you can persevere in the face of difficulty (and stay positive and pleasant to work with while doing so).

Types of Interviews

There are, at Cambridge and for some Oxford subjects, several different types of interview that you can be called for. **Every applicant will have at least one subject interview.** Applicants to some courses may also have a **general interview**, especially if they are applying for an arts subject. Either way, you will be asked questions that touch on the course you are applying to study. It may be useful to **look at your interviewers' teaching backgrounds and published work** as this could potentially shed some light on the topics they might choose to discuss in an interview. However, there is absolutely no need to know the intracies of their research work so don't get bogged down in it. Interviews tend to open with easier and more general questions and become more detailed and complicated as you are pushed to explore topics in greater depth.

GENERAL INTERVIEWS

A general interview is a get-to-know-you session with senior admissions tutors. This is your chance to demonstrate a passion for Oxbridge; that you have understood the Oxbridge system, have a genuine interest in being a student and could contribute to Oxbridge if you were admitted. These are more common for arts and humanities applicants, but all applicants should nevertheless be prepared for a general interview.

➢ This will be less specific than the subject interview. The interviewers will focus more on your personal statement, any essays you may have submitted or have completed on the day of the interview and may discuss your SAQ form if you are applying to Cambridge.

➢ One of the interviewers may not be a specialist in the subject you've applied for. Don't be put off by this – you aren't expected to have any knowledge of their subject.

➢ Ensure that you have read your personal statement and any books/journals that you've claimed to have read in your application. You will seem unenthusiastic and dishonest if you can't answer questions regarding topics and activities that you claim to know about. Remember that it is much better to show a good understanding of a few texts than to list lots of texts that you haven't properly read.

➢ Read and re-read the essays you have submitted. Be prepared to develop on the ideas you have explored in them. Remember, that the interviewers may criticise what you've argued in your submitted essays. If you believe in it, then defend your view but don't be stubborn.

➢ You will be normally be asked if you have any questions at the end of the interview. Avoid saying things like "*How did I do?*" – Instead use this as an opportunity to show the interviewers the type of person you are e.g. "*How many books can I borrow from the library at one time?*"

What type of questions might be asked?

The three main questions that are likely to come up in an Oxbridge interview are:

➤ *Why Oxford/Cambridge?*
➤ *Why this subject?*
➤ *Why this college?*

You may also get asked more specific questions about the teaching system or about your future career aspirations. This is also be the time for discussing any extenuating circumstances for poor exam-results and similar considerations.

To do well in a general interview your answers should show that you understand the Oxbridge system and that you have strong reasons for applying there. Thus, it is essential that you prepare detailed answers to the common questions above so that you aren't caught off guard. In addition, you should create a list of questions that could potentially be asked based on your personal statement or any submitted work.

Worked Questions

Below are a few examples of how to start breaking down general interview question- complete with model answers.

Q1: How did you choose which college to apply for?

This question is a good opportunity to tell the interviewer about yourself, your hobbies, motivations and any interesting projects you have undertaken. You can demonstrate that you have read about the College thoroughly and you know what differentiates your College from the others. The decisive factors can include a great variety of different things from history, alumni, location in the city, community, sport clubs, societies, any positive personal experiences from Open Day and notable scholars.

This is a warm up question – an ice-breaker so just be natural and give an honest answer. You may not want to say things like "*I like the statutes in the garden*". The more comprehensive your answer is the better.

Good Applicant: I chose which college to apply for based on a number of factors that were important to me. First of all I needed to consider how many other students at my college would be studying the same subject as me; this was important to me as I want to be able to engage in conversation about my subject with my peers. Secondly, I considered the location of the college as I wanted to ensure I had easy access to the faculty library and lecture theatres. Thirdly, I am a keen tennis player and so looked for a college with a very active tennis society. Finally, I wanted to ensure that the college I chose would feel right for me and so I looked around several Cambridge colleges before coming to my conclusion.

This response is broken down into a set of logical and yet personal reasons. **There is no right answer to this question** and the factors which influence this decision are likely to be unique for each individual. However, each college is unique and therefore the interviewer want to know what influenced your decision. Therefore, **it's essential that you know what makes your college special** and separates it from the others. Even more importantly, you should know what the significance of that will be for you. For example, if a college has a large number of mathematicians, you may want to say that attending that college would allow you to discuss your subject with a greater number of people than otherwise.

A **Poor Applicant** may respond with a noncommittal shrug or an answer such at *'my brother went there'*. The interviewers want to see that you have researched the university and although the reason for choosing a college won't determine whether or not you get into the university, a lack of passion and interest in the college will greatly influence how you are perceived by the interviewers.

Q2: Why have you chosen to apply to study at 'Oxbridge', rather than another Russell Group university?

This is a very broad question, and one which is simply designed to draw out the motives and thinking behind your application, as well as giving you an opportunity to speak freely about yourself.

A **good applicant** would seek to address this question in two parts, the first addressing the key features of Oxbridge for their course and the second emphasising their own personality traits and interests which make them most suited to the Oxbridge system.

It is useful to start off by talking about the supervision/tutorial system and why this method of very small group teaching is beneficial for studying your subject, both for the discussion of essay work and, more crucially, for developing a comprehensive understanding for your subject. You might also like to draw upon the key features of the course at Oxford and Cambridge that distinguish it from courses at other universities.

When talking about yourself, a good answer could take almost any route, though it is always productive to talk about which parts of your subject interest you, why this is the case and how this ties in with the course at Oxford/Cambridge. You might also mention how the Oxbridge ethos suits your personality, e.g. how hard work and high achievement are important to you and you want to study your chosen subject in real depth, rather than a more superficial course elsewhere.

A **Poor applicant** would likely demonstrate little or no knowledge of their course at Oxford/Cambridge and volunteer little information about why studying at Oxbridge would be good for them or why they would be suited to it. It's important to focus on your interests and abilities rather than implying that you applied because Oxbridge is the biggest name or because your family or school had expectation you to do so.

Q3: What will you contribute to college life?

This is a common question at general interviews and **you need to show that you would be a good fit to the College** and that you are also really motivated because you have researched the college's facilities, notable fellows and alumni, societies and sport clubs etc. You can mention that you have looked at the website, talked to alumni and current students.

This question also gives the interviewer an excellent opportunity to learn about your personality, hobbies and motivations. Try to avoid listing one thing after the other for 5 minutes. Instead, you should try to give a balanced answer in terms of talking about the College and yourself. You should talk about your skills and give examples when you had to work in a team, deliver on strict deadlines, show strong time-management skills etc. You should also give a few examples from your previous studies, competitions or extracurricular activities (including sports and music).

Q4: Tell me about a recent news article not related to your subject that has interested you.

This can be absolutely anything and your interviewers just want to see that **you are aware of the world in which you live** and have a life outside of your subject. You could pick an interesting topic ahead of time and cultivate an opinion which could spark a lively discussion.

Q5: Which three famous people would you most like to be stuck on a dessert island with?

This is a personal question that might be used by your interviewers as an 'ice-breaker' – you can say absolutely anyone but try to have a good justification (and avoid being melodramatic). This is a really **good chance to show your personality and sense of humour**. This is also a good question to ease you into the flow of the interview and make yourself feel more comfortable.

Q6: Do you think you're 'clever'?

Don't let this one faze you! Your interviewers are not being glib but instead want to see how you cope with questions you may not have anticipated! You could discuss different forms of intelligence e.g. emotional vs. intellectual, perhaps concluding that you are stronger in one over the other.

Q7: What have you done in the past that makes you think you're equipped to deal with the stresses of Oxbridge?

The **interviewers want to hear that you know what you're signing up to** and that you are capable of dealing with stress. If you have any experience of dealing with pressure or meeting strict deadlines, this would be a good opportunity to talk about them. Otherwise, mention your time management skills and your ability to prioritise workloads. You could also mention how you deal with stress e.g. do you like running? Yoga? Piano? Etc.

Q8: Why are you sitting in this chair?

There are hundreds of potential responses to this type of question, and the interviewer will see this as a chance to get to know your personality, and how you react to unusual situations.

Firstly, **take the question seriously**, even if it strikes you as funny or bizarre. A good response may begin 'there are many reasons why I am sitting in this chair. There are lots of smaller events and causes that have led up to me sitting in this chair'. You might choose to discuss your desire to attend Oxbridge, the fact that you have travelled to the college to take your interview. You might choose to discuss the interviewer or college's taste and budget when it came to selecting the chair you are sitting on, as that determined why and how you have come to be sitting on that particular chair, rather than any other chair. You might then simply mention that you were invited by the interviewer to take a seat.

A weak response to this type of question would be to dismiss it as silly, or irrelevant.

Q9: If you could have dinner with anyone in the world, who would it be?

This is a fairly straightforward question to get in a general interview, so use it to show your personality and originality, and to talk about something you are really passionate about.

If you are asked a question like this, give an answer that is relevant to your application. This is not the time to start talking about how you are a huge fan of Beyonce and would just love to have dinner together! You should also avoid generic answers like "God".

If you would love to meet Obama and know more about him, consider what that would be like. Would he be at liberty to answer your questions? Might you not get more information from one of his aides or from a close friend, rather than the man himself? As this is a simple question, try to unpick it and answer it in a sophisticated way, rather than just stating the obvious.

Q10: What was the most recent film you watched?

This question seems simple, and appears to require a relatively short answer. However, a good candidate will use a simple question such as this as an opportunity to speak in more depth and **raise new and interesting topics of conversation**: "What I find particularly interesting about this film was…. It reminded me of….. In relation to other works of this period/the historical context, I found this particular scene very interesting as it mirrored/contrasted with my previous conceptions of this era as seen in other works, for example… I am now curious to find out more about… This film made me think about…etc."

Whilst it is extremely important to respond accurately to the questions posed by the interviewer, do not be afraid to **take the conversation in the direction led by your personal interests**. This sort of initiative will be encouraged.

Q11: How should we measure your success at the end of your time here?

This question invites you to show your potential and how diverse your interests are. There are three aspects of this question that you should consider in order to give a complete answer: "end of your time here", "measure" and "your achievements". You may want to discuss your hobbies and interests and potential achievements regarding various aspects of university life including academia, sport, student societies, jobs, volunteering etc.

Then you may want to enter into a discussion about whether there is any appropriate measure of success. How could you possibly compare sporting excellence to volunteering? Is it better to be a specialist or a generalist? This ultimately, comes down to your personal motivation and interests as you might be very focused on your studies or other activities (e.g. sport, music). Thus, multiple things would contribute to your success at university and your degree is only likely to be one way to measure this. Finally, it might be a great closing line to mention that getting your degree might not be the "end of your time here".

Q12: Why should anyone go to university?

This sounds like a very general question at first but it is, in fact, about your personal motivations to go to university. You don't need to enter into a discussion about what universities are designed for or any educational policy issues as the interviewer is unlikely to drive the discussion towards this in a general interview.

The best strategy is to **discuss your motivations**- this could include a broad range of different things from interest in a certain field, inspiring and diverse environment, academic excellence, opening up of more opportunities in the future and buying time to find out more about yourself etc. As it is very easy to give an unfocussed answer you should limit yourself to a few factors. You can also comment on whether people should go to university and whether this is good for the society.

Q13: How would you describe this painting on the wall to your friend on phone?

This question is very common and surprisingly difficult. **You can take a number of approaches**. Ensure that you have a concrete idea of the structure you will use to describe the painting. For example, you could begin with your personal feelings about it, then the colours and atmosphere the painting creates, then the exact objects, then their respective position and size. It does not matter which approach you take but this questions is designed to test your way of organising and presenting your ideas.

You could also comment on the difficulty of the task and argue that human language limits you from adequately describing smell, taste, sound, and vision. Modern language applicants may have read about Wittgenstein in which case they can reference his works on the limitations and functions of language here.

Q14: Which person in the past would you most like to interview, and why?

This is a personal question but try to **avoid generic and mainstream answers**. Keep in mind that you can find out much more about a particular period or area by speaking to everyday citizens or advisors for politicians or other important figures. It is much more important to identify what you want to learn about and then set criteria to narrow down the possible list of persons. This questions opens the floor for developing an analytical, quasi-scientific approach to your research.

Q15: Tell me about a recent news article that interested you.

Whilst this question may be asked at a general interview, it's a good idea to come up with something that is related to your course. Instead of going into technical detail with an interviewer who may be from a completely different discipline, it is better to give a brief overview of the article and then put it into broader context.

For example, an economics applicant may want to discuss the decision of the Swiss National Bank to discontinue the currency "ceiling".

Definition: The currency ceiling was a policy to peg the value of the Franc to the Euro at a rate of 1.2.

Reasons: At the beginning of the euro-crisis, investors turned away from the more risky Euro and started buying Francs instead which was then perceived as a stable currency. This resulted in the value of the Franc increasing with respect to other currencies, especially the euro. But this had a negative impact on the Swiss economy as a strong currency is not favourable for export.

Analyse the news: The decision of the National Bank to let the exchange change freely will certainly cause harm to the Swiss economy. On the other hand, it cost the National Bank a lot of money to maintain the 1.2 Franc:Euro exchange rate by buying Euros and selling Francs in the open market. And the Swiss National Bank had a large exposure to Euro, with its risks.

The answer should not be a complete analysis of the issue but an intuitive and logical description of an event. Then the interviews would most likely ask you to make recommendations or ask your opinion about the whole article.

Q16: Do you have political views?

In general, you should avoid expressing any very extreme views at all interviews. The answer *"I do not"* is not the most favourable either. This question invites you to **demonstrate academic thinking in a topic which could be part of everyday conversations**. You are not expected to present a full analysis of party politics and different ideologies. It doesn't matter if you actually have strong political views; the main point is to talk about your perception of what political ideas are present and how one differs from the other.

With such a broad question – you have the power to choose the topic- be it wealth inequality, nuclear weapons, corruption, human rights, or budget deficit etc. Firstly, you should **explain why that particular topic or political theme is important**. For example, the protection of fundamental human rights is crucial in today's society because this introduces a social sensitivity to our democratic system where theoretically 51% of population could impose its will on the other 49%. On the other hand, it should be noted that Western liberal values may contradict with social, historical and cultural aspects of society in certain developing countries and a different political discourse is needed in different countries about the same questions. Secondly, you should discuss whether that topic is well-represented in political discourse of our society and what should be done to trigger a more democratic debate.

Q17: One of the unique features of the Oxbridge education is the supervision system, one-on-one tutorials every week. This means heavy workload, one essay every week with strict deadlines. Do you think you can cope with this?

By this point, you should hopefully have a sound understanding of the supervision/tutorial systems. You should also be aware of the possibility of spending long hours in the library and meeting tight deadlines so this question should not be surprising at all. It gives you an opportunity to **prove that you would fit into this educational system very well**. Firstly, you should make it clear that you understand the system and the requirements. On average, there is one essay or problem sheet every week for each paper that you are reading which requires going through the reading list/lecture notes and engaging with wider readings around certain topics or problems. Secondly, you should give some examples from your past when you had to work long hours or had strict deadlines etc. You should also tell the interviewer how you felt in these situations, what you enjoyed the most and what learned from them. Finally, you may wish to stress that you would *"not only be able to cope with the system but also enjoy it a great deal"*.

Q18: If you had to choose to be a character from a novel, who would you want to be?

This question is an ice-breaker- the interviewer is curious to find out what type of novels you read and how thoroughly you are reading them. For example, if you say like Robin Hood, then explain his situation briefly as becoming an outlaw, resisting the authorities and aiding the poor and his fellow men. You can then continue and argue that it is rather difficult to decide if he was a positive or a negative character at the end of the day. Making decisions like he did with strong moral standing on who is bad and good person would make up for a great experience and learning a lot about human nature just as much as about me.

The main point is to be able to **give a very brief summary of the character**, (especially if you choose a less well-known work), and have a good and interesting justification for being them.

Q19: Should you be allowed internet access during this interview?

This is a classic open question for an insightful debate. The most important thing to realise here is that **Oxbridge education is about teaching you how to think** in clear, structured and coherent way as opposed to collecting lots of facts from the internet.

Internet access would provide each candidate with the same available information and therefore the art of using information to make sound arguments would be the sole decisive factor. On the other hand, the information overload can be rather confusing. In general, a braindump is not helpful at the interview as it does not demonstrate in-depth understanding and analysis of any problems. At the end of the day, it comes down to the individual candidate i.e. what would you look up on the Internet during the interview? Would you want to rely on unverified knowledge? How reliable is that information on the internet? How could you verify this information?

Q20: What achievement are you most proud of?

This is another chance to highlight your suitability for the course, so try to **make it as subject-relevant as possible**. *"I felt proud to be awarded first place in a poetry competition with a sonnet I wrote about..."* (if you're applying for English). *"I recently won the Senior Challenge for the UK Mathematics Trust.", "Achieving a 100% mark in my AS-level History and English exams – an achievement I hope to emulate at A2"*.

Of course, it is not easy to pick one achievement and this is not a question that you might have expected. You could also argue that you can't really compare your achievements from different fields e.g. your 100% Physics AS-level and football team captaincy. This will allow you to bypass the question's number limit and mention more than one achievement so that you have more opportunities to impress the interviewer.

Q21: When would you toss a coin to make a decision?

This question can be quite tricky and aims at revealing how you make decisions in your life, your understanding of abstract concepts, rationality and probabilities. You should begin with answering the question from your perspective, you can be honest about it but give a justification even if you never want to make decisions based on luck. Try to **give a few examples when tossing a coin could be a good idea**, or would cause no harm. Then you can take the discussion to a more abstract level and argue that once all yes/no decisions are made by tossing a coin in the long run the expected value should be fifty-fifty so you might not be worse-off at all and you could avoid the stress of making decisions (although this is very simplistic).

You could also reference the stock markets where high returns may be purely luck-dependent. On the other hand, **rational-decision making is part of human nature** and analysing costs and benefits would result in better decisions in the long-run than tossing a coin. In addition, this would incentivise people to conduct research, collect information, develop and test theories etc. As you see the question could be interpreted to focus on the merits of rigorous scientific methodology.

Q22: If you could change one thing in the world now what would you change?

This question tests your sound reasoning and clear presentation of your answer. **There is no right or wrong "one thing" to choose.** It is equally valid to choose wealth inequality or the colour of a double-decker bus if you argue it well! It should be noted that if you've applied for a social sciences, it is a better strategy to choose a related topic, to show your sensitivity to social issues.

Firstly, you should choose something you would like to change while demonstrating clear thinking, relevant arguments. Secondly, you are expected to discuss how and to what extent you would and could change it. Again, a better candidate would realise that **this is not necessarily a binomial problem** – either change it or not – but there may be a spectrum between these two extremes.

Q23: Where would you like to travel with a time machine first?

This is a question where you can really use your imagination (or draw on History GCSE or A-level). **You can say absolutely any time period** in the past or the far future but you must have a good reason for it. This doesn't necessarily need to be linked to your subject.

For example, *"I would love to see time when my parents were little children and see where and how they have grown up. This would allow me to better understand their nostalgic stories of the 'good old days'"*.

Choosing something personal or creative will make you stand out and you are more likely to get interesting questions from the interviewer if you are able to involve them in an intriguing conversation. It is also fine if you choose a standard period like the Roman Empire or Victorian Britain if you have a good reason.

General Interview Questions:

The following pages contain real examples of interview questions that our tutors were asked at their **general interview**. At first glance, they may appear rather obscure and intimidating. However, remember that you are unlikely to be asked these questions in series. They will only be asked because the topic being discussed naturally led to the question or if you alluded to it earlier. E.g. '*Why are flowers not green?*' may precede or follow a discussion of chlorophyll or the evolution of colour vision.

Thus, whilst going through these questions is excellent practice - ensure that you don't get too bogged down in the knowledge aspects of these questions. **Interviewers are far more interested to see what you can do with the knowledge you already possess**.

1. What do you expect to get out of this degree?
2. Why do you want to study [insert subject here]?
3. Why do you want to come to this college?
4. Have you been to this college before?
5. What makes you think this University will be the right fit for you?
6. Where do you see yourself in 10 years time? What about 20 years?
7. What extracurricular activities do you do?
8. How will you contribute to College life?
9. What do you know about the course structure?
10. What is your biggest weakness?
11. What is your biggest strength?
12. How will your experiences from the Duke of Edinburgh scheme benefit your future studies?
13. What makes you want to come to here when you would most certainly get a better result at any other university?
14. Oxford is very intense, how will you manage your time to deal with all of the work?
15. What did you read this morning?
16. What is the biggest challenge you've faced and how did you dealt with it?

17. Who was your best teacher? How have they influenced you?
18. What are your long term plans in life?
19. What are your top three skills?
20. Would you choose a party over an essay?
21. Who's the most influential: Obama, Merkel or Adele?
22. What colour best represents you?
23. What shape is man? What shape is time?
24. Why do things have names?
25. What international newspapers and publications do you read?
26. Can you hear silence?
27. How many golf balls can you fit in a Boeing 747 plane?
28. How many planes are flying over London right now?
29. How many letters does Royal Mail deliver every day?
30. How much should you charge to wash all the windows in London?
31. How many piano tuners are there in Europe?
32. India introduces a new population control policy to address the gender imbalance. If a couple have a girl, they may have another child. If they have a boy, they can't have any more children. What would be the new ratio of boys : girls?
33. Why are manhole covers round?
34. How many times per day do a clock's hand overlap?
35. You are shrunk down so you're the size of a matchstick and then put into a blender with metal blades. It is about to be turned on – what do you do?
36. You are given 7 identical balls and another ball that looks the same as the others but is heavier than them. You can use a balance only two times. How would you identify which is the heavy ball?
37. What is your favourite number?
38. Who am I? (Always read up on your interviewers!)
39. Is there any question that you wished we had asked you?
40. If you could keep objects from the present for the future what would they be?
41. Does human nature change over time?
42. Is there such a thing as truth?
43. What is a lie? How do I know what you just said isn't a lie?

44. If you could have one superpower – which one would it be? Why?
45. Who has had the largest influence on your life?
46. What is more important – art or science?
47. What are you looking forward to the least at this college?
48. If you were me, would you let yourself in?
49. Would you ever go on a one way trip to Mars? Why/Why not?
50. What do you think my favourite colour is? Why do you say that?
51. Define Success in one sentence.

SUBJECT INTERVIEWS

Subject interviews are where subject-specific questions are asked to test critical thinking and problem-solving skills. These interviews are very likely to follow the format of tutorials/supervisions. You will be interviewed by one or two senior academics from the college you applied to. They will be experts in the subject you've applied for and will ask academic questions around a central theme. **The questions are intended to be difficult** so as to push you and test your critical thinking abilities in a learning situation. You are not meant to know the answers, but to use what your existing knowledge to offer creative and original thoughts to address the questions.

Here are some general tips to keep in mind:

➢ Apply the knowledge you have acquired at A-Level and from your wider reading to unfamiliar scenarios.

➢ **Stand your ground if you are confident in your argument**- even if your interviewers disagree with you. They may deliberately play the devil's advocate, to see if you are able to defend your argument.

➢ However, if you are making an argument that is clearly wrong, and are being told so by the interviewers - then concede your mistake and revise your viewpoint. Do not stubbornly carry on arguing a point that they are saying is wrong.

➢ Remember, making mistakes is no bad thing. The important point is that you address the mistake head on and adapt the statement, with their assistance where necessary.

➢ The **tutors know what subjects you have studied at A-Level** so don't feel pressured to read EVERY aspect of your subject.

In the chapters that follow, each subject is discussed in detail – including common types of questions and model solutions to previously asked interview questions. This book is not intended to be an exhaustive list of all that you need to know for your Oxbridge interview (if that's even possible!). Instead, it is designed to guide your learning by exposing you to the style and difficulty of questions that might come up and how to best approach them.

THE SCIENCES

BIOLOGY & MEDICINE

There is a large degree of overlap between the biological sciences and Medicine at Oxbridge. Thus, biologists may be asked straight biology questions, medical questions, or questions from a related subject, such as chemistry.

Contrastingly, medical interviews at Oxbridge are much more likely to focus on the human side of biology (physiology, pathology, pharmacology etc). One of the medical interviews maybe a 'general' one- similar in style to the classical medical interviews (with questions like "*how do you deal with stress?*" etc). This latter style of interview is beyond the confines of this book. The advice that follows is applicable to both biology and medicine applicants due to their similarity.

In general, you'll be **tackling a large question with many smaller sub-questions** to guide the answer from the start to a conclusion. The main question may seem difficult, impossible or random at first, but take a deep breath and start discussing different ideas that you have for breaking the question down into manageable pieces.

The questions are designed to be difficult to give you the chance to **show your full intellectual potential**. The interviewers will help guide you to the right idea provided you work with them and offer ideas for them to steer you along with. This is your chance to show your creativity, analytical skills, intellectual flexibility, problem-solving skills and your go-getter attitude. Don't waste it by letting your nerves overtake or from a fear of messing up or looking stupid.

For biology, the questions will usually take one of **five possible forms** based on the skills necessary to 'think like a biologist':

➢ Observation-based questions ("Tell me about this…")
➢ Practical questions ("How would you determine that…")
➢ Statistical questions ("Given this data…")
➢ Ethical questions ("Are humans obligated to…", "What are the implications of…")
➢ Proximate causes (mechanism; "How does…") and ultimate causes (function; "Why does…")- usually both at once.

The questions also have recurring themes because they are important for biological theory and research: Natural and sexual selection, genetics and inheritance, human body systems, global warming and environmental change, and general knowledge of plants, animals, bacteria and pathogens.

Medical Ethics

Medical applicants are commonly asked medical ethics questions so it's well worth knowing the basics. Whilst there are huge ethical textbooks available– you only need to be familiar with the basic principles for the purposes of your interview. **These principles can be applied to all cases** regardless what the social/ethnic background the healthcare professional or patient is from. The principles are:

Beneficence: The wellbeing of the patient should be the doctor's first priority. In medicine this means that one must act in the patient's best interests to ensure the best outcome is achieved for them i.e. 'Do Good'.

Non-Maleficence: This is the principle of avoiding harm to the patient (i.e. Do no harm). There can be a danger that in a willingness to treat, doctors can sometimes cause more harm to the patient than good. This can especially be the case with major interventions, such as chemotherapy or surgery. Where a course of action has both potential harms and potential benefits, non-maleficence must be balanced against beneficence.

Autonomy: The patient has the right to determine their own health care. This therefore requires the doctor to be a good communicator, so that the patient is sufficiently informed to make their own decisions. 'Informed consent' is thus a vital precursor to any treatment. A doctor must respect a patient's refusal for treatment even if they think it is not the correct choice. Note that patients cannot <u>demand</u> treatment – only refuse it, e.g. an alcoholic patient can refuse rehabilitation but cannot demand a liver transplant.

There are many situations where the application of autonomy can be quite complex, for example:

➢ **Treating Children**: Consent is required from the parents, although the autonomy of the child is taken into account increasingly as they get older.

➢ **Treating adults without the capacity** to make important decisions. The first challenge with this is in assessing whether or not a patient has the capacity to make the decisions. Just because a patient has a mental illness does not necessarily mean that they lack the capacity to make decisions about their health care. Where patients do lack capacity, the power to make decisions is transferred to the next of kin (or Legal Power of Attorney, if one has been set up).

Justice: This principle deals with the fair distribution and allocation of healthcare resources for the population.

Consent: This is an extension of Autonomy- patients must agree to a procedure or intervention. For consent to be valid, it must be **voluntary informed consent.** This means that the patient must have sufficient mental capacity to make the decision and must be presented with all the relevant information (benefits, side effects and the likely complications) in a way they can understand.

Confidentiality: Patients expect that the information they reveal to doctors will be kept private- this is a key component in maintaining the trust between patients and doctors.

You must ensure that patient details are kept confidential. Confidentiality can be broken if you suspect that a patient is a risk to themselves or to others e.g. Terrorism, suicides.

Ensure that you don't immediately give an answer – consider both sides of the argument (pros and cons) and discuss them in detail before arriving at a balanced conclusion.

Worked Questions

Below are a few examples of how to start breaking down an interview question, complete with model answers.

Q1: Why are fewer human females colour-blind than would be expected from the incidence in males?

[Extremely clear-headed] **Applicant**: Well, I know that women are much less likely to be colour-blind than men. Why don't I start by defining colour-blindness and working out why there is a gender difference using Mendelian inheritance, and then think about mechanisms of colour-blindness which may not be accounted for in this method. I noticed you specified females in relation to males, so I'm going to suggest that whatever **this mechanism is sex dependent**.

Now being this clear-headed is unlikely to happen when put on the spot, but shows that the question can be broken down into sub-parts, which can be dealt with in turn. At this point the interviewer can give feedback if this seems like a good start and help make any modifications necessary. The applicant would realise that colour-blindness is inherited on the X-chromosome and the second female X-chromosome may help compensate. Although a single defective X-chromosome would lead to colour-blindness in having two defective X-chromosomes does not necessarily mean that a woman would be colour blind as the defects might be opposites and therefore cancel each other to lead to normal colour vision. The details are unimportant, but the general idea of **breaking down the question into manageable parts is important**.

The interviewer is not looking for a colour-blindness expert, but someone who can problem-solve in the face of new ideas. Note that this is a question about Proximate Causes in disguise; although the question begins with '**Why**', it is actually asking '**How**' or which **mechanism** is causing this discrepancy.

A **Poor Applicant** may take a number of approaches unlikely to impress the interviewer. The first and most obvious of these is to say "We never learned about colour-blindness in school." and make no attempt to move forward from this. The applicants who have done this only make it worse for themselves by resisting prompting as the interviewer attempts to pull an answer from them, saying "fine, but I'm not going to know the answer because I don't know anything about this", or an equally unenthusiastic and uncooperative responses. Another approach which is unhelpful in the interview is the 'brain dump', where instead of engaging with the question, the applicant attempts to impress or distract with an assortment of related facts: "Colour-blindness mainly affects men. You can be completely colour-blind or red-green colour-blind. Many animals are colour-blind, but some also see a greater number of colours." Having gotten off to this start isn't as impressive as a more reasoned response, but the interview can be salvaged by taking the interviewer's feedback on board. Many of these facts could start a productive discussion which leads to the answer if the applicant listens and takes hints and suggestions from the interviewer.

Q2: Are humans ethically obligated to stop global warming and environmental change?

This is a question about Ethics. To answer a question like this, the important thing is not to have a strong opinion that you defend to the death, but to be able to discuss the different viewpoints based on different understandings of right and wrong, and always with a sound understanding of the underlying issues- both scientific and humanitarian.

One way to break down this question would be to **consider whether an ethical obligation extends only to other humans or to other organisms** as well, and whether it applies in any situation or only when contributing to a situation that wouldn't occur naturally. Similarly, one could also discuss whether humans as a whole are obliged to halt global warming or just a select few members of the human race. Showing an ability to think flexibly about abstract concepts is always good, but don't forget to then argue for the different cases using knowledge of past and present climate and environment, as this is the subject-relevant part of the question.

For instance, as you are a scientist, don't waste time discussing if climate change is a reality – the scientific community has already reached a consensus. However, if you would like to argue against an ethical obligation instead, discuss the natural climate variations which have occurred on Earth in the past. Use probable climate-change driven events, like the Permo-Triassic extinction when 96% of species died out 250 million years ago, to argue that humans have no ethical obligation to save other species from anthropogenic extinction, because **even without human presence there are climate-driven extinctions.** Or argue the opposite, that despite past extreme environmental change being a reality, humanity is pushing the Earth further than it has ever sustained humans, and that we are obligated to do our part to leave a habitable Earth for people in other parts of the world and the future. Alternatively, argue completely that there can be no ethical obligation because everyone **contributes to the problem in their own way**, and everyone will face the consequences, or that only those who contribute more than they suffer are in the wrong for dumping their consequences onto others. Whichever argument you put forward, be sure to include scientific examples so that your discussion doesn't veer away from the question.

Remember that climate change is not the same as global warming, and your discussion could include pollution (trash, toxins, chemicals, light and sound pollution, etc.), agriculture and monoculture, invasive species, hunting and fishing, deforestation and habitat fragmentation, or any of the other issues beyond the Greenhouse Effect which effect the environment.

Similarly, global warming is not just about fossil fuel use and carbon dioxide, but a range of gases and their effects on weather, ocean acidity, desertification, pathogen spread, etc. Show that you have a deeper understanding of these issues than you could get from skimming the headlines of the Daily Mail.

Q3: Why is DNA stored inside the nucleus rather than in mitochondria?

This is a question mainly about Ultimate Causes. While you could attempt to answer this by explaining proximate causes, **how** DNA is used and that it can't be in mitochondria. By giving reasons like "transcription occurs in the nucleus so it has to be there" you would be missing the important **why** part of this question. It is asking for an ultimate reason, in this case for the evolutionary history which led mitochondria to have their own separate reproduction. Although **you are unlikely to know about this in detail**, it is important that you engage with this part of the question so that the interviewer can guide you.

Applicant: DNA can't be stored in the mitochondria because the mitochondria are genetically separate from the host cell. When the cell replicates its DNA and divides, the mitochondria separately replicates its own genetic material and reproduces to populate the new cell. The reason for the mitochondria having separate and distinct genetic material not identical to that of the host cell has been proposed to lie in the evolution of eukaryotes. The **Endosymbiotic Theory** suggests that cell organelles, particularly energy producing chloroplasts and mitochondria, were originally separate prokaryotes that were engulfed by larger prokaryotes. They are believed to have begun a symbiotic relationship where perhaps the host cell receives energy and the mitochondria receive a safe environment for reproduction. As this symbiotic relationship evolved, the cells have exchanged some genetic material to coordinate their life-cycles and now cannot survive independently. This explains both the distinct genetic material of mitochondria and the double membrane which surrounds them in the cell – one the original prokaryotic membrane and one from being engulfed by the host. If **they were originally a separate organism** this explains why cell DNA cannot be stored there.

Q4: How would you find out what function a gene has in humans?

This is a question about the practical applications of genetics and experimental techniques – it is asking you to use your knowledge of genetics and research methods to come up with some practical ways of answering this. There are many ways you could answer this question, so take an approach that will allow you to use many examples which show off your knowledge, experience or extra reading about this subject.

If you only know about Mendelian genetics, you could suggest searching the genome (mention a technique if you know it, such as PCR) of relatives to a person known to have the gene to see if those with the gene share traits. **Even if you have no other suggestions, point out the flaws with this idea** – that it may not be possible to gene function may isolate this way because:

➢ The gene would need to be active.
➢ Any trait it contributed to would need to be single locus to really see an effect.
➢ It could produce a hidden condition that isn't apparent in a pedigree
➢ The gene could be essential and thus present in all relatives
➢ The sample size is so low making spurious correlations very likely
➢ This would only be a correlation study and not an experiment that determined cause and effect (experiments requiring human breeding are, at best, inconvenient).

If you are more familiar with genetics you may have other ideas; perhaps a cross-species survey looking for the gene in other species to judge its age and specificity to human life, or knock-out genetics with a closely related species possessing the gene to see if its presence is vital or has a direct effect. The gene could be added to a bacterial genome using plasmids to see which protein is produced. No matter what your answer is, the important part of this question is to take a practical and self-critical approach which plays to your individual knowledge base.

A **Poor Applicant** would disregard that the question is asking for a practical solution and instead tell the interviewer about the general function of genes, or would ignore the specifics of the question- treating it as if it could be solved through Mendel's pea-flower approach. A poor applicant would not be self-critical and would not point out the flaws and limitations of their proposed ideas.

Q5: What evidence would you like to conclude that there is life on Mars?

Applicant: I would want to know what is meant by 'life'- whether it means something Earth-like, or a more general definition. Then I would want either direct or indirect evidence. Direct evidence would be observing life itself, and the indirect would be observing some marker for this life based on how it was defined. Thus, I'll **start by thinking about how I would define life and then think about potential markers for it**.

This is a practical question that aims to set out what the hypotheses would be for future experiments. It is not about describing one precise experiment, but how you would design a series of experiments. With that in mind, it's important to ensure that suggested evidence is precisely-defined, observable and measurable or quantifiable and repeatable because these features open the door to a great variety of experiment types. Thus the response *"I'd like to see something that's alive"* isn't quite detailed enough. You can suggest something which is currently impossible, such as wanting to observe a specimen drilled from one kilometre down on Mars, but should include some practical ideas as well.

One approach would be to define life as an **ability to create chemical disequilibria**. Through respiration and other basic life functions, organisms shuffle electrons and molecules and create small disequilibria that are later used to power life functions (consider photosynthesis and the shuffling of electrons from donors to acceptors using sunlight to power the process). The surface and atmosphere could be studied for disequilibria, starting with those associated with life on Earth.

There are many other possible approaches, but the general idea is to define the question more specifically and then suggest **possible evidence** which could be found in a range of experiments. You should suggest multiple experiments as it is necessary to have a sizeable data-pool before reaching a conclusion on such a broad question.

Q6: Why don't we have more than two eyes? Why do we only have one mouth?

This is a question that involves disentangling ultimate and proximate causes. When answering this question it is important to show that you can approach a question from a variety of perspectives, including both **Proximate Causes** about **how** the **mechanism** influences the observed condition, but also **Ultimate Causes** about **why** this may be and what **function** this serves- particularly from an adaptive standpoint.

For a complete answer to this question, both types of cause are important. Take a moment to consider this from a few perspectives:

➤ A mechanistic approach through which eyes and mouths work.
➤ An evolutional approach by considering adaptation and fitness/survival and its impact on biological designs.
➤ An anthropological approach by considering evolutionary history and how our ancient ancestors influence the bodies we have today.

How many eyes and mouths we have is a matter of trade-offs. One eye provides an image of the surroundings, but **depth perception is only possible with two or more**. The slightly different angle from each eye allows us to determine how far away each object is. A very close object will project a very different image in each eye, while distant objects will look the same. The brain is then able to compare the differences in the images in order to estimate distances.

Having an extra eye and being able to integrate the two images is metabolically expensive energetically as a significant amount of neural processing is required. The gains from coordination in capturing prey and escaping predators offsets these costs, allowing for the second eye. A third eye could be helpful as it would allow **vision ahead and behind** simultaneously. However, each additional eye would be increasingly costly as its image would need to be integrated with the other eyes. Thus, the gains from escaping predators or spotting prey wouldn't be offset.

However, you might also point out that given rampant obesity and other signs that humans have great amounts of spare energy, so it would now make sense to have an extra number of eyes. Similarly, for common prey the metabolic costs of an additional eye could be offset by increased survival.

A mouth is the point of access to the digestive system and only one is required to ingest nutrients. Thus, having more mouths means would increase the rate at which we could ingest food. However, a larger mouth could achieve similar results, so the energetic costs of growing a second fully-functioning mouth are not supported. In addition, introducing another mouth would increase the **risk of infections**.

There is another dimension to this question than the **how** and **why**- the **was**. Humans can't just grow another mouth or gazelles another eye, because our ancestors did not have these. We have no genes to produce this extremely complex and divergent phenotype. It does not matter whether the prey would benefit from the third eye or not- they just can't grow one instantly because the path to that design is too difficult to attain from the present two eye setup.

In general, it is not easy to make such drastic physical changes (even over long periods of time). For example, consider the opposite case: if our ancestors had evolved a three-eye-system. The species would be more likely to become extinct rather than transform to a two-eye-system.

A **Poor Applicant** would miss the point of this question- it is not to delve deeply into the workings of 3D vision and the digestive system, or even into trade-offs in adaptation that lead to limits on designs. The point is to show that **there are many perspectives which must be integrated** to fully consider a question as complex as this.

Q7: How is DNA like sheet music?

A question like this is a chance to demonstrate lateral thinking and show you can abstract and relate concepts you are familiar with. In any comparison question, you should **directly relate one thing to the other**. For example:

➤ DNA consists of different patterns of amino acids; Sheet music consists of different pattern of 12 notes.
➤ DNA describes the order in which mRNA should be produced; sheet music describes the order in which the music should be played.
➤ DNA and sheet music can both contain instructions on how and when to repeat sections.
➤ Mistakes in reading DNA can result in harmful mutations – mistakes in reading sheet music can result in a ruined melody/chord.
➤ Mistakes in reading DNA can sometimes be beneficial and lead to useful mutations; mistakes in reading sheet music can also rarely make the piece better than it was originally written.

Q8: What is your favourite protein?

This question allows you to demonstrate your enthusiasm for the subject. **All answers are perfectly acceptable** as long as you can justify them. Do not waste a question like this on an answer which doesn't show either specific biological knowledge.

For example, you might like **haemoglobin** because of it is very important as it facilitates oxygen transfer, or because there are many interesting diseases associated with it e.g. Sick Cell, Thalassaemia. Alternatively, you might like **insulin** because of its importance in blood glucose homeostasis or relationship in diabetes.

Q9: What is the significance of the Hayflick Limit?

Firstly, if you do not know what the Hayflick Limit is, ASK! It is impossible to answer this question if you do not know this technical definition. The Hayflick Limit is the theoretical limit to the number of times a normal human cell can divide. A good approach to this question would be to start by **defining the Hayflick Limit** and suggesting proximate reasons for its existence e.g. shortening telomeres with each cell division until they reach a critical length. Then, if you have any suggestions for ultimate reasons, discuss those e.g. older DNA is more mutated, so older cells are less healthy and less related to the original than younger cells. If you have time, you could show an interest in biological issues by discussing some implications you may know about deriving from this topic, referencing articles or other media e.g. documentaries or the highly recommended TED talks available online.

Examples of things that are relevant would be the stability of clones derived from mature DNA, the possibility of immortality with finite cell rejuvenation, or problems with cancer cells that exceed the Hayflick Limit. You aren't expected to have any significant knowledge of these – the interviewers would guide you throughout the process.

Q10: Why is the liver on the right side of the body?

This is another classic question about **disentangling ultimate and proximate causes**, mechanisms and functions. The actual answer doesn't matter - only that you can show that are able to approach biological questions from different perspectives. You could take a proximate mechanism approach and argue that there is a reason the liver can only work in that position - perhaps it needs to be in a specific orientation to allow the other organs to fit into the human body in this right-hand configuration.

From an ultimate perspective you could argue there is an evolutionary advantage to this configuration. Maybe it is advantageous to have the vital liver on the opposite side of the body to the equally vital heart in case of severe injury to one side. You could take an evolutionary history approach- that there is no advantage to having the liver on the right, but some ancient ancestor had a right-left asymmetry with right-hand organs which became the liver. The important part of this answer is to show you are not locked into one perspective, but that you can see the variety of biological factors which may be at work.

A last example to drive this point home, would be the question *"why are flowers usually never green?"* You could argue this from a proximate perspective- that flowers aren't photosynthetically active and thus don't have green chlorophyll. Alternatively, you could approach it from an ultimate perspective- flowers are meant to be attractive to pollinators and thus need to stand out from the foliage. Therefore, their functionality would be diminished if they were green.

Q11: Why do humans have two ears?

This type of question is often asked because all good candidates should be able to arrive at the correct answer (even if they haven't heard of it before). Therefore, it is useful to **talk through your thought process**, which will also allow the interviewer to guide you if necessary. A good place to start is to recognise that there must be a distinct evolutionary advantage of having two ears, so it must allow for functions that are not possible to the same extent with only one ear.

Having two ears allows you to **compare differences in stimuli**. How could comparing the sound you hear in each ear be useful? The properties of this sound would include amplitude, frequency and timing – why would these differ between the ears?

If sound is coming from one side of the head then it would reach one ear before the other, so timing of the sound would differ between the ears. Similarly, the amplitude would also differ between the ears if the source was not equidistant from them. Finally if a moving sound source is closer to one ear than the other, then its frequency will differ between the ears (an extrapolation of the **Doppler Effect**).

Therefore, a comparison of the timing, amplitude and frequency of sounds in each ear provides the brain enough information to allow **sound localisation**, which is a powerful evolutionary advantage.

Q12: In one word, how does the brain work?

The challenge of this question is that the brain is such a complex organ that **no single word could ever summarise how it works**. It is important to make it explicit to the interviewer that you recognise this. Secondly, you need to recognise that the question is about '*how*' the brain works, so the best answers will talk about a process and not simply the architecture that allows it to work. For example, answering '*plasticity*' would be more appropriate than answering '*synapses*' or '*circuits*'. Whatever word you choose, the crucial thing is that you try to reasonably justify your answer.

A good student who chose '*plasticity*' might then say: 'this is because plasticity at the synaptic level encompasses processes like long-term potentiation and long-term depression. These are crucial in how the neural circuits that underlie brain function develop. Thus, they're ultimately responsible for modulating how one neuron responds to another neuron's firing and so how the circuits as a whole function. The crucial role of plasticity has been demonstrated in numerous brain functions; including learning, memory, emotions, sensation and the recovery from injury'.

Q13: Is cancer inevitable?

This question is purposefully vague, so it is up to you to **specify what you think they are asking**. It also gives you scope to pick an angle for your answer through which you can best demonstrate your knowledge. You could take a '**nature vs. nurture' approach**, discussing how there is a genetic component to cancer that predisposes to or protects vs. cancer.

You should make it clear that it is the predisposition to cancer that could be considered inevitable, not cancer itself. **Mention any examples** you may know of, such as the association of mutation in the BRCA1 gene with breast cancer.

In general, cancer is a disease of ageing and **the risk of most cancers increases with age**. Thus, one could argue that if most people lived long enough, they would eventually get some type of cancer. Alternatively, you could argue that whilst getting cancer is inevitable at the moment (like getting an infection), medical advances may change this in the future. The important thing is to **define the question so that you are able to tackle it** rather than giving a one word response.

Q14: What is the point of 2nd messenger systems?

You may have learned about this topic in A-levels, but may not have thought about *why* it is the way it is. The interviewer would give you a quick explanation of 2nd messengers if you hadn't heard of them before. Again, they are interested in how you deduce your answers logically and using first principles.

It is useful to think about why secondary messenger systems would have evolved and what **alternative systems** are conceivable. One such alternative is signalling chemicals that pass into the target cells and interact directly with effector proteins (such as steroid signalling). What advantages are conveyed by having an extra step in the signalling cascade?

This is best thought about in the context of an example, such as the cyclic adenosine monophosphate (cAMP) system and gives you an opportunity to display what you know about these systems. Having a system that requires binding of a primary messenger (e.g. acetylcholine) to a cell surface receptor (e.g. G-protein coupled receptors) allows for signals to be determined by receptor density to a certain extent. Similarly, a variety of **intracellular signalling** can affect the levels of secondary messenger, allowing even finer control of the ultimate intracellular signal and response.

Perhaps most importantly, second messengers help to amplify the cellular response. For example, a single molecule of Acetylcholine (primary messenger) can results in millions of downstream 2nd messengers. This setup **allows cells to react to small stimuli very rapidly**.

Q15: What is the greatest medical advance of the last 100 years?

There is no single right answer for this question- you just need to be able to justify your response. It is a good idea to pick something you may have read a little about, so that you can **add detail to support your answer**. Some good options include antibiotics, population-scale vaccines (smallpox, polio and MMR are good examples), evidence-based analysis (placebo controlled, blinded, randomized controlled trials; meta-analysis), advances in blood typing/banking/infusion.

For example, "I think that the development of a huge array of antibiotics since the discovery of penicillin is perhaps the most important medical advance in the last 100 years. This is because bacterial infections are very common and affect most of us at some point in our lives. Before antibiotics, even very small infections could be life threatening. The discovery of antibiotics represented a paradigm shift in medicine whereby a huge number of very harmful infectious diseases (such as tuberculosis, diphtheria, typhoid) became treatable. Furthermore, antibiotics made surgery a lot safer, by reducing the risks of post-operative infection.

Your answer to this question may **determine future line of questioning** for the remainder of the interview so choose carefully! For example, this particular response may lead to a discussion of how antibiotic resistance develops or why multi-drug resistant bacteria are a problem.

Q16: A drug is given orally in regular repeated doses. The drug is eliminated from the blood by the kidneys, but not all of it is eliminated before the next dose is given. Draw what you might expect to see on a graph of drug concentration in the blood against time, over several repeated doses.

You haven't been given enough information to allow you to draw the graph accurately e.g. the rate of absorption, the rate of elimination and the time between each dose. However, you can still **draw the general shape** - as the drug is absorbed from the gut, the concentration of drug in the blood (called plasma drug concentration, or C) will rapidly increase.

When the majority of the drug has been absorbed, the **rate of drug elimination will exceed the rate of absorption**. Thus, there will be a turning point where C starts to decrease. C will continue to drop until the next dose.

Since the dose isn't fully eliminated, the lowest value of C will still be greater than zero. It will then again rapidly increase because the new dose is being absorbed.

Therefore, over several successive doses, C will become progressively greater to eventually give a graph shaped like below:

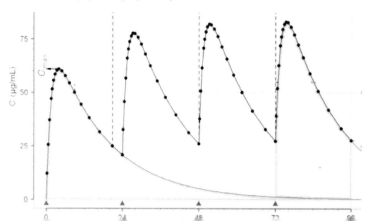

Q17: The 'nocebo effect' is a phenomenon where patients feel negative effects such as pain, nausea, and discomfort in response to a drug that is known to be physiologically inert. What could this tell us about how patients respond to treatments?

A good place to start with answering this question is to make it clear that you understand the difference between the 'nocebo effect' and negative iatrogenic side-effects produced by treatments. The key difference is that there is no physiological reason for the side-effects with the nocebo effect. You can then **compare this to the well known 'placebo effect'**, where positive effects are experienced in response to 'drugs' (often completely inert sugar pills), despite there being no physiological explanation for this.

It is thought that the placebo effect is due to the patient's expectation of positive effects from the drug. Therefore, you could suggest that in nocebo, it is likely that some expectation of negative side effects could precipitate the perception of these negative side effects. Both these effects show that there is a **psychological aspect** to how patients respond to their treatments. This is very important when doctors consider how to manage patient expectations about how a treatment will affect them. It introduces an interesting ethical dilemma about keeping patients fully informed about the potential negative side effects of a treatment – it is important to let patients know the risks. However doing this could cause them to experience negative side effects due to the 'nocebo effect'.

Q18: Why is negative feedback necessary for the human body to function?

You will know of examples of negative feedback from A-level Biology, such as homeostatic mechanisms like **temperature control** and the maintenance of steady **blood glucose levels** using insulin and glucagon. Although it's good to start by describing the role of negative feedback in these processes, it is crucial that you go on to discuss **why** homeostasis is necessary in the first place.

At the **system level**, you can discuss how using negative feedback to keep such parameters within a small range allows for larger physiological responses to relatively small changes in the environment. At the **cellular level**, the internal environment must be tightly regulated by negative feedback to allow enzymes to function efficiently e.g. temperature and pH.

A poor candidate would just list examples of negative feedback rather than discussing its significance.

Q19: What do the adrenal glands do? What would happen if they were hyperactive?

Your ability to answer this question will depend on if you know what hormones are produced by the adrenals and what their function. Again, the interviewer will prompt you if you get stuck. The adrenals produce catecholamines such as adrenaline and noradrenaline as well as other steroid hormones like cortisol and aldosterone. Therefore, a 'hyperactive' adrenal gland would produce excess amounts of these hormones.

Catecholamines increase heart rate and cause peripheral vasoconstriction. So increased catecholamine production from a hyperactive adrenal gland would lead to all of these features. You could also think about what would cause the adrenals to be 'hyperactive' e.g. an adrenal tumour or increased stimulation from the nerves innervating the adrenal gland.

Similarly, if you were aware of the effects of increased steroid hormones, then you should describe what actions they have and what would happen if there were increased production of them.

NB: This is an interesting area of clinical medicine and if you're interested in endocrinology – you are advised to do some background reading on *Cushing's Syndrome* and *Conn's Syndrome*.

Q20: What diseases do you think we should screen for?

This **ethical question** gives you an opportunity to demonstrate an understanding of resource allocation and knowledge of any screening programmes that you are aware of. You can discuss how it is important that the resources are used to achieve the most benefit for the most people (utilitarian argument). This is often measured using **quality adjusted life-years** (QUALYs) by the **National Institute of Health and Care Excellence** (NICE). They perform these calculations in order to decide if screening is appropriate. So for screening to be appropriate and cost-effective:

➤   The disease must be an important health problem.
➤   The disease should be treatable.
➤   There should be a simple screening test for the disease.
➤   The test should have low false positive and false negative rates.
➤   The test should be cost effective.

You could then offer your opinion on which diseases would satisfy these criteria. For completeness, current screening programmes include:

➤   Pap smears vs. Cervical Cancer
➤   Mammograms vs. Breast cancer
➤   Faecal Occult blood test vs. Colorectal cancer
➤   Foetal blood tests for Down's Syndrome

Biology & Medicine Interview Questions

52. How does a cheetah run so fast?

53. Why is the structure of an elephant's foot the way it is?

54. How is a horse's leg adapted to running?

55. Why do you want to be a vet/doctor?

56. How does respiration differ between fish and mammals?

57. What is your favourite animal?

58. How does an electron microscope works?

59. How does the leg respond to reflexes? What would happen if you stimulated both the sensory and motor neurons at the same time?

60. How can mutations cause an RNA or DNA to be longer or shorter?

61. How would you find out which colours a rat can distinguish? What about an octopus?

62. Why does the brain:body ratio of moles and bats differ?

63. I see from your personal statement that you do a lot of sports. What effects does lactic acid have on the body and brain?

64. What can you tell me about this skull?

65. Female deer appear to select their mates based on the size of their antlers. The older deer's have bigger antlers. How would you confirm this experimentally?

66. When competing for mates, male deer engage in "show-fighting", and the loser eventually backs down. Is there an evolutionary advantage to this, rather than fighting to the death?

67. How do dolphins regulate their body temperature in cold and warm water?

68. How many petrol stations are there in Europe?

69. How many molecules of gas are in the room?

70. How many sulphate ions would you expect in a 0.5 litre aqueous sulphuric acid solution at pH 2.0 assuming it was completely dissociated?

71. Draw the structures of as many compounds as you can think of with the formula C_4H_8O, with an emphasis on the different chemical groups that may be involved.

72. What do you know about the bonding in a benzene ring?

73. An ice cube is floating in a glass of water. What happens to the water level when it melts?
74. How is aspirin synthesised? What organic reaction takes place?
75. Draw the full chemical structure of DNA.
76. Why are diamonds so expensive?
77. What is entropy?
78. Why are bacterial infections easier to treat than viral infections?
79. Does the molecular structure of glycine change with pH?
80. How long is a gene?
81. How many genes are in a cell?
82. Give an example of when specialist biological knowledge has helped a global issue.
83. Was Lamarck right?
84. How would you mass produce insulin?
85. How would you tell if a mouse could differentiate between the smell of an apple and the smell of chocolate?
86. Should all stem cell therapy be legalised?
87. If senses work only because our brain interprets electrical signals, what is reality?
88. How many guinea pigs would you use in an experiment?
89. Is euthanasia too broad a term to use? What are the different types of euthanasia?
90. Should patients always have complete autonomy?
91. How much money should the NHS spend on palliative care?
92. Why do some people describe the NHS as the 'crown jewel of the welfare state'?
93. How well can we compare public and private healthcare?
94. Should patients with a terminal illness be able to use an experimental drug, even if it has not yet been rigourously tested?
95. What is a clinical trial and why are they so important?
96. Will 3D printing revolutionise medicine?
97. Why are cancer cells more susceptible to destruction by radiotherapy than regular cells?
98. If you had £1billion to spend on a specific area of research, what would it be and why?

99. What is the most significant medical breakthrough in the last 10 years?
100. What is an ECG and how does it work?
101. How could you justify the legalisation of ecstasy?
102. Should every hospital have an MRI machine?
103. What are the ethical implications of genetic screening from birth?
104. Should placebos be used in hospitals? What about GP-surgeries?
105. How would you differentiate between salt and sugar without tasting them?
106. What do you understand by the words perception, self-awareness and consciousness?
107. If a psychologically ill person commits a crime, are they a criminal?
108. If you had to give human rights to one of either chimpanzees, dolphins or elephants, which would you choose?
109. How many litres of blood does your heart pump in your lifetime?
110. Why do men often go bald, but women rarely do?
111. Why is there no cure for the common cold? How does the flu vaccine work?
112. Why do the atria contract before the ventricles?
113. Why do we need ATP? Why not just release energy from glucose directly?
114. What is DNA fingerprinting and why is it used in forensics?
115. What is normality?
116. Has the enhancement of medical knowledge destroyed human evolution?
117. How can we cure global warming if environmental measures fail?
118. Why do leaves have stomata on their bottom and not top?
119. Why are so few flowers and animals coloured green?
120. Radiation can cause cancer yet we use radiotherapy to treat cancer. What could explain this apparent paradox?
121. How would you find out what function a gene has in humans? What about in plants?
122. What is the Red-Queen effect? What is its significance?
123. What is your favourite pathogen?
124. What is the difference between bacteria and viruses?
125. How does a caterpillar transform into a butterfly?

126. Why do some habitats support higher biodiversity than others?

127. Why do so many animals have stripes?

128. Here's a cactus. Tell me about it.

129. If you could save either the rainforests or the coral reefs, which would you choose?

130. Is it easier for organisms to live in the sea or on land?

131. Why do lions have manes?

132. Ladybirds are red. So are strawberries. Why?

133. Would it matter if tigers became extinct?

134. Why do cats' eyes appear to 'glow' in the dark?

135. Why are dogs the most common type of pet?

136. How does a fridge work?

137. How do stem cells become specialised?

138. If money was no barrier, how would you scientifically prove life on Mars?

139. What is a neurotransmitter?

140. Why are infectious diseases no longer the biggest killer in the UK?

141. What is a gene?

142. Why can you stay balanced whilst cycling, but not on a stationary bike?

143. Why did $E = mc^2$ change the world?

144. What are the problems with the current taxonomy system?

145. Draw a graph of how a bacterial population changes over time and one for human population. Why is there a difference?

146. I have just injected myself with an unknown substance. Work out what it is doing to my body by asking me simple questions. (Answer= it blocked the function of motor neurons).

147. How would you measure the mass of nitrogen in this room?

148. What is the most important technology available in medicine?

149. Is humour a useful skill for a doctor?

150. If you lived in the 18th century, how would you prove that different areas of the brain have different functions?

151. Why is glass transparent but the sand that it's made from not?

152. Will the population of mankind ever stop increasing?

153. Why do people have different gaits when they walk?

154. How do you measure blood pressure?

155. Talk about a piece of recent scientific research. Why was it important and how could it be improved?

156. How could you measure how much blood is in your body right now?

157. What did you have for breakfast?

158. Describe and draw a Volume/Pressure curve of a balloon and compare it to workings of the lung.

159. You are with a nurse who takes blood and makes a labelling mistake on a patient who has needle phobia. What do you do? What do you say to the patient and what do you say to the nurse?

160. Describe how the human nose is adapted anatomically and physiologically to perform its function?

161. How would you classify diseases?

162. What do you understand by the term 'apoptosis'?

163. Why is the heart so well adapted to performing its role?

164. What are QALYs?

165. Draw a schematic diagram of the heart and tell me about the circulatory system.

166. Interviewer places a skeleton foot on the table. What is this?

167. Is this a left or right foot? How do you know which side the foot is?

168. How do you know it is a foot and not a hand?

169. Describe the processes that occur at a synapse.

170. What causes the common cold?

171. What is cerebral palsy?

172. What is an amino acid?

173. How do amino acids bond to form a peptide?

174. Please look at this picture (brain slice after a stroke). What does it show?

175. What are the two main types of stroke?

176. What can cause strokes in young patients?

177. What are fluid balance charts used for?

178. What are the most important characteristics of a good doctor?

179. Is it more important to be competent or compassionate?

180. What will you do if the senior doctor is not at the hospital and you have to perform a life-threatening procedure for the first time to save someone's life?

181. Are disabled lives worth saving?

182. Why can't you breathe underwater through a 1 metre straw?

183. What is the difference between meiosis and mitosis?

184. Genes- why are we not more like bananas?

185. Why do we need lungs?

186. Why are people obese?

187. How does a bird fly?

188. What is the relationship between flow through a vessel and its diameter?

189. What is a pulse?

190. Why do you drown faster in sea water than fresh water?

191. How does blood get back from your feet to your heart?

192. Why is blood red when you bleed even though your veins actually look blue?

193. How can you stand upright and balanced even with your eyes closed?

194. How would you break the news to a farmer that his cow has died?

195. Explain the respiratory system using this snorkel.

196. What is the point of cellular compartmentalisation?

197. How true is it to say that the modern meal is the culmination of a long journey away from biology?

198. What are the effects of cocaine on cerebral and coronary blood flow?

199. Which is better adapted- a human or a chimpanzee?

200. What is the best way to tackle the obesity epidemic?

201. How would you stop the spread of Ebola if you were in charge?

202. How much of human behaviour is genetically determined?

203. Why is sustainability so difficult to achieve?

204. What are the dangers of an ageing population? Is ageing a disease?

205. Do we actually need a brain?

206. What does the kidney do?

207. Why does our heart best faster when we exercise?

208. What else do doctors do apart from treating patients?

209. If you have the money to do either 1 heart transplant or 100 hip replacements? Which one would you do and why?

210. Discuss the ethical dilemma of Huntingdon's disease when one family member knows they have it and don't want anyone else to know.

PSYCHOLOGY

A psychologist will likely be asked questions on biology, experiment design or statistics and data-handling. The interviewers understand that some applicants may not have studied psychology before – be prepared to explain why you think you want to study psychology and show through extra-curricular reading or activities how you've fostered your interest.

The questions below are specific to psychology, but **there is no guarantee that 'psychology' questions will be asked** in a psychology interview. Be prepared to answer questions that are open-ended, require some knowledge of popular psychology topics (e.g. well-known psychiatric conditions), require you to demonstrate an interest in psychology, require you to design experiments or metrics, and that show you can use statistical or other objective approaches to answer subjective questions. Remember that **neuroscience is a part of psychology**, so you may be asked about cognitive functions or sensory systems.

Worked Questions

Below are a few examples of how to start breaking down an interview question, complete with model answers.

Q1: How do babies learn?

There are a number of different ways this question could develop, and it is open-ended enough that it is possible to steer towards areas of particular knowledge or interest. Taking a neurological approach could mean discussing neuronal mechanisms involved with learning and memory (e.g. forging new synapse connections). It could also involve discussions of cognitive pathways, for instance the functioning of normal versus impaired language centers in the cortex, and language acquisition.

Taking a psychological approach could involve discussing **normal human developmental milestones** and **Piaget's learning stages**. It could also involve a discussion of different types of conditioning (e.g. Pavlov), and how feedback from consequences and rewards influence behaviour. A social psychological discussion may include how individuals take cues from parents and society to learn (though remember the question specifies babies). This is also a chance to discuss any recent research encountered, for instance a new study showing that mother rats lastingly pass down their specific fears to their babies through the scents they emit when reacting to specific triggers.

Q2: What is the best way to measure intelligence?

This is a question about metrics, and there are several ways you could start this answer off. You could **define intelligence** in some way you like, and then set up some systems for measuring that definition of intelligence, or you could start by discussing the concept of intelligence and suggest some ways to constrain both the definition and level of intelligence simultaneously. For instance, you could define intelligence as a set of mental abilities, such as logic, spatial awareness, numeracy and memory and suggest tests of each ability. Or you could mention current intelligence metrics and discuss which abilities they measure and ignore, whether they are representing different societal ideas about intelligence and intelligent figures, and if they work cross-culturally and through time.

For example, using IQ testing as a starting point you could discuss the different types of questions it presents and which people will score high and low (e.g. spatial questions can be a large component of some versions of the test and men often have better spatial reasoning skills). You could discuss some of its advantages (e.g. that it scores on a bell curve with 100 at the center to normalize a sample of test-takers) and disadvantages (e.g. that it is not an absolute scoring system so comparisons may be false). You could discuss related effects, such as the **Flynn Effect** (apparent rising of IQ over time as modern test takers score above average on older IQ tests), and whether these work in the favour of these tests as valid metrics.

Remember that however you argue, you are not setting out to defend a personal viewpoint, but are discussing the strengths and weaknesses of a number of definitions and metrics from different perspectives, including recognizing those ways of thinking which may be Western-centric.

Q3: Are psychiatric diseases like schizophrenia more to do with nature or nurture?

This is a classic nature-nurture question with a psychology twist. A good way to start this question is to define nature and nurture as the genes inherited from parents and the environment exposed to during development. At this point you can showcase some knowledge of schizophrenia; you could perhaps cite the rates of incidence in relatives of schizophrenics versus the general population, or some adoption studies monitoring the incidence of the disease in children raised by their schizophrenic parent or by unaffected adoptive parents. If you have no knowledge of schizophrenia you could **ask if you can generalize** the question to similar psychiatric disorders.

To continue, you might want to discuss the different ways you could be affected by nature and nurture. For instance, you could inherit genes that directly predispose you to schizophrenia or to conditions which make you vulnerable to schizophrenia, such as a related condition or a neurotransmitter imbalance, etc. You could also be **epigenetically affected** through the impact of schizophrenia on lifestyle, for instance leading to damaged DNA in gametes or the transmission of phobias and anxieties in DNA, as has been shown possible in some recent studies. For nurture, you might want to mention in vivo effects of drugs and alcohol or stress and poor nutrition on a developing baby, and after birth, the effects of having an ill parent, such as poor care or trauma as infant, learning bad habits by imitation or other conditioning to an unhealthy mental state, or having a generally bad childhood potentially leaving an individual more disposed to psychiatric conditions. The important part of this question is **breaking down the effects of nature and nurture** in a thorough discussion, rather than demonstrating perfect knowledge of schizophrenia.

Q4: What is synaesthesia? What is its significance?

The first part of this question would allow you to show that you have taken an interest in psychology, particularly if you haven't studied psychology at school, and the second part would show how you reason about the brain. Synaesthesia is a famous neurological abnormality where **stimulation of one sensory or cognitive pathway leads to the automatic stimulation of another**, particularly one not usually associated with the first, for instance the letter 'S' may always seem red or the number '1' may sound like the note middle C. Synaesthesia is a favourite of popular neuroscientist V.S. Ramachandran. If you haven't heard of synaesthesia, say so, you can still answer the second part of the question. Synaesthesia is thought to be caused by **cross-activation of brain regions**, so the most common forms hint at which brain regions are adjacent. This can be then be used for cortex mapping. It also may hint at which cognitions and sensory concepts are processed in similar ways, as the prevalence of some forms and directions of synaesthesia over others may suggest that those cognitions and sensory concepts are encoded similarly in the brain.

Q5: How do we know what we don't know?

This question is designed to push you to think in the abstract, to show that you can work on a problem where all definitive answers are off the table and to see what unique thoughts you can have. Any approach to this question will be individual and rely on your ability to think originally. Some ideas you might want to consider in your answer, if you are stuck, are distinguishing between individual and societal knowledge (e.g. knowing what you don't know by comparing to other members of society), or specific instances of **definable ignorance versus an overall lack of knowledge** (e.g. not knowing someone's phone number versus not knowing there is a great concept in our understanding of physics completely untouched, such as quantum mechanics in the 19th century). You could also take a neurological approach, discussing how the brain fills in gaps in knowledge automatically to reconcile reality to what the brain 'knows', perhaps citing an instance where this malfunctions and renders a situation unknowable.

For instance in anosognosia, where, for example, people suffering a paralyzed limb believe that they are not paralyzed due to a failure in reconciling the dissonance between the command to move a paralyzed limb and the visual feedback that no movement is occurring. Whatever the approach to this question, it is important to show an understanding of the **different types of knowledge** and the different ways we can understand knowledge, both in our own minds and academically.

Q6: Which animal is the most conscious?

This question is clearly aiming at consciousness and our understanding of it, which is known to be the "hard question" of psychology. It is important to define whether by animal the interviewer means only animals or only non-human animals. Should it be the first, the interviewer does not necessarily expect a "right" or a "wrong" answer, it is very difficult to assess whether a chimpanzee or a dolphin is "more" conscious than the other. Indeed, it is very difficult to assess the consciousness of anyone that is not us, even our fellow human beings: the only reason we assume they are conscious is because they tell us so.

A good answer would take into account the **difficulties of defining consciousness** and assessing it in non-verbal creatures. It is also important not to get confused and equate consciousness with intelligence: there might be a good reason to believe that a monkey is "more conscious" than a goldfish, but it is necessary to define the relationship between intelligence and consciousness and not conflate the two. Should the interviewer include humans in the question, it might be worth discussing the **evolutionary importance of consciousness**, how it may have developed to humans and whether "proto-consciousness" can be found in animals. Again, a few sentences highlighting the difficulties of defining and assessing consciousness are needed.

Q7: Does IQ accurately reflect intelligence?

Intelligence is a complicated construct that most people have an opinion of, which makes it difficult to discuss in psychological terms. The question seems to be aiming at two things: first, provoking a discussion on our understanding of intelligence, the many different things it can mean, and how it can mean different things to different people. For example, in some cultures, intelligence may be regarded as something different than what many people in the Western world equate with intelligence. Indeed, upon inspection there might be a large divergence in what individuals within a culture believe intelligence to be. Some issues that may come up are whether there is one intelligence or many, whether intelligence is learned or inherited, whether intelligence can change over time. The second point the question is trying to get at, which is closely related to the previous points, is regarding the **measurement of intelligence**. If you know about IQ and how it is quantified, here is your opportunity to demonstrate your knowledge, always taking into consideration however, that you have to answer the question and not get side tracked. If you do not know about much about IQ, it is your opportunity to deduce what it is from an intelligent conversation: if you had to invent a way to measure intelligence, how would you do it? **The interviewer will help you if you get stuck**, and once you do it try to steer back the conversation to see if the new method wholly covers what you believe is intelligence, examining what the possible pitfalls may be.

Q8: What does activity in the brain really mean?

This question is double edged: on one hand it is an opportunity to demonstrate your knowledge in different brain scanning techniques. If you know a little about functional magnetic resonance imaging, magnetic resonance imaging or other methods to scan for brain activity, here you have the opportunity to demonstrate your knowledge and discuss them. If you happen to not know much about brain scanning methods at the point this question is asked, do not panic for the interviewers are more interested in **how you engage with difficult issues** rather than looking for any concrete knowledge that you may or may not have.

It is indeed a bit of a philosophical question: if we see brain activity in a certain brain region during a certain task, what does it really mean? In many experiments people are told to do a certain task while their brain activity is measured, and certain inferences are made based on the outcome. For example, the **amygdala has become known as the fear centre** of the brain for its strong activity during fear related stimuli. But does this tell us that amygdala activation is both necessary and sufficient for experiencing fear? The brain is an **extraordinarily interconnected system**, is it really possible to isolate individual parts? More importantly, is it possible to isolate psychological processes, such as fear or attention? Just because we subjectively feel that they are isolatable does not mean that they actually are.

Q9: What type of personality does a world leader require?

This sort of question may arise as a prompt to discuss personality, or as an interesting discussion point in places where students are able to study both psychology and politics. Given the priority on psychology, it would be recommended that the answer begin with a **definition of personality**, what it means, what people usually understand it to mean, and perhaps on how it can be measured. Once you feel you have covered your bases, it would be interesting to incorporate the answer as to what a world leader would require. World leaders, be it in business or politics, generally need to be **charismatic and able to convince people** to work for them. Does this mean that they have to have a highly empathetic personality? On the other hand, these leaders often have to make difficult decisions that involve considerable sacrifices. Does this mean they need a **particular sort of empathy** that helps them understand individuals but not care too much about them? If we assume so, how does this fit into the personality structures that exist? How would one measure this? World leaders are generally thought to be intelligent: is intelligence part of a personality?

Q10: Are subjective reports from people who have experienced psychedelic drugs a good way to understand cognition?

In the early days of psychology, a lot of research was performed on subjective reports of individuals. The problem with this research was that it was difficult to verify and confirm, and was not objective due to its very nature. Psychological research then attempted to move on to more objective measures, such as behaviour, which many people believe was a very important step towards establishing the validity of psychology as a science. On the other hand, interesting psychological constructs, such as consciousness, are very difficult to experiment on objectively. Drugs are interesting because by chemically altering the way the brain works, experimenters can make deductions about how the brain works. For example, most **psychotropic substances alter time perception**, which could be used to determine whether time perception depends on a specific part of the brain, or whether it is a broader function involving several parts of the brain. In addition, if a particular substance affects both certain types of vision and certain types of movement, it could be assumed that the two are somehow linked together. That being said, there are ethical questions raised by a reliance on psychotropic substances in a research setting, such as their almost ubiquitous illegality or their effect on health, which should be taken into account before research is done in this way.

Q11: What can people with autism teach us about the way we think about others?

Autism spectrum disorder is characterised by a wide variety of cognitive and behavioural symptoms, most characteristically problems in social issues. For example, people with autism are often thought to be highly interested in routines and numbers (e.g. a train schedule) whereas they seem to show very little interest towards other human beings, or other games children like to play, like role playing games. By studying the problems that people with autism have, we can perhaps get an insight in how healthy people think about others. It is well known that people with autism have trouble **identifying and understanding human emotion** from a very early age.

This can tell us many things, perhaps the most important of which is the realisation that it is surprisingly intuitive and easy for us to perform highly complicated tasks such as understanding what other people are feeling and why. By studying the development of autistic children, and identifying the errors that they make compared to the errors of healthy children we might be able to identify the mental processes that are behind our intuitive social appraisals and understand at what point and why they start to differ.

Q12: Why do we know that we think?

This question can be answered in a vast variety of ways, my answer will approach it from an evolutionary psychology point of view. First of all, I would like to point out that it is possible to dispute the premise of the question: we indeed know that we think, but often we overestimate exactly how aware we are of our mental processes. Psychology researchers looking at decision making have discovered that human beings are quite unaware of how they come to decisions, and how extraneous factors, such as the irrelevant number they had been presented earlier can affect their decisions. This is important, for one could also argue it is better to ask: "why do we think we know that we think".

Nonetheless, it is safe to assume that **we do indeed have a certain degree of awareness of our own thoughts**, and I propose two reasons why this may have developed. First, this awareness may have developed in human beings because it helps us understand why we behave in the way we do, which facilitates complex tasks like making tools or solving problems (i.e. I am looking for sharp stones so I can make an arrow that can kill an animal which I can then eat). Secondly, humans are highly social animals, and knowing why we do things may help us understand why others do things, which can provide us with a competitive advantage.

Q13: Is asking people about their personality a good way to find out about their personality?

First of all it is necessary to distinguish what the question means by personality. The construct of personality is defined in a myriad of ways, but it is generally believed to be a group of individual characteristics, usually thought to be relatively stable over time, which can be used to predict and explain behaviour. Taking that into account, most personality tests, such as the Big 5, take the approach of asking individuals a set of questions and scoring the answers in order to place the individual along different dimensions of personality or in different groups. This has some merits: the resulting values are quite stable over time (if you take the same test a week apart you get the same result), between individuals (if you take the test and a good friend takes the test answering he or she thinks you would, you can expect the results to be quite similar) and can be used to predict behaviour to a certain extent.

However, there are a few downsides to asking people questions to determine their personality. First, it **assumes that people are aware of what their personality is**. Cognitive psychological research, particularly in decision making, has demonstrated that people are very unaware of many things we would intuitively consider to be consciously accessible information. Secondly, it assumes that people will answer accurately questions relating to personality (they may be biased to answer in a certain way, or to please the person asking, or to stick to cultural norms). Other, new methods, such as those which rely on using behavioural footprints online, have recently become increasingly accurate in predicting the personality of individuals.

Q14: Do different people behave similarly in similar situations?

This question is hinting at the person situation debate in psychology, in which psychologists long debated whether an individual's personality or the situation is more predictive of behaviour. On one hand, influential studies like Stanley Milgram's electrocution experiments and Phillip Zimbardo's Stanford prison experiment showed that ordinary individuals are prone to act in extraordinary ways in certain circumstances, supporting the claim that the situation is more important than the person. On the other hand, as many other researchers pointed out, not even in those experiments did everyone behave in the same way, and there are various reasons to believe that the methodology of the study did not quite support the arguments made by the original researchers. For example, people who are keen to participate in a "prison experiment" are likely to be different than most people. Of course, it seems to be true that both factors matter: both the person and the situation.

Overall, different people often behave similarly in similar situations because **in most cases it makes sense to do so**: if we had to think explicitly about what to do every time we do something, everything we do would involve a significant amount of effort. Therefore it makes sense to copy others or follow certain behavioural schemas in many situations, not least because it is expected from us by other people. That being said, it is fairly evident that different people do tend to behave differently in the same situation, which is perhaps evidenced by the range of different behaviours interviewers witness in the interview setting.

Q15: Why do we sometimes hear things that are not there and how is this related to schizophrenia?

What we perceive the world to be is not so much what is actually out there but rather the reality that our brain constructs out of our sensory inputs: our vision, our hearing, our tactile input, etc. This is an extraordinarily complex process, as **there is a lot of noise in the world** and our brain is constantly engaged in separating the useful information from the less useful information, and to do so it often makes inferences, such as assuming that an unheard word was based on the context.

In some cases, these inferences are incorrect, even for healthy individuals, for example when one wrongly thinks someone said your name. Importantly, these inferences are dependent on a considerable amount of prior beliefs, such as what sort of word fits in a particular sentence or what sort of things people say.

Schizophrenics are known to sometimes have auditory hallucinations, often appearing in the form of persecutory voices. It is possible that schizophrenics hear voices that are not there because they have trouble making the correct inferences, perhaps confusing their own internal beliefs with outside stimuli. In this case, **auditory hallucinations might be the product of a highly effective but imperfect system** (hence the mistakes made by healthy individuals) which is incorrectly calibrated in the case of schizophrenia.

Course-Work Interviews

When applying to do Biological Natural Sciences (including Experimental Psychology) at Cambridge, or possibly Biology or Psychology at Oxford, an applicant may be asked to submit course-work and called for a course-work interview. Usually in the morning on the day of the interview, this work is submitted and read by the interviewer. The work is used as a basis for discussion of research and experimental methods and analysis.

The interviewer may open by asking for a summary of the piece of work, of the methodology behind it, and the results obtained. They may then ask some follow-up questions related to the work, or the subject matter. This part of the interview will be very individual and depend on the nature and subject of the work submitted.

After the discussion of the work, the interviewer will probably guide the conversation toward some questions about experimental methods and analysis to test the applicant's ability to think like a scientist. For example:

Q16: How would you test if a rat can differentiate colours?

Answering this question would involve suggesting model experiments and how to analyse the data. Perhaps the rats could be presented with **different-coloured tiles**, and when they step on one of the colours they receive a treat. As the tiles are removed and replaced in new positions, the number of times the rats stepped on the food-giving colour could be counted, and this data analysed for a significant correlation. The point of these questions is to suggest different ideas, and to show an understanding of their strengths and weakness and an ability to use data usefully.

Q17: Data shows that bats and moles have the same size and body weight but different sized brains. How could you explain this?

Those of you knowledgeable about bats may immediately think of their brain-power-demanding echolocation, and it's OK to say this idea, but remember to think like a scientist and make sure you aren't jumping to conclusions. This is a chance for you to ask testable questions which may constrain the answer. Ask first: Which brain is bigger? Is the whole brain bigger or is one part, such as the cortex, disproportionately large? Then perhaps: Is it the brain which is too large/small for the animal's body size, or the body which is too large/small for the brain size. You might then use specific knowledge of mole (e.g. lives in dark) and bat (flies) life-habit, and of brain function in relation to size to give all of the possible justified answers to these questions, and maybe **design simple tests to rule out certain answers or favour others**.

Psychology Interview Questions

211. What is involved in phantom limb syndrome?
212. Why haven't you applied for Medicine?
213. How can you treat phantom limb syndrome?
214. Explain why perception of pain might rise steeply as stimulation increases and level off at the top (shown a graph).
215. How would you create a model of the human brain?
216. What makes a face special?
217. Tell me something interesting about one of the Oliver Sacks books you read.
218. Why does experimental psychology appeal to you?
219. Shown some data from a possible psychology experiment - how would you go about interpreting this?
220. Could we ever make a computer as complex as the human brain?
221. What aspects of psychology interest you most?
222. Are our phenotypes due to nature or nurture?
223. Do you think children are born with their IQ naturally, or can this be developed?
224. What is consciousness? How do you know if you are conscious?
225. Can fishes hear sound?
226. Where does neuroscience begin and psychology end?
227. What does heroine do to the brain?
228. To what extent do you agree with Freud?
229. Can machines make decisions?
230. Should a chimpanzee have human rights?
231. Should interviews be used for selection?

PHYSICAL SCIENCES

The core of a subject interview in the physical sciences, mathematics or engineering is almost certain to be technical questions based on the subject material. Usually these are not the odd or general questions that Oxbridge is rumoured to pose, but precisely defined questions that **test your technical knowledge of your subject and your ability to apply it**. The problems may be new or push problem-solving skills further than school questions, but for most questions it will be clear what the task is and you will have to use knowledge from school to get to an answer.

There is no absolute formula for how to approach these questions, as they will are highly subject to change and the method for one isn't transferable to others. A general point is to never give up – once you are there at the interview all you can do is try your hardest; giving up means certain failure. Nevertheless, this doesn't mean you shouldn't prepare! By working through the questions in this book, you'll get a much more comprehensive understanding of what admissions tutors are looking for as well as the style & difficulty of the questions you might get asked.

Remember that you may have interviews in other related subjects - not just for the subject you are applying for. This is particularly important if you've applied for Natural Science at Cambridge, so read all the relevant sections to ensure you don't get caught out.

Unusual Questions

Beyond questions relying on specialist knowledge, you may be asked questions to test your reasoning and problem-solving skills. These may test numeracy, logic or estimation abilities, where you are expected to rely on your wits rather than anything specific you learned in school. **Estimation questions are particularly important for scientists and engineers** as they show a command of skills essential to these disciplines. Solving an estimation problem requires an ability to co-opt general day-to-day knowledge, and most importantly, to use simplifying assumptions and where possible correct for these. For any science or engineering problem it is never possible to account for every variable- assumptions must be made (e.g. 'assuming no air resistance'). The ability to make sensible and helpful assumptions without radically changing the problem is essential to all work in science. Though applicants are often warned about 'weird' questions, even an unexpected question will almost certainly be relevant to the subject or the ongoing discussion in an interview.

Worked Questions

Below are a few examples of how to start breaking down an interview question, complete with model answers.

Q1: How did the Ancient Greek astronomer Aristarchus determine how much further the Sun is from the Earth than the Moon is?

This question is already giving you a big hint by mentioning the moon – asking you to compare two linear distances, Earth-Sun and Earth-Moon, already suggests that this may be a question about triangles. You may be given the second hint you need by your interviewer, if your mind hasn't already wandered to the most apparent lunar phenomenon – the phases of the moon.

This may have seemed like a random or difficult question at first, but once you have brain-stormed and are thinking both about triangles and about the phases of the moon, how to answer this question may be obvious. If you still aren't sure what the phases of the moon have to do with this question, consider why they occur (and don't say something stupid like 'the shadow of the Earth on the moon', because what is a lunar eclipse?). Draw a diagram of how the phases of the moon work including the sun, Earth and moon in the figure. Recognize that there is a time (quarter-moon) when Sun-Moon-Earth forms a right-angle. Remember also that **the sun and moon can be in the sky together**, and at this time you can measure the angle Sun-Earth-Moon. Work out the Sun-Earth distance using a sine function of the angle and the Earth-Moon distance.

Aristarchus found distance Sun-Earth to be more than 40 times Earth-Moon, which is more than an order of magnitude too small, but is the right method. End with a discussion of which assumptions your model made (e.g. the sun is close enough that the angle of light on the moon and Earth is measurably different) and what the sources of error for Aristarchus would have been (e.g. the sun is very bright so hard to measure, it's hard to say when exactly it is quarter-moon, the measured angle would be very close to 90 degrees, etc.).

Q2: How much does the Earth weigh?

This is a fantastic illustration of the power of simplifying assumptions. It is possible to **get extremely close to the correct answer with no specialist knowledge**. Consider this approach:

Method 1:
I'm going to use $Mass = Density \times Volume$
The interviewer would tell you that the Earth's radius is approximately 6,000 Km.
Thus, Volume of the Earth $= \frac{4}{3}\pi r^3 = \frac{4}{3} \times \pi \times (6,000,000)^3$
You can approximate π to 3 to give: $V = 4 \times 216 \times 10^{18} \approx 10^{21} \ m^3$

The majority of the Earth core is made up of Iron and since that is very dense, it probably contributes the most to the Earth's average density. I know that the density of water is 1,000 kg/m^3 and I'll assume that iron is 10 times as dense as Water.

Thus the average density of Earth $\approx 10^4 kg/m^3$

Therefore, the Mass of the Earth $\approx 10^{21}$ x $10^4 = 10^{25} kg$

Method 2:
A good physics student should also be able to use the fact that the moon orbits the Earth to calculate it's mass.

Since the moon is approximately the same distance away from the Earth during it's orbit, the **resultant force acting on the moon must = 0.** Thus:

Gravitational Attraction between Moon and Earth + Centripetal Force = 0

$$\frac{Gm_1 m_2}{r^2} + \frac{m_2 v^2}{r} = 0$$

$$\frac{Gm_1 m_2}{r^2} = \frac{m_2 v^2}{r}$$

$$\frac{Gm_1}{r} = v^2$$

Therefore, Mass of the Earth, $m_1 = \frac{v^2 r}{G}$

At this point, the interviewer would probably stop you as the only thing stopping you from proceeding is knowing the moon's velocity and the distance between the Earth and moon.

A harsh interviewer may not give these to you immediately in which case you might have to use some general knowledge- e.g. it take light one second to travel from the moon to Earth.

Thus, $r = 1$ x 3 x $10^8 = 3$ x $10^8 m$

If you assume that the moon has a circular orbit, you could also use this to calculate the moon's velocity:

$$Orbital\ Velocity = \frac{Orbital\ Distance}{Time\ for\ one\ Orbit} = \frac{2\pi r}{1\ month}$$

$$v = \frac{6\ x\ 3\ x\ 10^8\ metres}{1\ x\ 30\ x\ 24\ x\ 60\ x\ 60\ seconds} = \frac{1.8\ x\ 10^9}{2.6\ x\ 10^6}$$

$$= 0.7\ x\ 10^3 = 700\ ms^{-1}$$

Finally: $m_1 = \dfrac{v^2 r}{G} = \dfrac{(700)^2 x\ 3\ x10^8}{6.67\ x\ 10^{-11}}$

$$m_1 = \frac{4.9\ x\ 10^5 x\ 3\ x10^{19}}{6.67} = \frac{15\ x\ 10^{24}}{6.67}$$

$$= 2.25\ x\ 10^{24} kg$$

[Real Answer: $6\ x\ 10^{24} kg$]

Q3: What are the odds that two members of a five person family share a birthday?
This is a probability questions that is testing two things: 1) basic numeracy, in this case a grasp of probability, 2) the ability to interpret words into equations. This second point is very important to physical scientists, engineers and mathematicians alike, but particularly to physicists and engineers who must throughout their degree take real-world problems and interpret them as equations which can be solved mathematically, so being able to demonstrate this ability is essential. It is also necessary to **make simplifying, yet not strictly true, assumptions**, such as that all birthdays are equally likely (babies are more likely to be born on days favourable for tax reasons, and less likely to be born on 'unlucky' dates).

To solve the problem consider the complementary case, that no one shares a birthday. The likelihood of the second person not sharing the first person's birthday is 364/365, the likelihood of the third person not sharing either of the first two birthdays is 363/365, etc. As the events are independent they are multiplied to find the overall probability that none share a birthday, about 97/100. The chance that any do share a birthday is thus 3/100.

Q4: Three prisoners stand in a line. They can look at the men ahead, but cannot turn to see those behind themselves. A hat is placed on each man's head from a bag they are told contains three red and two green hats. If any man can say the colour of his own hat, which he cannot see, all three will go free, and if any man gets the answer wrong they will all be executed. The third prisoner gives no answer when asked, and neither does the second, but the first man says, "I know the colour of my hat." What colour did he say?

This is a classic 'Hat problem' logic puzzle. In answering this question you can show that you can approach a problem logically and methodically, and choose an appropriate method which will lead to an answer. You can also demonstrate that you can interpret and extract the important pieces of a chunk of verbal information.

One approach is to list and eliminate the possible hat combinations given the problem statement. There are eight possible hat combinations for three people: RRR, GGG, RRG, GGR, RGR, GRG, GRR and RGG. GGG is not possible as there are only two hats, leaving seven options. The third prisoner can see the two in front of him, but remains silent. If both hats he could see were green he would know that his is red, so it cannot be RGG (assuming prisoner three is on the left). Prisoner two can see prisoner one. If the first prisoner had a green hat the only options remaining would be GRG and RRG, either of which gives prisoner two a red hat. He remains silent, so these are eliminated. All remaining options (RRR, RGR, GRR, GGR) give the first prisoner a red hat so he says, "My hat is red."

Practising these questions is both easier and harder than subject-related questions. If you struggle with using logic and reasoning, these questions may be very difficult for you, even with practice. On the other hand, they are **easy to practice and make-up in day-to-day life**, and if you get the reasoning skills down, you can apply them to many questions. As you go about your day ask yourself little questions to practice: How much does that tree weigh? How many gumballs in that machine? Or get yourself a book of riddles and logic problems and have a go on the way to school. You may already be familiar with shorter version of this type of question from Thinking Skills Assessment (TSA) practice.

Experimental Interviews

The specific interview types and testing procedures vary from college to college, but it is possible that a physical scientist or engineer will be called for an Experiment-based interview or a course-work interview. This type of interview is **based on experimental work done at school**. The applicant will submit a project or Experiment Logbook written at school, or be asked to bring it to the interview. The interviewer will ask questions using this work as a basis.

This type of interview can go in many directions, as it is personalized to the student. Be prepared to discuss a favourite experiment or one of the interviewer's choosing. A discussion of an experiment may start with your description of the aims and general method. You may be asked detailed questions about the methodology. It is likely that you will be asked about your conclusions and discussion. This is not the time to try cover up your mistakes or make your conclusions seem exceptional. This is your chance to be self-critical and correct your own mistakes and errors to show that you are capable of thinking like a scientist. Don't worry about pointing out your own errors to your interviewer – they have almost certainly already noticed them, and this is your chance to show that you noticed them too and would know how to improve if you had another chance. When pointing out mistakes, highlight the ones that you wouldn't make again because you have grown as an experimenter or because you later realized a flaw in the methodology. Don't point out your own sloppiness or laziness, that time you rushed the experiment because you wanted to leave or got the wrong answer because you couldn't be bothered to get out your ruler and calculator.

The discussion may diverge from your own work to general questions about experimental design or theory questions about topics covered. If asked about designing your own experiments have many suggestions and critique your own ideas. The point of these questions isn't to come up with the perfect experiment, but to **show that you can have original ideas** and that you can see the strengths and weakness of different approaches.

CHEMISTRY

In your chemistry interview, your knowledge of a range of topics could be tested, as well as your ability to apply your understanding of specific cases to other situations. The questions could be drawn from any part of the curriculum, so there is no way to revise just the area you will be tested on. There is no specific way to prepare for the example types of questions given in this chapter, or the similar styles of question that could be derived from other parts of the curriculum. The important thing is to have a **sound understanding of not just specific instances you have rote-learned for exams, but the chemical principles that underlie them**. When you do your revision for your interview, make sure you always ask why certain results are achieved – don't just learn that a certain compound is less reactive, make sure you know why that is. If you don't know, then ask your teacher about the underlying principles, or even better, try to figure out the answer yourself to practice this way of thinking.

For instance, you could be asked questions about chemical formulae and their relation to structure and physical or chemical properties. For this style of question you may be asked to **draw the chemical formula** for an ionic compound and a covalent compound, and then asked to draw the formula for something in-between like Al_3O_6. You could also be asked to draw in detail each atom with electrons and describe their distribution in the shells and Bohr's theories explaining this behaviour.

Alternatively, you could be asked to draw an organic compound from the formula and asked about the physical properties you would expect. This could be a compound you are expected to be familiar with. Then, you could be asked to draw other compounds with similar properties, or how you would alter the original compound for a new property. You could be given a made up chemical formula and asked to draw a suggestion for how it may be structured to have certain properties. You could be asked about the **nature of any bonds**, or how properties might change for enantiomers.

Your knowledge around the subject might be tested by asking about a well-known case, such as Thalidomide or hydrocarbon fractionation. Moving away from chemical structures and properties, you could be asked **calculation-based questions**, such as molar equations or thermodynamics (entropy and enthalpy, reaction rates, phase changes, etc.). Given the nature of the interview, you are unlikely to get an in depth calculation-based question.

However, knowledge of these topics might be necessary to answer questions such as: How would you balance these reactions? Which reaction would proceed faster? Which reaction would you expect to occur spontaneously? Would you expect either to reach equilibrium? Which conditions would you change to change your answer? The important thing is not to have the right answer, but to show you can reason through unfamiliar examples using your knowledge of the principles.

As it is an experimental subject, your knowledge of experimental techniques and examples could be tested. Make sure you **revise the material and methods used in experiments and practicals**, in case you are asked specific questions about designing an experiment or interpreting results. An example of this is being asked to design an experiment to identify an unknown organic acid. This might involve an understanding of titration curves for mono-, di-, and tri-protic acids and how to generate them in the lab, or a number of other topics you may have covered in experiments.

As an extension of this, be familiar with the techniques that were used to discover the facts and theories in your textbooks, you could be asked how they were discovered or how you would verify they are true.

One Maths question is also likely to come up in the interview. Maths represents a significant portion of most Oxbridge science courses and skills like sketching, differentiating and integrating are skills that will be necessary throughout much of your scientific education. Thus, it is advisable to also read the mathematics section in this book.

Worked Questions

Below are a few examples of how to start breaking down an interview question, complete with model answers.

They are by no means an exhaustive list, but they give a sense of how A level material can be used as a basis for questions that require independent thought and problem-solving skills. Use these examples as a guide of what topics to revise and the style of questions that may arise.

Q1: How was the composition of the sun determined?

This is a common example, so you may be expected to be somewhat familiar with it. Don't be discouraged if you are not though, the interviewer may be even more impressed if you can reach a reasonable answer all on your own. The gist of this question is to use spectral analysis and knowledge of the theories underlying it to determine the sun's composition using its own light. Spectral analysis is based in Bohr's work – as light passes through an atom, the energy in the photons passes to the electrons in the outermost shell, shifting them to higher energy levels. As they return to their original position they release the energy.

Since energy levels in the atom are discrete, from **Einstein's photoelectric effect** the energy is known to produce a specific frequency of light. The atoms which make up the sun are being constantly energized to plasma, so the frequencies they would have emitted as their electrons returned to original positions are absent from the spectrum of light the sun emits. By comparing the spectra emitted by known elements to the gaps in the sun's spectrum, it is clear that hydrogen and helium are the main elements. This question only relies on basic knowledge of vital chemical principles, but requires the applicant to use these in practice, and being familiar with common experimental techniques is helpful.

Q2: You receive a small sample of a human bone of unknown age and place of origin. How might you constrain these parameters?

Hopefully, seeing the word 'age' instantly makes you think **'isotopes'** - this is a question about radiometric dating and isotope fractionation. To answer the first part, you might want to start with a description of isotopes and radioactivity and write an expression for radioactive decay. But, the question asks for something more — it is pushing you to **explain experimentally** how you determine the age. This includes choosing an appropriate isotope system (in this case Carbon has an appropriately long half-life) and describing how mass spectrometers are used to find isotopic ratios. This is a difficult question if you have no knowledge of experimental techniques, but even if you don't know the specifics, show that you understand the difference between general theory and practice.

The second part of this question, the place of origin, is a chance to show you have cross-subject knowledge, or to show you can have ideas even when you are out of your depth. One sample answer is to look at the ratio of Carbon-12 and Carbon-13. Recent bones from North America will contain more C-13 relative to C-12 than European bones because of the much greater use of corn. Those with biology knowledge may remember that corn is a C4 plant which takes in a higher proportion of C-13. This is just one example that shows how you can integrate your specific knowledge base into an original answer.

Q3: Which of the two molecules below is more acidic? What factors make this the case?

This question is introducing the candidate to the idea that the **concept of acidity** can be applied to more molecules than just the classic "acids" you learn at school.

A good candidate would first define acidity:

$$HA \rightleftharpoons H^+ + A^-$$

Then need to **highlight the key reactive areas** on each of the molecules and assign how each of the molecules would behave when behaving as an acid. In this case both molecules form $RO^- + H^+$ as the products. The crux of this problem is that the stability of MeO^- is greater than $(Me)_3CO^-$ which is because the O^- is more stable in A.

Methyl groups are electron donating groups and in molecule (B) there are three Me groups pushing onto the carbon bonded to the oxygen therefore this carbon is more electron rich than molecule (A) so destabilises the O^-. Therefore, the equilibrium for molecule (B) in water is more shifted towards ROH rather than RO^- so molecule A is more acidic than molecule B. A good candidate will also then link this to equilibrium constants.

$$K_a = \frac{[H_3O^+]_{eq}[A^-]_{eq}}{[HA]_{eq}}$$

This question should not be too difficult - good students would be expected to give a comprehensive answer that synthesises multiple chemistry principles from the A level syllabus. This question tests how comfortable people are with these principles and if they can use them in different scenarios.

Q4: How do these two molecules react? Draw the mechanism.

This should be a really simple question to start with. The candidate should acknowledge the rich area of electron density in the alkene will attack a Cl atom in the symmetrical Cl-Cl causing the bond to break and form a Cl⁻ anion.

Then the candidate needs to explain **why the double bond breaks** in such a way to leave the positive charge on the carbon with one Me group and one Cl atom, this is because the Me groups are electron donating so push electron density onto that carbon and stabilise the positive charge. Also need to comment that F more electronegative than Cl therefore the Cl-C bond is less polar.

The route that is normally taught in A level is that the Cl⁻ anion then quenches the positive charge which is then localised on that carbon and forms the product. This however is not strictly the case. A standard candidate should be able to answer this question, the second part however will assess a standard candidate compared to a good one.

Q4b: The reaction drawn above is actually not complete. What else can quench that positive charge instead of the Cl⁻ ? Explain the new path mechanistically.

Here the candidate should recognise that the Cl⁻ anion is not the only nucleophile and actually the Cl atom in the molecule can actually donate a lone pair of electrons and stabilise the reactive intermediate. It forms a **cyclo intermediate** with the positive charge now more delocalised but strictly speaking primarily localised on the Cl atom. A good candidate will remark that this intermediate happens almost immediately when the carbocation is formed because **intramolecular reactions happen faster than intermolecular reactions**, as intermolecular reactions require a collision between the two molecules.

This cyclised intermediate is then attacked by the Cl⁻ anion and relieves the steric strain of the 3 membered ring. The reaction still takes place on the same carbon because it has a lower activation energy than if the ring was opened up the other way. This forms the same product as in the original reaction mechanism. This question is a typical example of taking what a student already should know and analysing something a bit deeper.

Q5: Ketones and aldehydes in aqueous solution are typically hydrated following the mechanism below. The extent a ketone/aldehyde is hydrated is dominated by numerous factors. Discuss the extent of hydration of each of the molecules below and order them from most hydrated to least.

The addition of water is reversible and happens via proton transfer. The candidate should recognise the thermodynamic stability of the carbonyl versus the hydrate, which will determine the percentage of hydrate at equilibrium. This reaction is under thermodynamic control. The candidate should first discuss the percentage of hydrate for **an aldehyde vs. a ketone**.

Ketones are less likely to be hydrated than the equivalent aldehyde, this is because of greater steric hindrance in molecule (B) vs. molecule (D). There is repulsion between the two Me groups as they are so close in space when the hydrate is formed as they are forced together on forming a tetrahedral hydrate. This causes the equilibrium to be towards the starting material for molecule B.

For molecule C the candidate should acknowledge that there is a lot of strain in cyclopropanone, the C=O forces the molecule to be in the same plane and the bond angles to be very small. With the addition of water to molecule (C) the steric strain is released and it can form a more stable tetrahedral molecule with an increased bond angle of $109.5°$. Therefore the equilibrium   constant   for   this   reaction   is   extremely   large. For molecule (A) the candidate should comment on the effects of three Cl atoms, which are electron withdrawing groups due to being more electronegative than C. The inductive effect of the Cl atoms increases the reactivity of the C=O (a larger δ^+ on the C) as less electron density on neighbouring carbon atom (CCl_3) and so the water is even more strongly attracted the C in C=O and therefore has a large hydration constant.

Therefore the ordering is as follows: C, A, D, B

The discussion here is more important in some respects than the ordering. But it is also testing candidates' ability to assess the dominance and importance of different factors. It would also be advisable that the candidate draw out the whole mechanism as this will show that they understand how this reaction happens and also will actually help them answer this question.

Q6: Explain mechanistically how this reaction happens?

The candidate needs to analyse what will attack the acid, "H^+", i.e. what is the best nucleophile in the system. The Br-Br bond is not going to break by itself so it is not that so has to be the ketone. The lone pair of electrons on the oxygen attacks the H^+.

The resulting molecule can be stabilised by losing the relatively acidic proton alpha to the C=O. Thus creating an enol, ketones in acidic condition are always in equilibrium with their enol form. The stability and where the equilibrium lies depends on the molecule. The enol form however can go on and actually productively react with Br_2.

This molecule here can then attack Br-Br. Like with electrophilic addition, the electron density is going to come from the double bond and break the Br-Br sigma bond. In this instance there is an additional driving factor, the lone pair on the oxygen can feed into the double bond and kick start the reaction with Br_2.

At this point the candidate is basically there and just needs to point out that Br⁻ can attack the protonated ketone and form the product. This reaction step is not in equilibrium. Unlike the enolisation, once the enol has reacted with Br₂ it is irreversible..

Q7: Order these atoms in decreasing first ionisation energy: Al, Ba, S, O, P and Mg.

It is first necessary to **define first ionisation energy**: X(g) + e⁻ -> X⁻(g). The candidate should remark that O and S are both in group 16, Mg and Ba are both in group 2 Al and P are in the same row as each other as well as S and Mg. Recognition of this will help the candidate compare each of the atoms and have a nice structure.

There are two factors playing each other off in this question and the candidate has to weigh them out. The first factor is that in general the ionisation energy across a period increases, due to an increase in effective nuclear charge. The nucleus is becoming more positively charged with the increase in protons and the outmost electrons are experiencing a similar shielding affect as they are filling up the same principle quantum number. The valence electrons are attracted more strongly and pulled in closer to the nucleus. The other factor here is that the first ionisation energy decreases as you go down a group. Although the nuclear charge increases, the valence electrons are shielded by the greater number of inner electron shells. Thus, the **valence electrons are further away from the nucleus**.

A **poor candidate** may get confused at the last point and predict that the ionisation energy increases down a group, the interviewer will check to see that they are comfortable with these two factors.

With this you can thus conclude that O will have a higher first ionisation energy than S and Mg will have a higher first ionisation energy than Ba. Ba is last because the first ionisation energy means that a valence electron is removed from 6s orbital which is much more shielded than for Mg [He]$3s^2$ which loses an electron in 3s, [Ar]$3s^2$. You can also conclude that Mg has a lower ionisation energy than Al, [Ar] $3s^2 3p^1$ which in turn has a lower ionisation energy than P and S, P [Ar] $3s^2 3p^3$ and S [Ar] $3s^2 3p^4$.

The last factor that needs to be deduced is comparing P and S. P $3p^3$ vs S $3p^4$. The candidate needs to recognise that whilst S has a larger **effective nuclear charge** than P, in fact the first ionisation energy for P is larger than that of S. p energy level is comprised of 3 orbitals, p_x, p_y and p_z, Phosphorus had 3 electrons each in the three respective p orbitals, Sulphur $3p^4$ has 2 single electrons and one orbital has paired electrons. This is a less favourable electronic configuration, undergoing ionisation removes the **electron-electron repulsion** and so rather favourable.

The order is therefore: O→ P → S→ Mg → Al → Ba.

Q8: Draw the shapes of the following molecules: CH$_4$, PF$_5$, SF$_6$, ClF$_3$ and SF$_4$.

The logic for working out each of these shapes is the same. First work out the **valence electrons** on the central atom. This tells you the area of negative charge around that atom. Then work out how many electrons each other atom gives to the central one – in single covalent bonds it is 1 electron that is being donated. Pair the electrons up and work out the number of areas of negative charge around the atom and then this will indicate the shape of the molecule.

The first 3 molecules should be quite easy and will test to see if the candidate understands the basic principles; which can then be used to solve the latter molecules.

CH₄: Carbon 4 electrons, 4 x 1 e⁻ from each H. Therefore 4 areas of negative charge, no lone pairs. So the shape is tetrahedral.

PF₅: P 5e⁻ , F 5 x e⁻ so 5 areas of negative charge so trigonal bipyramidal.

SF₆: S 6e⁻ , F 6 x e⁻ so 6 areas of negative charge so octahedral.

ClF₃: Cl 7e⁻, F 3 x e⁻ , 5 areas of negative charge , two of which are lone pairs, so is a trigonal bipyramidal structure but lone pair –lone pair repulsion greater than bond pair – lone pair and bond pair – bond pair therefore the two lone pairs take up more room, creating a "t-shaped" molecule

SF$_4$: S 6e$^-$, F 4 x e$^-$, so 5 areas of negative charge, this time one lone pair of electrons. Candidate should remark that the lone pair of electrons goes in the equatorial position as is statistically further away from all other bond paired electrons. Again this shape is based on trigonal bypramidal but is called a "see saw" molecular structure.

Q10: Why are metals, in particular transition metals, coloured?

Octrahedral splitting for transition metals:

Candidates may comment on the following features:

➤ **Changes in oxidation state** lead to different colours - as the oxidation state changes so does the configuration of electrons in the d-orbitals.
➤ The **absorption of white light** can lead to different colours. In aqueous solution the d-orbitals split into two, but are still relatively close together. When certain wavelengths of light are absorbed, electrons in lower energy levels are excited to higher ones as they have the right energy match. The remaining photons then pass through and cause the metal to be coloured.

> The **shape of the molecule** affects the colour as it results in different electron arrangements in the d-orbitals. I.e. tetrahedral complexes are different colours to that of octahedral.

> The **nature of the ligand** itself will affect the colour – the greater the splitting of the d-orbitals, the more energy will be needed to promote electrons in the lower d-orbitals to the higher ones.

> The **wavelength of light**: shorter wavelength absorption means that the colour of the complex will tend towards the blue end of the spectrum.

Q11: Draw for me and describe a phase diagram for a hydrocarbon, pointing out key characteristics of the graph and what you can deduce from it.

A Phase diagram shows the melting, boiling and sublimation curve of a substance and also the triple point. Candidate should end up discussing all of the points highlighted below on the graph. The important thing to note is that **the substance is in equilibrium between gas and liquid**. If they do not know what one is the examiner may draw the graph and then expect the candidate to analyse it. A question on differentiation may also be asked to calculate the melting point.

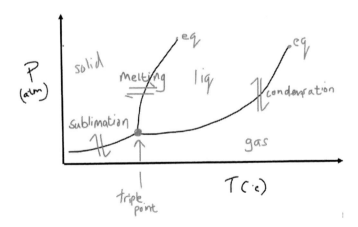

Q11b: what would this diagram look like for water?

This is slightly discussed at A level so shouldn't be too challenging, but the phase diagram may not have been drawn before. The key thing to note is that ice takes up more volume than water (liquid), this is due to hydrogen bonding. This intermolecular force is very strong and favourable and causes the H_2O molecules to align themselves in a certain arrangement so each molecule can have two hydrogen bonds each. **When ice melts, these hydrogen bonds are broken** and so the water molecules can get closer together. This should then lead to the negative gradient of the melting equilibrium line.

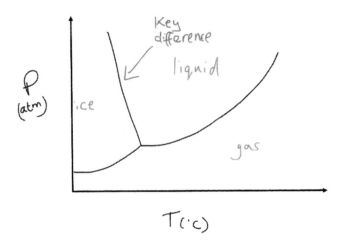

Q12: Describe for me what a ball in a 2D box (or well) would be like if it could only move along the x axis and was between two infinitely high potential energy walls. Therefore only potential energy is applicable on the ball. What would happen to the ball?

The candidate should start by drawing a potential well drawing the y axis and noting that it has infinite potential energy. The ball (analogy of a particle in a 1D box of Schrodinger's equation) can only move in the x axis direction and since only potential energy is acting on the particle it will vibrate back and forth.

Key things for candidates to note are that **the ball will not be able to move out of the 2D box,** when it approaches the y axis there is an infinitesimally large potential force acted on it and thus is repelled. Also note that the balls potential energy would stay at the same level since no other force is acting on it.

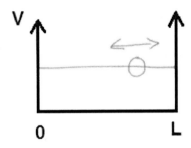

Q12b: Where is the ball statistically most likely to be found inside this potential well?

Here we are treating the ball as a particle and therefore if you label the x axis say 0 to length L then the most probable place of finding the ball would be in the middle of the box i.e. L/2. This is applying a classic physics principle in what is a **quantum physics problem**. The ball passes through the middle the most and so is therefore most likely to be found here.

Chemistry Interview Questions

232. Draw the structure of Al_3O_6.
233. How do the double bonds in this hydrocarbon affect its solubility?
234. Can you draw an alkane where every carbon atom is in a different NMR environment?
235. Can you think of any ways that playing in your school band would make you better at chemistry? What is wrong with the periodic table?
236. Compare and contrast electronegativity and ionisation energy.
237. Why is life carbon based and not silicon based?
238. The nucleus and electrons are oppositely charged. Why do electrons not crash into the nucleus?
239. What is the significance of bonding in benzene?
240. How do you make aspirin?
241. What is the difference between diamond and graphite?
242. What is the cause of le chatelier's principle?
243. What does pH stand for?
244. Estimate the mass of oxygen in this building.
245. What determines whether an acid is 'strong' or 'weak'?
246. What is your favourite element? Why?
247. Why are the transition metals so colourful?
248. How many isomers of C_4H_8 can you draw?
249. Why are the transition metals good catalysts?
250. How many moles of water are there in this bottle of water?
251. What is the density of air in this room? What about outside? What about in Beijing?
252. What's the difference between entropy and enthalpy?
253. How do glow sticks work?
254. Why does food taste better when it's hot?
255. You have 30 seconds to name as many functional groups as possible.
256. Why do we use water to dilute solutions?
257. Compare and contrast hydrochloric acid to phosphoric acid.
258. Why is Vandium so special?
259. Where does chemistry end and physics begin?
260. Can you change an endothermic reaction into an exothermic one?

PHYSICS

Depending on which college you have applied for, the day of your physics interview will look different. At most Oxford colleges the day will start with a general meeting with all physics applicants to go through the day's events and expectations, before having **Subject Interviews**. At any college you may sit a short test; the questions you choose to answer in the test may form the foundation of the interviews later. Try to view these tests positively – they are letting you choose your strongest topics for the interview. Test or not, you will have one or more subject interviews for physics, and you may have an interview in a related subject, such as maths or chemistry (particularly if you're applying for Natural Sciences), an **Experimental Interview** or a **General Interview**.

Questions in a physics interview may take a few forms, but are most likely to be detailed and technical physics problems drawn from a range of topics you may have studied at school. There may also be more general questions which use basic physics concepts and reasoning skills to solve a physics-related problem, or there may be general questions testing numeracy, logic and estimation skills.

Most questions asked at interview will be open-ended technical questions and may be quantitative or qualitative. You will need to use your knowledge of maths and physics to attempt problems that may be quite different from those you have encountered at school, and the point is not to solve the problem perfectly, but to show you are able to use your understanding of maths and physics concepts to create expressions which model physical systems. Many questions are also intended to test your physical intuition, whether you can get the right 'feel' for a system and its parameters, and whether you can tell if equations make physical sense.

While there are many topics that could come up in the interview, some are more prevalent, and most questions will involve a generally similar approach. Mechanics questions appear to be favoured over other topics, particularly questions about gravitational systems ('If you jumped into a tunnel running straight through the centre of the Earth to the opposite side, what would happen?') and projectiles ('If you aimed a gun at a monkey hanging from a branch, and it let go at the exact moment you fired, would the bullet hit the monkey?'), but waves and lenses also come up often ('How would the fringe pattern from a Double Slit experiment change if you put a sheet of glass against the slits?'), as do a range of physics-related questions about computers, engines ('How do wind turbines work?'), refrigerators and the like ('How would you create artificial gravity in a spaceship?').

Questions about electronics and magnetism are less common, but if you have covered these topics in school, be prepared to answer questions, as you should be for any topic you've covered.

No matter the question, there is a standard approach to questions about physical systems that is nearly always applicable.

Always start by making a **quick sketch** and giving a qualitative assessment of the situation (what does your common sense tell you the likely outcome will be – you are setting out a hypothesis to test with the next steps); there are almost no questions where this is unhelpful, and even if it proves to be unnecessary for the question, it shows the interviewers you have a good standard approach to physics problems.

State any assumptions you are making as you go along (infinitely small points, no air resistance, parallel rays of light, etc.). Next, expand your sketch to a full labelled diagram, including all bodies and the forces/energies/etc. from different bodies.

Evaluate how these forces/etc. work together in this system and which are most relevant – think about what type of questions it is, whether you are dealing with momentum, gravitational forces, conservation of energy (use the information given in the question as a tip, sometimes whether you are given distances, velocities, energies, etc. can tell you what type of question you are dealing with).

Write expressions for the forces/etc. you have marked on you figure; always work with variables, only substitute numbers where absolutely necessary or where it will greatly simplify expressions.

Return to the question statement to remind yourself what the precise aim of the question is before writing equations using the expressions from your figure.

Even if you can't reach a final answer, you've showed you know how to approach a physics question. This approach can be used for a range of questions so is a good go-to method.

To answer the questions at interview, there are a range of specific skills you may need to practice beyond general problem-solving. You will need to know how to make **quick and simple sketches**, both for physical systems and for changes in physical quantities relative to each other (e.g. velocity-time diagrams). You will need to be able to demonstrate that you can interpret words to figures and figures to equations.

You will need to be able to work in the abstract, using variables rather than numbers, and it is helpful if you can apply calculus concepts to physics, for instance considering acceleration as the second derivative of displacement with respect to time, which allows you to work more freely and generally when writing expressions. It is uncommon, though possible, to be asked to derive well-known equations ('Find an expression for the distance between fringes generated by Young's Double Slit apparatus'), and you can be asked to find general expressions for a certain system, but most commonly you will be asked to **show you can use physical and mathematical expressions** to model reality.

You will need to demonstrate that you have physical intuition for building models and that you can explicitly recognize the assumptions and limits of your models. Some questions may be even more open-ended, testing how you apply physics to more general physics-themed problems.

An interviewer may reasonably expect a physics applicant to have **general knowledge of physics fields** (e.g. astronomy), and **popular current research topics** (e.g. the hunt for exoplanets). Particularly if an applicant has expressed any interest in space in the personal statement, it would not be impossible for a question such as 'How are exoplanets detected?' to be asked at interview. It would be quite difficult to reason yourself to the answer that planets in orbit gravitationally shift their stars, moving them closer and further from the Earth and creating a Doppler shift in their light which can be used to make a basic description of the planet. However, with interviewer guidance this may be possible. It would be helpful, though, to have a basic understanding of this and other popular research topics to pull ideas from.

Finally, one Maths question is also likely to come up in the interview. Maths represents a significant portion of most Oxbridge science courses and skills like sketching, differentiating and integrating are skills that will be necessary throughout much of your scientific education. Thus, it is advisable to also read the mathematics section in this book.

Worked Questions

Below are a few examples of how to start breaking down an interview question, complete with answer outlines and model answers.

Q1: The track for a high-speed train can be modelled as a very long beam (the rails) supported by an elastic foundation. The vibration of the rails away from a moving train is governed by the following partial differential equation:

$$EI\frac{\partial^4 y}{x^4 \partial} + Ky + M\frac{\partial^2 y}{\partial t^2} = 0$$

Q1 (i) Look at this equation and tell me about the structural behaviour associated with each term.

This is a very interesting question because it tests concepts related to mechanics, stresses and strains, and calculus.

Recommended Approach:
It should be obvious that y corresponds to vertical displacement. This suggests that the term to the right – with mass M times the second time derivative of y (i.e. acceleration) – corresponds to inertia for vertical motions.

The middle term is simply Hooke's Law, describing the elastic foundation. (K is the stiffness of the foundation.)

However, the term on the left is tricky, so most people would find it hard – but don't worry, it's meant to push you so you shouldn't feel scared. This is meant to test you and push you to think outside the box.

Let's break down the problem: E is Young's modulus, relating stress to strain. Although this is not part of the A-level syllabus, it is worth reading up a little about it. The symbol I corresponds to the second moment of area. And finally, there is the fourth derivative of y with respect to x.

The answer is that this is the bending stiffness of the beam. The interviewers will prompt you along the way and hope that you come to this result.

Q1 (ii) If a train runs at constant speed V and only the steady-state deformed shape of the track is required, do you think this partial differential equation can be reduced to an ordinary differential equation?

Recommended Approach:
This might seem very tricky but it is actually quite an easy question! Have a look below at how it can be approached, simply by understanding the relationship between distance and velocity:

$$\frac{d}{dt} = V \frac{d}{dx}$$

This means we can replace $M \frac{\partial^2 y}{\partial t^2}$ with $MV^2 \frac{d^2 y}{dx^2}$

We are now left with an ordinary differential equation that can be solved without difficulty.

Q2: The diagram to the right shows an idealisation of a tapered concrete chimney. It is desired to represent the dynamic behaviour in the fundamental mode by an equivalent single-degree-of-freedom system, using the approximate mode shape. In this context, think of dynamic behaviour as its response to a disturbance, and single degree-of-freedom simply means it can only move in 1 direction.

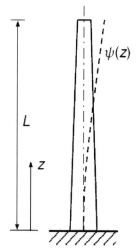

$$\Psi = \frac{(3\lambda^2 - \lambda^3)}{2} \qquad Where \; \lambda = \frac{z}{L}$$

Q2 (i) What are the boundary conditions in this scenario?

This is a question that tests your ability to think intuitively on the spot. Kinetic constraints are not taught explicitly at A-level, but the knowledge required to come up with them should not be beyond you – especially with prompts and hints from the interviewer. (Remember, the interviewers are not there to see what you CAN'T do; they are there to see what you CAN do. If you're struggling, ask them for a bit more information to help you along.)

Recommended Approach:
Firstly, let's deal with the boundary conditions. We expect the slope at $z = 0$ to be zero because the beam is fixed into the ground*.

The displacement will also be zero at z=0. You will be expected to come up with this using your intuition, but the next two boundary conditions are not immediately obvious (although you will hopefully be able to get to them after a few hints from the interviewer).

The shear stress* and bending moment are zero at z = L.

Q2 (ii) Do you think the assumed mode shape satisfies the kinematic constraints of the problem?

This is another way of asking whether the boundary conditions in (i) are satisfied.

Given that $\Psi = \frac{(3\lambda^2 - \lambda^3)}{2}$ and $\lambda = \frac{z}{L}$ → $d\lambda = \frac{dz}{L}$

Differentiate:

$$\Psi' = \frac{1}{2L}(6\lambda - 3\lambda^2)$$

$$\Psi'' = \frac{1}{2L^2}(6 - 6\lambda) = \frac{3}{L^2}(1 - \lambda)$$

$$\Psi''' = -\frac{3}{L^2}$$

z = 0 corresponds to $\lambda = 0$. Clearly, we must have ψ=0 at λ=0 in order for the displacement to be zero, i.e. for the first boundary condition to be fulfilled.

Likewise, the first derivative of ψ corresponds to the slope. This, too, must be zero at λ=0.

This next part is the tricky bit: the shear stress is the third derivative and the bending moment is the second derivative. But don't worry – this is beyond what you'd be expected to know, so the interviewer will help you along. We can test these boundary conditions at z = L:

$\lambda=0 \rightarrow \psi = \psi' = 0$　　　　　: Both Satisfied
$\lambda=1 \rightarrow$　: $\psi'' = 0$ Satisfied but $\psi''' = 0$ Not Satisfied
Check Normalisation: $\lambda = 1 \rightarrow \psi = 1$

The "check normalisation" simply refers to the fact that the displacement is non-zero at $z = L$.

Conclusion:
The mode shape is NOT ideal but represents a reasonable compromise between accuracy and ease of use. In short, we have *assumed* a mode shape that *might* correspond to the deformation of the chimney. This allows us to analyse the problem, and thus to work out the values of interest – displacement, slope, etc. – to a reasonable level of accuracy.

Additional Tips:
➢ Do some research on the differences between simply-supported, fixed-ended, and free-ended structures.
➢ Search online for shear stress and try to understand what is going on conceptually.

*Q3: **Cavitation** is the formation of vapour cavities in a liquid – i.e. small liquid-cavitation-free zones ("bubbles" or "voids") – that are the consequence of cavitational forces acting upon the cavitational liquid. It usually occurs when a liquid is subjected to rapid changes of pressure that cause the formation of cavities where the pressure is relatively low. When subjected to higher pressure, the voids implode and can generate an intense shockwave.*

A therapeutic ultrasound transducer is to be designed to deposit heat without producing cavitation. The desired peak heating rating is $16 W/cm^3$. At 1 MHz, the cavitation threshold of tissue is determined to be 2 MPa (peak rarefractional pressure). Assume linear propagation, plane wave relationships, sound speed 1500 m/s, density $1000 \ kg/m^3$, and specific heat $3700 \ J/(kg \ K)$.

Q3 (i) For 1 MHz ultrasound, determine the value of tissue attenuation at which heat can be generated without producing cavitation.

This question is particularly important for Physics candidates, as it explores concepts related to wave propagation and energy. It is also relevant for mechanical/biomedical engineering candidates.

Recommended Approach:
Step 1: Find the intensity, using the maximum value of pressure (which is the pressure that causes cavitation) and the values of density and speed that would be given to you.

Peak allowable pressure: $\widehat{p} = 2$ MPa

$$I = \frac{1}{2} \frac{\widehat{p}^2}{\rho_0 c_0}$$

$$= \frac{1}{2} \frac{(2 \times 10^6)^2}{1.5 \times 10^6}$$

$$= \frac{4}{3} \times 10^6 \frac{W}{m^2}$$

Step 2: Rearrange the expression for the heating rate to obtain the attenuation α. Np is the dimensionless unit Neper, which is commonly used to express the attenuation.

Heating rate: $Q = 2\,\alpha\,I$

$$\alpha = \frac{16 \times 10^6 \ W/m^3}{2 \times \frac{4}{3} \times 10^6 \ W/m^2}$$

$\alpha = 6 \ Np/m$

Note: You would be given all the formulae above. The symbol I refers to the intensity.

Q3 (ii) Using the value of attenuation from part (a), determine how much extra heating could be realized if the frequency is increased to 4 MHz. Account for the frequency dependence of both attenuation and cavitation.

Recommended Approach:

At 4MHz, cavitation threshold will double. Therefore α will quadruple. Thus, $\alpha = 24 \, Np/m$

$$\dot{Q} = 2 \times 24 \frac{Np}{m} \times \frac{(4 \times 10^6 \, Pa)^2}{1.5 \times 10^6 \, Pa} = 256 \text{ W/cm}^3$$

Thus, there is a sixteen fold increase in heating rate.

You will be told the relationship between frequency and pressure and between frequency and attenuation, although the latter might be discernible, intuitively, to some candidates. Pressure is proportional to frequency squared, so the pressure doubles. The attenuation is directly proportional to frequency and hence quadruples.

Conclusion:

A small change in frequency can lead to a very large change in the heating rate.

Q3 (iii) If the pressure were increased to generate cavitation, what are the advantages and disadvantages with respect to heating?

Increasing the pressure to produce cavitation will result in higher heating rates and shorter treatment times, as the cavitation bubbles do work on the tissue. Disadvantages are that controlling cavitation is difficult and so the heating rates are unpredictable. If cavitation grows out of control, it will grow towards the transducer, shielding the target region: this will mean very little therapeutic effect at the focus and damage in undesired regions.

Q4: In a BOD (biochemical oxygen demand) test, a 50 ml sample of treated sewage is placed in a 300 ml bottle. The bottle is then completely filled with clean water at 20°C containing inorganic nutrients and dissolved oxygen at a concentration of 9.0 mg/litre. After 5 days storage at 20°C the dissolved oxygen concentration in the bottle is measured and found to be 4.5 mg/litre.

Q4 (i) Calculate the five day biochemical demand (BOD5) of the sewage. If the deoxygenation coefficient of the treated sewage at 20°C is 0.25/day (to base e), calculate the ultimate BOD of the treated sewage.

This question is related to environmental/chemical/production engineering and several applied physics topics.

Solution:

	Volume (ml)	Oxygen Concentration (mg/litre)	Oxygen Mass (mg)
Effluent sample	50	0	0
Clean water & nutrients	250	9	2.25
Mix at 5 days	300	4.5	1.35
Oxygen consumed	50	18	0.9

The ultimate BOD is 18 mg/litre.

The key to this question is to work out the mass of oxygen consumed **by the 50 ml sample.** It is trivial to obtain oxygen masses from oxygen concentration given that we know the volumes. A simple subtraction will then give the mass consumed to 0.9 mg. Finally, we need to multiply by 20 to get the amount that would be consumed by a 1 litre sample.

Q4 (ii) What are the implications of this result? Why is BOD important? What harm can be caused?

The point here is that the microorganisms in the sewage will consume oxygen in a river or stream once it enters it. This means, often, there will be insufficient oxygen for the fish to survive. The impact is usually strongest quite a distance downstream from where the sewage is disposed, as the biological processes involved take a long time.

Q5: Discuss the use of sedimentation in waste water treatment and derive a formula for the overall removal of solids from wastewater in a rectangular sedimentation tank.

The second part of this question is very good for testing the student's understanding of core concepts related to physics or engineering. The first part is aimed at those interested in environmental/chemical engineering or similar topics within physics.

Recommended Approach:

Sedimentation is used for the following:
➢ To remove grit and course solids.
➢ To remove finer organic solids in primary settling tanks.
➢ To remove sludge from the effluent from trickling filters and the activated sludge process.

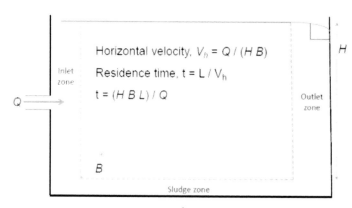

Idealised settling tank

Horizontal velocity, $V_h = Q / (H\,B)$

Residence time, $t = L / V_h$

$t = (H\,B\,L) / Q$

Inlet zone

Outlet zone

Q

H

B

Sludge zone

L

To reach sludge zone at the end of the tank: $V_s = H/t$

But $t = BHL/Q$

Thus, $V_s = Q/BL$

I.e. Settling velocity $V_s > V_o$ the hypothetical upward velocity- the overflow rate V_o.

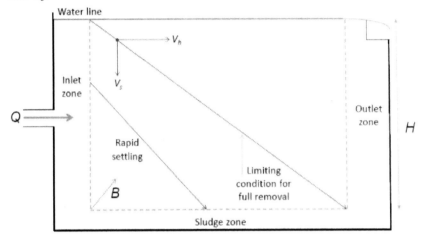

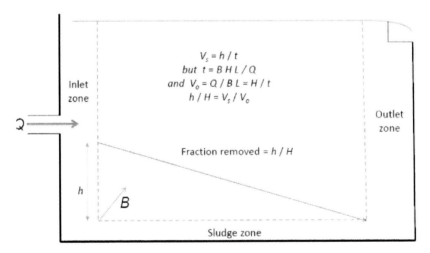

$$Overall\ removal = (1 - x_o) + \frac{1}{v_o} \int_0^{x_o} V_s dx$$

Q6: Determine the forces acting on all the bars below, and label them on a sketch.

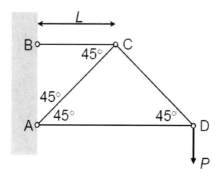

This question tests general mathematical skills, such as resolving forces, in addition to mechanics. Mention how this might be asked at interview. The interviewer could give you a diagram like this and ask you to simply resolve the forces. Some people like to talk through every step, while others like to work on it a bit first before telling the interviewer their working. Although both are fine, any approach where you aren't talking through your working constantly risks going off track, without giving the interviewer a chance to steer you back.

Solution:
Work with one joint at a time. Starting with D, resolve for the forces vertically.

This gives: $CDcos45 = P$
Thus, $CD = P\sqrt{2CDcos45}$
Next, resolve horizontally at D.

This gives $AD = -P$
Employ the same method at joint C.

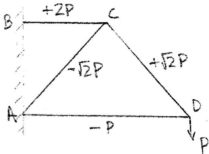

The key here is equilibrium: the net force and moment at each joint is zero.

We stay away from joints A and B because we don't know the reaction forces, so we avoid having to deal with them.

Q7: A pulsating sphere radiates spherical waves into air, where the frequency is 100 Hz and the intensity is 50 mW/m² at a distance of 1 m from the centre of the sphere. The sphere has a nominal radius of 10cm.

Q7 (i) What is the acoustic power radiated?

Comment: This tests your understanding of how power vs. energy, and how this can be related to wave theory.

Solution:
$\dot{W} = I \times 4\pi r^2$

$= 50 \, mW \times 4\pi \times (1m)^2$

$= 0.628 \, W$

The symbol I is the intensity, which is given in the question.

Q7 (ii) How are sound waves different to electromagnetic waves?

Sound needs a medium to propagate through, unlike electromagnetic radiation which can propagate in a vacuum.

Q8: The resolving power of a light microscope can be calculated by:
$Resolution = \frac{0.61\lambda}{n sin\emptyset}$

Q8 (i) Define each term in the equation.

λ is the wavelength of the light used.
n is the refractive index.
$\emptyset$ is half the angular width of the cone of rays collected by the objective lens.

Q8 (ii) Explain why better resolution can be achieved by illuminating the sample with violet light.

The frequency of violet is higher than visible light:

$$c = f\lambda$$

This means the wavelength of violet is greater. This, in turn, means the resulting resolution is smaller.

N.B. Smaller resolution is better!

Q9: The linear dispersion equation for water waves on constant depth is:

$$\omega^2 = kg \tanh(kd)$$

Starting from the dispersion equation, show that for waves on deep water the phase speed is twice the group velocity but that for waves on very shallow water the phase speed and group velocity are equal. w is the angular frequency, k the wave number, g gravity, and d depth below water.

This question tests calculus and algebraic manipulation.

Solution:
As d tends to infinity, the tanh term tends to 1. This leaves $w^2 = kg$. The phase speed, which is w/k, is therefore g/w. (Formulae would be given.)

The group velocity, $\frac{dw}{dk}$ is $\frac{g}{2w}$

To get this, simply differentiate w with respect to k and then substitute back in for k.

For shallow water, d tends to zero and tanh(kd) tends to kd.

This leaves $w^2 = k^2 gd$.
Next, take square roots to get $w = k\sqrt{gd}$. The phase velocity, w/k, is $\sqrt{gd}$.
Differentiate to find $\frac{dw}{dk}$: this, too, is $\sqrt{gd}$.

Q10: What is meant by wave breaking? Indicate the important parameters that determine wave breaking on a natural beach.

This question is related to hydraulics and coastal/offshore/geotechnical engineering, but the second part is really just a test of intuition.

Recommended Approach:

Waves break when the water particles begin to move faster than the wave celerity.

(Note: The group velocity of a wave is the velocity with which the overall shape of the waves' amplitudes – known as the modulation or envelope of the wave – propagates through space.)

Wave breaking depends on the following:
➤ Bed slope
➤ Local water depth
➤ Offshore wave conditions.

Physics Interview Questions

261. How did the Greek astronomer Aristarchus determine the distance to the sun?

262. How much is the mass of nitrogen in this room?

263. The titanic weighed over 50,000 tonnes. Why did it not sink earlier?

264. If a sand timer was turned over onto a weighing scale, would there be any fluctuations in the weight displayed as the sand fell through?

265. If you have a helium balloon on a string in a car, and the car accelerates, what happens to the balloon?

266. How can a plane fly upside down?

267. Explain the different between entropy and enthalpy.

268. How would you go about calculating the number of atoms in the world. What information would you need to calculate it and given this data work out the answer.

269. An alkane has 750 carbon atoms. Given the length of a carbon-carbon bond and a carbon-hydrogen bond calculate the total length of the molecule.

270. Draw the shape of the molecule B_2H_6.

271. Calculating the speed at which a coin will hit the floor when dropped from a certain height above the ground.

272. Suggest a method of storing large amounts of hydrogen.

273. Integrate $y = cos2x + sinx^2$

274. Why did the Titanic initially float? Why did it split into two?

275. What is centrifugal force? How do you measure it?

276. Why does 'heat rise'?

277. How do forest fires spread so quickly?

278. How can light be both a wave and a particle?

279. What safety mechanisms prevent a plane from being damaged by lightning?

280. How would you weigh the Earth?

281. Why was 2011 an incredible year for physics?

282. What is the area of your skin?

ENGINEERING

Engineers can expect to have a few **Subject Interviews** and possibly a **General Interview**. Questions may be detailed maths and physics questions, general questions testing estimation, logic and numeracy skills, questions about physical situations where the applicant may display the ability to 'think like an engineer', or questions about the subject and applicant. An engineer may be asked to sit a test before the interview with topics such as pure maths, mechanics and electricity. Discussing the answers given in this test will then be the starting point for the interview, so try view tests positively, as they may allow you to choose your strongest topics for the interview.

The subject interviews are technical interviews with questions usually centred in physics and maths, but which may also have an engineering twist. Remember, a question aims to test your ability to apply maths and physics concepts in practice and your **ability to think about designs and real-life imperfections**, while showing enthusiasm for engineering. You will need to be fluent in expressing core mathematics and physics concepts mathematically. Since engineering is not a subject usually taught at school, the interview will also test how quickly you think and assimilate new ideas and how you apply your foundation knowledge in new situations. All of these skills are vital for engineering students.

The **questions you will be asked will likely be too difficult for you to answer outright**, so you will need to approach each question methodically to help you build from your base knowledge to an answer, with guidance from the interviewer. When given an engineering question (e.g. 'How would you design a gravity dam?'), a helpful first step is to repeat it back in your own words to make sure you have digested what your task is (e.g. 'How would I design a free-standing dam utilizing only gravitational forces?'). A good second step is to draw a quick sketch of the system and make a qualitative/descriptive assessment of the situation (e.g. 'The dam would need to be able to withstand the force of the water without falling over and have some measures to prevent this').

Once you have sketched the system, write some simple maths and physics expressions to model the system. These will often be for mechanical or electronic forces and energies, because engineering is a practical design subject at heart, so real systems are often considered. Use the expressions you jot down to set up equations describing the system if possible, or if you aren't sure, give a verbal assessment of how the expressions dictate how the different elements of the system will interact.

Make sure to explicitly **recognise any assumptions** you are making; while in physics these assumptions may be largely ignored, in engineering it is not always possible to ignore simplifying assumptions (e.g. no air-resistance when designing an airplane), so you must be aware of which assumptions you make in order to recognize how they may fail in the real world.

An engineer needs to be able to recognize potential problems to a system, including those which you may not have considered previously in school (e.g. sliding, seepage, non-plastic behaviour, uneven surfaces, etc.). Once you have a working model, address potential problems. Don't be afraid to poke holes in your own model – **your interviewer will already have noticed the weaknesses in your ideas**, they are more interested in whether you will!

Many questions will be similar in style to those for physics interviews, so it may be useful to read the section on **Physics** above as well. Despite the emphasis on maths and physics in the interview questions, don't forget that you are in an engineering interview, and need to think like an engineer, not like a physicist. You may even be asked a question such as 'What are the differences between Physics and Engineering?'

Any applicant to engineering should be prepared to discuss their choice of subject. Interviewers are aware that students won't have studied engineering before, so applicants should be able to justify their interest in the course, as well as demonstrate an interest in the subject though extracurricular reading, projects, internships, etc. An applicant may also be expected to demonstrate an interest in the subject through well thought-out answers to questions about the role of engineers in society.

Maths represents a significant portion of Engineering; skills like sketching, differentiating and integrating are skills that will be necessary throughout much of your scientific education. Thus, it is advisable to also read the mathematics section in this book.

Worked Questions

Below are a few examples of how to start breaking down an interview question, complete with model answers.

Q1: (i) Could you explain what is meant by osmotic pressure?

Recommended Approach:
Always start by drawing a diagram of some sort, if applicable.

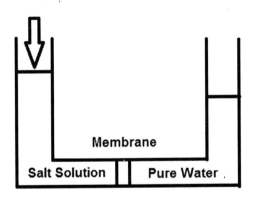

In the above schematic drawing, the osmotic pressure is the minimum pressure exerted on the salt solution that prevents pure water from moving through the semi-permeable membrane and entering the salt solution.

Q1 (ii) The molecular weight of NaCl is 58.5. What is the concentration of physiological saline (0.9% w/v NaCl solution)?

This is a question aimed at anyone who might have stated an interest in chemical/manufacturing/systems engineering in their personal statement. However, as with most Oxbridge interview questions, the interviewer is testing your intuition; the question is therefore appropriate for any engineering or applied sciences discipline.

Recommended Approach:

w/v corresponds to the mass of solute (g) times 100, divided by the volume of solution (ml). (Note: You would be told this if you were not studying Chemistry to A-level.)

We are told that the w/v concentration is 0.9. Assuming a 1000ml volume of solution (as we write concentration as moles/litre), this implies 0.9=mass $x\frac{100}{1,000}$. Therefore mass = 9g. We are also given the molecular weight = 58.5.

$\frac{9}{58.5}$ = 0.154 moles/litre.

*Q2: Positive autoregulation (PAR) occurs when the product of a gene activates its own production. PAR is a common network motif in transcription networks but occurs less often in the E. coli network than negative autoregulation. (**Network motifs** are patterns in transcription networks that occur more often than at random. **Transcription** is the first step of gene expression, in which a particular segment of DNA is copied into RNA by the enzyme RNA polymerase.)*

In positive autoregulation, a gene product activates its own transcription. A model which takes the following form has been proposed:

$\frac{dx}{dt} = \beta + \beta_1 x - \alpha x$

Q2 (i) Explain the different terms in this equation.

This question is aimed at students who might have mentioned biomedical/bioprocess/cellular/tissue engineering in their personal statement. However, the calculations involved are related to calculus and therefore could be asked to all engineering applicants, especially if this is the interviewer's field of interest.

$\frac{dx}{dt}$: The production rate of x

β: Basal Transcription rate

β_1: Transcription rate on activation

α: Degradation/Dilution rate

You are not expected to know the technical terms, e.g. "basal transcription rate". However, it should hopefully be intuitively obvious that the **basal rate** is the **rate of continuous supply** of some chemical or process. Like this, try to explain what you think is going on qualitatively.

N.B: Brush up on transcription, translation, etc., if you have mentioned anything related to this topic in your personal statement.

Q2 (ii) What is the condition so that the steady-state concentration of x is positive?

Recommended Approach:
Steady-state simply means the derivative with respect to time is zero. Rearranging the terms, we get the following:

$$x_{ss} = \frac{\beta}{\alpha - \beta_1} > 0 \text{ Requires } \alpha > \beta_1$$

Q2 (iii) How do you think we might try to quantify the response time of this reaction?

Recommended Approach:
The response time is actually defined as the time to reach half of the steady-state concentration.

$$T_{\frac{1}{2}} = \frac{\ln 2}{\alpha - \beta_1}$$

An equally acceptable answer would be to solve the differential equation and find the time constant.

Q2 (iv) When might positive autoregulation be biologically useful?

Recommended Approach:
Positive autoregulation is important for processes that take a long time, such as developmental processes, due to its slower response time. However, instabilities can arise with positive autoregulation. Negative autoregulation, on the other hand, is typically more robust and leads to a faster response.

Q3: Explain how nanotechnology might be exploited for preventing and reversing chemical and microbiological contamination of water.

This is very topical at the moment. Think of the properties associated with nanotechnology and how these are relevant to answering the question, e.g. the precision that nanotechnology introduces.

The recent introduction of nanotechnology holds great promise preventing and reversing the effect of water contamination.

1) **Remediation**. The very high reactivity of nano-scale iron in terms of inducing redox reaction is being used for dehalogenating ubiquitous contaminants such as TCE. It is also being used to immobilise toxic heavy metals such as mercury.

2) **Detection** of contaminating chemicals (organics and metals). Nano-scale sensors are available which prove real time *in situ* measures of the presence of chemical contaminants and microbial pathogens.

3) **Nano-filters** with pore size ranging from 0.001-0.0001μm are effective for removing pesticides.

4) **Nanomaterials** such as <u>silver</u> and <u>titanium</u> have huge potential for killing microbial pathogens in water. The nano-scale is <u>non-toxic</u> and only becomes toxic when it is activated with UV, which causes the short-lived free oxygen particles which are toxic. The nano-scale silver damages the cells membrane negatively impacting on respiration and penetration, thus disrupting metabolite transfer.

5) **Magnetic nanoparticles** have the potential to <u>attach to cells for targeted kill and removal,</u> as well as isolation of strains that could be exploited in biodegradation.

Q4: Tell me a bit about the potential of plants for improving soils damaged by anthropogenic activity.

This is also very topical – particularly within civil engineering, where an understanding of the soil properties are crucially important to the design of the structure.

The way plants can improve soils that have been damaged by industrial activity is by **fixing carbon and pumping this out of the roots**. This improves the **nutrient status** of the soil, **stimulates beneficial activities** and encourages the migration of new plant species which contribute to the cycle of **soil recovery**.

➢ **Phytoextraction**, extraction of toxic metals out of the soil by plants that are then harvested.
➢ **Phytotransformation**, plant uptake and degradation of organic compounds within the plant.
➢ **Phytostabilisation**, roots exudates precipitate the pollutant heavy metals and in the process making them less bioavailable and toxic.
➢ **Rhizofiltration**, uptake of metals into the plants
➢ **Phytovolatilisation**, plants evapo-transpiration of metals such as mercury and hydrocarbons.
➢ **Vegetative cap**, rainwater is evapo-transpired by plants to prevent leaching contaminants from disposal sites.

Try to describe the engineering/physics principles at play behind some of these, if possible, too. What are the properties of toxic heavy metals? What features of soil do you think would be desirable in a civil engineering context? How might slope instability be prevented? Etc.

Q5: If intrinsic rates of contaminant degradation in a habitat are slow, what engineered interventions can be applied to stimulate microbial bioremediation of the site and how do they work?

This question will take most candidates by surprise. It is certainly effective in getting the candidate to think out of the box and apply engineering concepts to solve real world problems.

The most common reasons for slow degradation include:

The **concentration** of the **contaminant** is so **high** it kills those cells that could potentially degrade them. In the case of soils this problem can be overcome by **diluting** contaminated soil with clean soil or another substrate, such as **saw-dust**. **Bioslurping** is another approach that is commonly used. (Bioslurping combines the two remedial approaches of bioventing and vacuum-enhanced free-product recovery. Bioventing stimulates the aerobic bioremediation of hydrocarbon-contaminated soils. Vacuum-enhanced free-product recovery extracts LNAPLs from the capillary fringe and the water table.)

There is **insufficient oxygen** to stimulate the favoured aerobic mode of biodegradation. In deep groundwater aquifers this can be alleviated by **sinking wells** and **injecting air** or **oxygen release granules**.

There are **insufficient microbial populations** with the **genetic capacity** to degrade the contaminant or resistant to the toxicity of co-contaminants. This is a rare situation, which when it does occur can be overcome by **bio-augmentation of specific selected populations** originating from culture collections, other sites and even genetically modified. These can be injected into soils or introduced into sunken wells in the case of aquifers.

Heterogeneity of contaminant distribution on the site. In this case, the contaminant is present unevenly as hot spots, at such high concentrations they kill or inhibit all the cells present. Alternatively other spots are clear of all contamination or present at such low concentrations, that degradation activity is not expressed. This condition can be alleviated by several physical mixing approaches, including **electrokinetics**, a technique of using direct electrical current to remove organic, inorganic and heavy metal particles from the soil by electric potential. The use of this technique provides an approach with minimum disturbance to the surface while treating subsurface contaminant

Q6: The diagram below shows a simple model of a two-storey steel moment-resisting frame building. Write down the equations of motion for free vibrations.

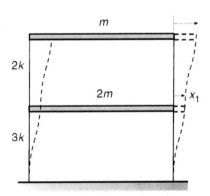

This question tests mechanics, a topic that is almost certain to play an integral part of a physics/engineering interview.

Recommended Approach:
Step 1: Treat the two storeys separately. (You will most likely need prompting with this.)
Step 2: Resolve forces for each storey, bearing in mind that the forces must cancel at the point where the cut is taken.

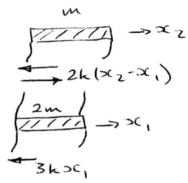

Step 3: Write out the equations.

$$m\ddot{x}_2 = -2k(x_2 - x_1)$$

$$2m\ddot{x}_1 = 2k(x_2 - x_1) - 3kx_1$$

Step 4: Write in the equivalent matrix form.

$$\begin{bmatrix} 2m & 0 \\ 0 & m \end{bmatrix} \begin{bmatrix} \ddot{x}_1 \\ \ddot{x}_2 \end{bmatrix} + \begin{bmatrix} 5k & -2k \\ -2k & 2k \end{bmatrix} \begin{bmatrix} x_1 \\ x_2 \end{bmatrix} = 0$$

Q7: A cell suspension is concentrated in a batch MF process from 1% to 10%. Due to an effective back-shock method the flux remains at 100 1/m²h. The fermentor has a volume of 1m³ and the membrane area is 1.5m². Calculate the batch processing time assuming that the membrane has rejection of 100%.

Although this question is referring to a cell suspension, it could apply to any engineering process or system.

Solution:
Solids retained 1 x 1% = V j x 10% m³. This implies V j = 0.1.

Therefore, final volume = 0.1 m³.

Change in volume =1 - 0.1 = 0.9m³ = Throughput of membrane

$Flux = 100\ lm^{-2}h^{-1} = 0.1\ m^3m^{-2}h^{-1}$

$Time = \dfrac{Throughput}{AxFlux} = \dfrac{0.9}{1.5 \times 0.1} = 6h$

Q8: I'm going to ask you about a cell culture medium that contains two types of cells, A and B, in a ratio of 1:3 by numbers. The mean cell doubling time is 6 hours for type A cells and 8 hours for type B cells under the prevailing cultivation conditions. What is the expected ratio of type A to type B cells in the culture after four days?

This question would be well-suited to any discipline of engineering/physics.

Solution:
Step 1: Note that the growth rate is to the power of 2.

$N_A = 1 \times 2^{4 \times \frac{24}{6}} = 65{,}536$

Step 2: Note that both species will double 4 or 3 times a day.

$N_B = 3 \times 2^{4 \times \frac{24}{8}} = 12{,}288$

Step 3: Note their different concentrations.

$\dfrac{N_A}{N_B} = 5.3$

Q9: I'd like you to draw a diagram, briefly outlining the main components in the signal pathway of a diagnostic ultrasound imaging system. Also, if you can, explain what is meant by time-gain compensation (TGC).

This might appear to be a biomedical engineering question, but it is really testing your electronics.

Recommended Approach:
Time-gain compensation refers to the use of increasing amplification of the beam formed RF signal received with increasing time of flight, to account for the fact that the signal emanating from greater depths within tissue will have experienced greater attenuation both on transmit and on receive.

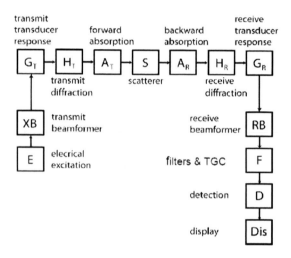

From an engineering point of view, what ultimately limits your ability to image deeper and deeper into tissue?

As the imaging depth is increased, the echo **signal received** by the imaging array eventually **drops** below electrical noise levels. The only option is then to **start increasing the transmit signal amplitude** so as to achieve greater signal-to-noise ratio on receive, but this can only be done up to a point. As the amplitude is increased, two non-linear phenomena (**non-linear propagation and acoustic cavitation**) cause transfer of some of the energy carried out by the transmitted pulse into higher harmonics, where it is readily absorbed into heat. Furthermore, cavitation activity occurring in the propagation path will **shield the region of interest deep within tissue**, causing a further reduction in signal-to-noise ratio.

Q10: Specify typical procedures for the collection and transportation of soil samples from the site for triaxial testing.

This question is related to civil/geotechnical engineering.

Recommended Approach:
Know the main differences between using triaxial testing, the cone penetrometer test and the shear vane test. No need to know any of the details, but no harm being familiar with the different methods. This displays your enthusiasm and shows that you have carried out research beyond you're A-level syllabus.

Install bore-hole to 8m depth using auger or light percussion drilling rig with clay cutter. Collect sample by driving a U 100 sample tube into the ground. If the clay is soft and sensitive consider using a Shelby tube instead. In this case the tube is careful jacked into the soil at the base of the borehole. The sample tube is removed from the ground and brought to the surface. The ends of the sample are waxed and the tube wrapped in plastic. It is then transported to the testing lab.

Describe two of the main sources of error in the determination of undrained strength using the triaxial test. How can these errors be minimised?

The restraining effect of the **membrane** surrounding the sample **increases the radial stress**. This can be accounted for by applying a **correction** to the measured deviator stress.

Small samples (e.g. the 38 mm diameter samples that are often used) may not provide an appropriate **representation** of the **soil fabric** and any **fissure** that may be present. Conduct the test on larger samples instead.

Engineering Interview Questions

283. How does Earthquake-proofing work?

284. You create a circular hole in a sheet of metal and then heat it up. What happens to the size of the hole?

285. Why do large ships like aircraft carriers not sink despite weighing several thousand tonnes?

286. What are the difficulties with building a bridge that connects the UK and USA?

287. What is the significance of superconductors?

288. What limits the size of a computer chip?

289. How do aeroplanes fly? Why can some fly up-side down?

290. What would be your first invention?

291. Derive the equation that links voltage, charge and capacitance.

292. Fast bowlers in cricket can 'swing' and 'reverse-swing' the bowl. What allows this to happen?

293. Why do windmills never appear stationary?

294. What is the strongest naturally occurring material? How is it cut into shapes?

295. How does an airplane fly?

296. Are engineering bridges more stable on concrete or on soil? Why?

297. Derive the formula for the area of a circle.

298. What are the main assumptions that we make when we model potential flow?

299. What is Moore's law? What limits how small computers can get?

300. How do aeroplanes fly? Why can some planes fly upside down?

301. How do you tell if a website is busy because it has lots of visitors or because it is hosted in Australia?

302. How do trains go around bends?

303. What is the difference between a gun and a rifle? What advantage does a spinning bullet have?

MATERIAL SCIENCES

Material Science interviews generally follow the formula of: one maths question, one mechanical reasoning question, one materials-based question. Thus, you are strongly advised to also read the mathematics section in this book.

Materials Science is a hands-on subject and requires an ability to explain and visualise potentially abstract concepts clearly; sketching is therefore encouraged (you will be given a pen and paper).

It should be stressed that, while specifics are given in the answers below, the interviewers are rarely looking for you to arrive at a correct final answer. They simply want to see how you approach unfamiliar and potentially daunting problems, and how you reason. The interview aims to achieve one thing: to **determine if you have the intellectual capacity, creativity and curiosity to thrive in the tutorial system**.

Finally, skills like sketching, differentiating and integrating will be necessary throughout much of your scientific education. Thus, it is advisable to also read the mathematics section in this book.

Worked Questions

Below are a few examples of how to start breaking down an interview question, complete with answer outlines and model answers. The answers are by no means exhaustive; the points given could be used by the interviewer as prompts and to encourage lengthy discussion of certain topics.

Q1: What should we build a fusion reactor out of?

This question emphasises the multidisciplinary nature of material science. A well-read candidate who's keeping up-to-date with the biggest recent scientific news will know that a fusion reactor uses the process of nuclear fusion to produce energy which we can use on the electrical grid.

This knowledge is not presumed though and so this definition can be given as an initial prompt. From there, a good answer should **split the question into two distinct parts**.

The first is based on the physics of nuclear fusion. Fusion involves bringing together nuclei to create an element with higher atomic number. This involves overcoming the electrostatic repulsion of two positively charged nuclei, and so requires huge temperatures and pressures (a good candidate might give the example of hydrogen fusing in our sun to give helium and the energy which powers our earth). A prompt may be given to explain that fusion reactors use deuterium and tritium rather than hydrogen nuclei as this gives the most efficient release of energy. Thus the candidate would be expected to say that the products of such a reaction are α-radiation and high-energy neutrons.

The second part of the answer should take the environmental conditions which arise in the first part of the answer (i.e. high temperature, high pressure, α-radiation and high-energy neutron bombardment) and use these to decide upon issues which come with materials selection. High temperature might suggest the use of ceramics (higher melting points than metals); high pressures might suggest the use of metals (more ductile than brittle ceramics). Strong candidates, after prompting, may be able to explain the effects of **α-radiation and high-energy neutron bombardment** on any materials used. α-radiation are just helium nuclei; these could penetrate a metal lattice structure and form helium gas bubbles; the effect of these bubbles on the strength of the metal could be likened to the difference in strength between an Aero chocolate bar and a Cadbury Dairy Milk bar. High-energy neutrons displace atoms in the metal lattice, leading to the formation of dislocations; dislocations are the reason for plastic deformation; simply put, more dislocations means more deformation which isn't great for the structural integrity of our fusion reactor.

Q2: I give you a vial with a black powder in it. I tell you the sample is pure and made of carbon. How do you determine what the black powder is?

There is a lot of scope in this question for a good candidate to make use of knowledge of characterisation techniques learnt in both Chemistry and Physics. A good answer will give solid reasoning for employing each technique plus knowledge of what the technique involves, rather than covering as many techniques as possible. A by no means exhaustive list of potential techniques is given below:

➢ Heating to **determine melting** point (good candidates might suggest that there's the possibility the sample will sublime rather than melt).

➢ (Time-of-flight) **mass spectrometry**: the sample is ionised and accelerated using an electric field before being bent round a corner using a magnetic field. Heavier species fly slower; particles with a greater charge fly faster. We end up with a plot of relative intensities with respect to the mass-to-charge ratio (m/z) of each species.

➢ **Infrared spectroscopy**: infrared radiation causes covalent bonds to vibrate at characteristic frequencies. When the applied IR radiation is in resonance with the vibration of the bond then we know which bond is present.

➢ **Nuclear Magnetic Resonance** (NMR) spectroscopy: protons have a property called spin, which can be thought of as a tiny bar magnet. When an external magnetic field is applied, this determines the direction the spin "points" in. Switching off the magnetic field leads to the spin decaying to its previous unaligned state and giving off radio-frequency radiation in the process. The local environment of a proton spin (i.e. where the hydrogen atoms are in a molecule) gives detectable changes in this signal. A good candidate will note that if this is a pure carbon sample then there are no hydrogen atoms present and that ^{13}C NMR spectroscopy has to be employed instead.

➢ **Liquid Chromatography**: if the sample can be dissolved in a solvent then different methods such as thin layer chromatography (TLC), column chromatography, and high performance liquid chromatography (HPLC) can be employed. Different species have different retention times and so can be identified if we know what our stationary and mobile phases are.

➤ Being a pure sample made of carbon, candidates should be aware that this must be an allotrope of carbon (such as diamond). Not being transparent, it cannot be diamond, so could be graphite or amorphous carbon (allotropes candidates should have heard of). Leading on from graphite, the interviewer can prompt to suggest that the sample could be graphene, explaining what this is if need be. **Transmission Electron Microscopy** (TEM) could be employed on such thin samples.

Q3: What is a Formula-1 car made from and why?

A common favourite given the incredible engineering which goes into making such a car. Good candidates should identify the solution to such a question involves identifying the requirements of the materials given the environment they're in, and then choosing suitable materials whose properties fit the desired function. It is this principle on which Materials Science rests as a discipline.

The main focus of the answer should be the **chassis of the vehicle**, although given the general nature of the question, mention could be given for example to the rubber in the tyres (how vulcanisation affects how hard or soft they are and when you might want to use each type) and the metals used in the suspension (balance between strength and lack of plastic deformation).

An F-1 car needs to be light. **Carbon-fibre** has an excellent strength-to-weight ratio but is no good by itself on impact as it absorbs energy by bending before potentially splintering. Thus a metal support could go beneath an outer layer of carbon fibre. Light metals include aluminium and titanium (good candidates will consider which is easier to process and cheaper to make). But bulk metal is heavy. Therefore, we could employ a **hexagonal structure**; hexagons are strong (cite the example of a beehive) and the resulting large air gaps significantly reduce the mass of the structure.

Q4: The temperature in a jet engine can exceed 1500°C. This is higher than the melting point of the nickel-based superalloys which are used to make the turbine blades. Why don't the blades melt?

This should be an unfamiliar concept to most candidates. Three types of answer could be given, for which most candidates will probably need prompts:

➢ **Serpentine cooling**: the introduction of an internal system of cooling channels in the blade. Cool(er) air flows through the channels; heat transfers from the blades to the air. Suggestions of using liquid instead of gas are no good as the liquid will not withstand the heat and could also lead to corrosion effects. Comparing this system to the operation of a radiator shows an understanding of what's going on. Surface area of the channels should be increased, but too many channels will compromise the structural integrity of the blades.

➢ **Thermal barrier coatings**: a thin layer of highly heat resistive material could coat the outer surface of the blade. Good candidates should note such a material would be a ceramic. With prompts, the efficacy of this thermal barrier coating could be improved by increasing its surface area; this is achieved by giving the coating a fin-like structure (as seen in certain systems in the body, such as the lungs).

➢ Good candidates should comment on what a superalloy could possibly be. **An alloy is a mixture of metals** whose properties are different from its constituent elements. A metal melts when its atoms have enough thermal energy to break free of the lattice structure in which they find themselves. The addition of certain elements to a metal lattice may affect the movement of the atoms in the lattice (e.g. because of their differing size).

Q5: How does a touchscreen work?

A ubiquitous technology to which many of us never give any thought. Prior knowledge is not assumed, but insight can be gained into how this physical system works. There are two simple systems to consider:

Resistive screens:
These are made up of two conductive layers on top of the normal glass surface, which are separated by tiny spacers and through which passes a well-defined current. A scratch-resistant layer is applied on top of all this to keep the system safe. The upper conductive layer is flexible. When a local force is applied, this upper layer bends and comes into contact with the lower conductive layer, thus resulting in a voltage drop. A good candidate should note that one instance of stimulus requires two measurements, one in each of the x- and y-directions, and thus that a voltage is dropped separately across each of the x- and y-directions – the entire process taking a time shorter than is humanly perceptible.

Capacitive screens:
A conductive layer coats the top of the glass of the screen, and this is again covered with a protective layer. As above, the conductive layer has a well-defined current running across it but it is not flexible. Instead, when your finger touches this layer, its charge can be transferred at the point of contact to your finger which is capacitive (it can store an electric charge). This leads to a change in the flow of current and can be detected appropriately. Good candidates should suggest that this is why some touchscreens don't work when you are wearing gloves (as the material in most gloves cannot hold a charge).

Q6: What's so special about carbon?

A deliberately broad question, and impossible to answer in full in an interview. Candidates should draw from their Chemistry knowledge to talk about carbon's four valence electrons. These can bond with other carbon atoms in a dazzling array of ways to form many different structures. Organic chemistry arises because of carbon's ability to bond to itself and to other atoms: the building blocks of life as well as polymers (derived from the hydrocarbons of the oil industry) are built in this way. Focus should be kept on **carbon's ability to bond with itself** to give unique structural forms known as allotropes.

Candidates should be aware of diamond (all four electrons bonded in a tetrahedral structure, thus giving strength and transparency) and graphite. In graphite, only three electrons are used in bonding to give planar hexagonal sheets which interact weakly each other (van der Waals forces are weaker than covalent bonds) and so can slide over each other – hence why we use graphite as pencil lead. There is also a free electron in graphite which leads it to being an electrical conductor. With prompts, extend the conversation to graphene (single graphite sheets) and what properties it might have (electrical conductivity, strength etc.). Particularly strong candidates might be asked as well/instead to consider **fullerenes and carbon nanotubes** – what is unique about their electronic structures and what properties might these materials have?

Q7: Computer chips are intricate patterns of circuitry on silicon wafers, where the smallest features are of the order of 10nm. How do we make them? And how do we know we've made what we think?

Candidates should first identify that circuitry means "paths along which electricity conducts" – thus, this material should be a good conductor (suggestions of metals with their free electrons e.g. copper which is used in macroscopic circuitry, but gold and silver have higher conductivities). Hints and prompts should be given to engage in a discussion about likely never-before-encountered processes such as lithography, electron-beam milling, masking etc.

Masking involves the protection of certain areas with a material durable to the etching process – for example, a layer of gold may be sputtered onto the surface of the silicon and selectively covered where the circuitry will lie; an etch then gets rid of the non-protected gold before a further wash gets rid of the protective layer and leaves the desired micro-circuitry behind.

Characterisation of the product can be achieved using microscopy. Candidates should notice that **optical microscopy is of no use** for imaging the smallest features on these chips and so we have to move to electron microscopy (arguments for this citing the difference in wavelengths between electrons and photons are encouraged). Transmission electron microscopy (TEM) should be discounted as this requires extremely thin samples (which the microchip is not). Scanning electron microscopy (SEM) and scanning tunnelling microscopy (STM) can be used for topographical information. Strong candidates might spot that SEM can give both topographical information (from secondary electrons near the sample surface) and compositional information (from back-scattered electrons deeper within the sample).

Q8: I lay a Coke can on its side and balance a 2p piece on its edge on top. At what angle does the coin fall off?

An exact answer is not the aim of this question. Emphasis should be placed on the candidate setting up the problem well and **contemplating all variables** at each step, rather than diving in head first to get an answer. Making reasonable assumptions to help make the calculations manageable is an invaluable skill used everyday in the physical sciences.

Such preliminary assumptions might talk about the coin not falling flat on its face, the start velocity of the coin (is it given a push?) and the coefficient of friction between the coin's edge and the can's surface. How do we define the angle at which the coin falls off? How do we analyse the effect gravity has on the coin's velocity as it begins to roll? It is the candidate's ability to discover why this is a complex problem and then trying to solve it methodically using familiar mechanical concepts which is what should be looked for.

Q9: I place an apple in a bowl of water and find that it floats. How much of the apple is above the waterline?

Again, the interviewer is not looking for an exact answer; rather a methodical approach to a seemingly simple question. The topic of buoyancy requires consideration of an object's mass and volume, and so its density too. There are two approaches to this question.

In the first, the candidate considers the **Archimedean principle** that an object will sink in water until it has displaced an amount of water equal to its own mass (this is independent of the size or shape of the object). If the object has a volume greater than the volume of water displaced, then the object floats. The point of such a discussion is to get the candidate to say that how much of the apple is above the waterline is dependent on its density (which we are not told). Since it floats, it must be less dense than water. The closer its density to that of water, the more of it lies below the waterline.

The second approach involves looking at the forces involved. Gravity acts on the apple ($F = mg$) downwards. A buoyancy force acts to hold the apple up; this can be thought of as the force of gravity acting on the mass of water equal to the volume displaced by a fully submerged apple. Again this demonstrates the **dependency of the answer on the density of the apple** (the force of gravity is dependent on the apple's mass; the buoyancy force is dependent on the apple's volume).

Q10: I give you the definition of the hyperbolic sine function: $sinh(x) = \frac{e^x - e^{-x}}{2}$ *. Sketch sinh(x). Using only your sketch, sketch the derivative of sinh(x).*

Whilst Further Maths A-Level students should have come across hyperbolic functions, the teaching of sketching visually is generally poorly taught in pre-university education. It is an essential skill in the physical sciences.

To sketch sinh(x), candidates need only one building block: the sketch of e^x. Candidates should be encouraged to split the problem into bite-sized chunks. First, sketch e^x (intercepting the y-axis at 1; asymptotic along the x-axis for x→-∞; exponential increase to y = ∞ for x→∞). e^{-x} can then be sketched as a reflection in the y-axis. The latter then needs to be taken away from the former. This can be done by considering three key regions of the sketch: x=0, x→-∞ and x→∞. At the infinite extremities of the x-axis, we are subtracting y-values of infinity from zero and vice versa, to give y-values of -∞ and ∞ respectively. At x = 0, y = 1 is subtracted from y = 1 (or y=½ from y=½ if the candidate had already included this from the definition of sinh(x)) to give a point at the origin. The symmetry of the problem also tells the candidate that the gradient at the origin is 1. Using this information, the sweeping curve of sinh(x) can be sketched with its rotational symmetry of order 2.

Stronger candidates should then be asked to sketch the derivative of sinh(x) on the same set of axes **without carrying out any symbolic differentiation**. As previously mentioned, the gradient at the origin is 1. Again the x-axis extremities should be looked at. In both cases, the gradient is positive and exponentially increasing. The leap to sketching the derivative, cosh(x), with its reflection in the y-axis shouldn't be great.

The very strongest candidates might then be asked to divide their two sketches by one another: $\frac{sinh(x)}{cosh(x)} = tanh(x)$ before sketching its derivative ($sech^2(x)$). **All without algebra.**

Material Sciences Interview Questions

304. What is the difference between carbon and carbon fibres?
305. What is a space ship made of? Why?
306. This is graphene [shows a tube of graphene flakes]. Do you know what it is?.
307. How do you think you make it?
308. What do you think is special about it?
309. How would you build a lift to outer space?
310. What do you think it's made from?
311. Why is it made from those materials?
312. Differentiate $y = \sin x + \cos x + \tan x$
313. What is the dissociation constant of this reaction given these concentrations? Why is the dissociation constant important?
314. What are submarines made of? Why? Wouldn't a harder metal be better?
315. What are airplanes made of? Why? Wouldn't a less dense metal be better?
316. What is a polymer? Why are they so useful?
317. Why is gold such a valuable material?
318. What do we use to cut metals precisely?
319. What do we use to cut diamond precisely?
320. A new compound is found at a suspected alien landing site. How would you work out what it is?
321. What would you expect alien spaceships to be made of?
322. What is the difference between the material sciences course and engineering?
323. Derive the formula for the surface area of a sphere.
324. What is the strongest material in the world? How would you cut it?

MATHEMATICS

A mathematician may be called for a **General Interview** or several maths **Subject Interviews** which can be difficult to prepare for. Unlike other subjects, where an ability to think critically about the subject may be enough, maths interviews will require technical knowledge of all of the mathematics you have studied as well as an extensive complement of mathematical abilities and techniques.

Mathematics interviews will almost always take the form of questions outright testing if you are familiar with mathematical concepts and techniques. While there are several topics more likely to come up, **any topic covered in school until the day of your interview could come up**, and you would be expected to show that you can solve these problems. This section will give some pointers on which questions may appear and which techniques any applicant should be familiar with, but the only real way to succeed is by being incredibly skilled and intuitive in solving mathematical problems. These are perhaps not the most encouraging words for an applicant, but Oxbridge has an exceptionally high bar for mathematicians, and the reality is that only gifted mathematicians will be accepted. Given that you have gotten as far as interview, Oxbridge believes that you have the necessary technical knowledge of mathematics to interview successfully, so at this point you need only practice how to best present your answers and deal with the strange questions which may be asked (as well as revise all your school material!).

The form the interview takes can vary from college to college; you may or may not be asked to sit a test first, and if you are, this test is often used as a foundation for the interview, so the expectation is usually that the applicant will answer a few questions fully rather than all the questions on the test. The interview may build on the problems in the test or discuss techniques, etc. Try to view these tests positively – they are letting you choose your strongest topics for the interview. Test or not, the interviewers (usually) try to make the interview less frightening by **starting slowly with some easier questions and working up to some harder problems**.

The most popular topics that appear in subject interview questions are:

➢ Integration and Differentiation (e.g. differentiate $y = x^x$)
➢ Imaginary Numbers
➢ Trigonometry (e.g. Euler's Formula)
➢ Probability
➢ Combinatorics and Series

Any technically difficult question is almost certain to be about integration, differentiation, trigonometry and complex numbers in some combination.

The interview is much less likely to thoroughly test topics from earlier years in school, such as logarithms, solving lower polynomial equations or geometry, but knowledge of these is assumed to be basal to higher topics, so you may be asked questions which assume knowledge of these or an 'easy' starter question about one of these topics. Double-check you are still familiar with these topics; as you revise you can use them to make your own practice questions for some of the techniques discussed later, such as practice proofs (e.g. prove the Pythagorean Theorem is true or why $10^0=1$).

The advanced topics listed above would be used to test the ability of the applicant to solve problems of a high technical level, but mastery of important mathematical techniques and reasoning may also be tested. An applicant may be asked to demonstrate techniques on either advanced or rudimentary topics.

For instance, **proofs will almost never be required for advanced topics**. Interviewers will usually be testing how you think about concepts and present mathematical solutions, so **often ask deceptively simple questions**. Prove that there are an infinity of primes, prove that some given value is the sum of two squares, or prove than 4n-1 is a multiple of three, are examples of this type of question. This is not about demonstrating advanced knowledge, but about showing that you can use an appropriate method to approach a problem and present your solution in a logical way with proper use of mathematical language. You may be asked to prove something specifically by contradiction, so be prepared.

You may also be asked a similar style of question (e.g. Why is the product of four consecutive integers always divisible by 24?), but even when not asked to give a formal proof, present your answer well, laying it out in an attractive and logical way. The companion to proof questions, but for more advanced topics, are the 'Show that'/'Derive' questions. You could, for example, be asked to show that a trigonometric identity is valid or to derive an expression for differentiation from first principles.

The most common technique you will be asked to demonstrate is **graph sketching**. It is likely that you will first be given functions you are expected to be familiar with [e.g. e^x and sin(x)], and then some function combining these (e.g. $e^{\sin(x)}$), or a new function (e.g. x^x). You would be expected to find the intercepts, stationary points, asymptotes and maybe inflection points. Sketching is almost certain to come up, so check that you still remember how to sketch graphs for all the main types of functions and that you know how to combine functions when sketching graphs. It is probably safest to revise this from the basics, not just rely on memory of how each function looks.

It is not uncommon to be asked a question which tests your ability to interpret word problems as equations. These may be physics-type questions of the 'Two trains leave two stations heading for each other at…'-type, or probability or geometric questions, or any number of other problems which are simple to solve once the equations are set up right. Rarely, you might also be asked a question where you need to 'brain dump' in a constructive way. An example is 'Tell me what you know about triangles', where you need to think through your approach carefully in order to lay out what you know in an **appropriate order and a way which emphasizes the most important points**.

In general, the best preparation is to **revise all the topics you have studied at school**, taking particular note of the ones listed above. Make sure you understand how all these topics are constructed, both the specific derivations of concepts you have studied, and how mathematicians systematically added these ideas to the body of mathematical knowledge through methodical work and proofs.

Worked Questions

Below are a few examples of how to start breaking down an interview question, complete with answer outlines and model answers.

Q1(i): Do you know why $det(AB) = det(A) \, det(B)$?

The Fibonacci numbers are defined as $F_{n+1} = F_n + F_{n-1}$ with $F_0 = 0$ and $F_1 = 1$. Can you show that $\begin{pmatrix} F_{n+1} & F_n \\ F_n & F_{n-1} \end{pmatrix} = \begin{pmatrix} 1 & 1 \\ 1 & 0 \end{pmatrix} \begin{pmatrix} F_n & F_{n-1} \\ F_{n-1} & F_{n-2} \end{pmatrix}$?

The determinant can be thought of as the scale factor of the transformation. So when we write down det(AB), we can think of it as doing the transformation A and then the transformation B. The scale factor of a composition of transformation is the same as the product.

Once can also achieve this by doing the algebra on two general 2x2 matrices.

The first part follows directly from the definition of matrix multiplication, and then using the definition of the Fibonacci numbers.

The question seems to be guiding us to the fact that:

$$det \begin{pmatrix} F_{n+1} & F_n \\ F_n & F_{n-1} \end{pmatrix} = det \begin{pmatrix} 1 & 1 \\ 1 & 0 \end{pmatrix} det \begin{pmatrix} F_n & F_{n-1} \\ F_{n-1} & F_{n-2} \end{pmatrix}$$

Q1(ii): Hence show that $F_{n+1}F_{n-1} - F_n^2 = (-1)^n$

We know that the determinant of the first matrix is -1 so iteratively apply this identity and use the fact that for $n = 1$ the determinant is -1 to get $(-1)^n$.

Q1(iii): Can you think of an alternative way of showing this?

Alternatively induction works here, $F_{k+2}F_k - F_{k+1}^2 = (F_{k+1} + F_k)F_k - (F_k + F_{k-1})^2 = -(F_{k-1}F_{k+1} - F_k^2)$, as required.

Q2: A rectangle's four corners touch the edge of a circle. What is its largest possible area?

There are two ways to do this. Taking a **geometric approach**, consider the diagonals of the rectangle. We know that the diagonals of the rectangles pass through the centre of the circle. The diagonals form two angles, θ and $\pi-\theta$. The area of the inscribed rectangle is therefore $\sin \theta + \sin (\pi-\theta) = 2 \sin\theta$, either from the angle addition formulae, or just knowing that $\sin (\pi-\theta) = \sin\theta$. Thus this area is maximized when $\theta = \pi/2$, and this is a square. This area will then be 2.

Alternatively, you can **approach it computationally**. If we look at the circle $x^2 + y^2 = 1$ we know that the rectangle has vertices *(a, b), (a, -b), (-a, b), (-a, -b)*. Consider the *square* with vertices *($\pm$(a + b)/2, $\pm$ (a + b)/2)*. This has area $(a+b)^2$. Compare the area of this circle to the area of the rectangle, it has area *4ab*. But, $(a + b)^2 \geq 4ab$ (as $(a + b)^2 - 4ab = (a - b)^2 \geq 0$). Thus the square is bigger, and it only gets bigger when we consider the square projected out on to the circle.

Q3: What is integration?

Integration is two possible things: a good candidate will discuss both of them. Integration can be considered *the inverse of differentiation* or it can be considered a process to *find area*.

For the first, we know the fundamental theorem of calculus that states $\int f'(x)dx = f(x) + C$ where $\int$ is considered the indefinite integral (or $\frac{d}{dx}\int_a^x f(t)dt = f(x)$). Such a definition makes sense whenever what we are integrating has a closed form anti-derivative. However a candidate who has done S1 should be aware that there is no anti-derivative for $\exp(-x^2)$, and thus an approach to integration should be more flexible than simply computing the function that differentiates to it. Through-out such an explanation, a candidate may be asked to prove one variant of the fundamental theorem of calculus (they would probably be encouraged towards the second of these) and a proof should be given.

For the second, we have some notion of 'area' under a curve, typified by the area under rectangle, or the area under a straight line. Such an approach leads to the definition of definite integration, e.g., $\int_a^b f(x)\,dx$ is the 'area' under a curve. This may be made more precise, eg, a candidate may be expected to recall the trapezium rule (or lower/upper Riemann sums if these have been seen before), e.g., we can *approximate* the integral by taking sums of this form.

Q4: What is differentiation? Can you explain why $\frac{d}{dx}x^n = nx^{n-1}$?

Differentiation is the act of finding the gradient of a curve at a point, e.g., taking a curve and then considering its tangents. We then map x to the gradient of the tangent at this point.

More formally, we consider $\frac{f(x+h)-f(x)}{h}$, where we think of h as very small. This gives a *secant* of the curve, we then take h closer and closer to zero and come up with some notion of the limit. This is then defined to be the derivative.

$\frac{(x+h)^n - x^n}{h} = \frac{hnx^{n-1} + \frac{h^2 n(n-1)}{2}x^{n-2} + \cdots}{h} = nx^{n-1} + q(x)$ where q is some polynomial in x (and h). So, on taking h to be extremely small, the second term vanishes.

Note that for both of the above questions, attempting to define differentiation or integration in terms of its **action on polynomials**, e.g., in terms of what $\int x^n dx$ and $\frac{d}{dx}x^n$ is possible. However, one needs to be a lot more careful than one thinks one would have to be. It is possible that such a situation would not end well, eg, it is probably a poor candidate who attempts to define integration and differentiation in terms of x^n. Such an issue may also arise with questions of the type 'differentiate x^x', another staple interview question.

The response $x\, x^{x-1}$ is very incorrect and implies a misunderstanding of what differentiation is. (Bonus: $\frac{d}{dx}x^x = \frac{d}{dx}e^{x\log x}$ apply the chain rule with $u = x\log x$ to get $x^x(\log x + 1)$. Since $xx^{x-1} = x^x$ we (in fact) get a bonus, the 'wrong' answer is right if and only if $\log x = 0$, eg, $x = 1$. Thus it's incorrect everywhere, which is pretty bad).

Q5: Which is harder, differentiation or integration?

Both. You can think of either of as harder (and successfully argue it!) but the general rule is, for A level students integration is harder, for undergraduates differentiation is harder.

Differentiation is harder: The issue is that one can integrate a function such as *f(x) = 1* for $x > 0$ and 0 for $x > 0$. What you get is $\int_{-\infty}^{x} f(t)dt = t$ for $t > 0$ and 0 for $t < 0$ (and $t = 0$ at $x = 0$). This shows that we can integrate functions that have 'jumps' in them. We note that for both of the definitions of integration we have given above (including the one based on differentiation) this works, eg, the integral of $f(x)$ legitimately is this thing. So, there are functions you can integrate but not differentiate, eg, differentiation is harder.

Integration is harder: The issue here is that whenever you have a nice explicit function, e.g., $\tan\left[e^{-x^2}log(\sin x)\right]$ we could instantly write the derivative of this down. It's not a pleasant thing to do; however, it reduces to repeated applications of the chain rule and the product rule. So, any function with an explicit 'formula' (whatever that means) can easily be differentiated. This is different for integration: $\int e^{-x^2}dx$ is the most commonly known example. There is no expression of this integral in terms of elementary functions. This is because (ultimately) integration is not as algorithmic, substitution and by parts are *rules* that may simplify the integral, or may not.

A good candidate will pick one and argue it well (following the rough outline here, these are two most sensible interpretations of the question). The interviewer may prod the candidate in the other direction, eg, by drawing the function $f(x)$, or writing down e^{-x^2} and encouraging through.

Q6: What is the area of a circle? Prove it.

As to be expected, the area of a circle is πr^2, where r is the radius of the circle. At this point the interviewer would ask the candidate for a definition of π. One has various retorts: however there are two sensible ones. The first is that it is the ratio of the circumference of a circle to its diameter. The second is that it is the smallest non zero root of $\sin x$ (in essence, every other definition in terms of a trigonometric function is the same).

Again, various proofs exist of which two are now shown: If $x^2 + y^2 = r^2$ we have that $y = \sqrt{r^2 - x^2}$, where $\sqrt{}$ can take positive or negative signs. We take the positive sign, eg, we get the semi circle. Then the area of the circle = $2 \int_{-r}^{r} \sqrt{r^2 - x^2} \, dx$. We set $x = r \cos \theta$ and then $\frac{dx}{d\theta} = -r \sin(\theta)$, and the integral equals $2 \int_{0}^{\pi} r \sin(\theta) \sqrt{r^2(1 - \cos^2 \theta)} \, d\theta$. Then, since $\sqrt{(1 - \cos^2 \theta)} = |\sin \theta|$ we get that the integral = $r^2 \int_{0}^{\pi} \sin^2 \theta \, d\theta$. Integrating $\sin^2 \theta$ is a tricky business: however nothing that $1 - 2 \sin^2 \theta = \cos(2\theta)$ allows us to conclude that the area of the circle = $r^2 \int_{0}^{\pi} (1 - \cos(2\theta)) d\theta = \pi r^2$. (Here we are using that π is the smallest root of the sin function).

Another **integration based proof** is called the onion proof: you can consider the circle as a union of rings going outwards. Each ring has an area equal to the *diameter x a little bit*, so when we integrate we get that area = $\int_{0}^{r} 2\pi t \, dt = \pi r^2$. This proof uses that fact that π is the ratio of the circles circumference to its diameter. Although technically correct, it is not a particularly good proof as making all the intermediary steps precise is a gargantuan task.

Q7: If $f(x + y) = f(x) + f(y)$ and f is differentiable, what is $f(x)$?

If $g(xy) = g(x) + g(y)$ and g is differentiable, what is g?

If $h(x + y) = h(x)h(y)$ and h is differentiable what is h?

If $f(x)$ is differentiable, consider:

$$f'(x) = \lim \frac{f(x+h)-f(x)}{h} = \lim \frac{f(x)+f(h)-f(x)}{h} = \lim \frac{f(h)}{h} = f'(0).$$

So f has constant derivative, eg, $f(x) = Ax + B$ where $A = f'(0)$. Note that $f(x + 0) = f(x) + f(0)$, eg, $f(0) = 0$, and therefore $B = 0$.

For $g(xy) = g(x) + g(y)$, consider $g(e^u e^v) = g(e^{u+v}) = g(e^u) + g(e^v)$ eg, the function $G(y) = g(e^y)$ satisfies the first part. We thus have that $g(e^y) = Ay$, eg, $g(x) = A \log x$.

The same trick works for h, except consider $log(h(x))$. This is of the form Ax, eg, the solution e^{ax}.

This question is straight forward, however each stage requires somewhat of a jump. The candidate would be expected to *know* the answers, and then guided. The first step of using the derivative is not obvious, and there are various false starts a candidate could make (and various not so false starts). Obtaining that *f(0)* is good, using the fact that f is differentiable is good, writing down the Taylor Series works. Using the fact that f is differentiable is good, writing down the Taylor Series works. Using that $f(n) = nf(1)$, and $f(\frac{1}{n}) = \frac{1}{n} f(1)$ can be helpful too. The issue of "are there any functions other than the ones listed" is an interesting one, for such a function to exist it would have a lot of bad properties.

Questions 8-16 are fairly straightforward questions that might be asked at the start of the interview and wouldn't take longer than 2-5 minutes. They also frequently come up in science interviews e.g. Biology, Chemistry, Material Sciences, Physics and Engineering.

Q8: If x is odd, show that $x^2 - 1$ is divisible by 8.

$x^2 - 1 = (x - 1)(x + 1)$. If x is odd, $x - 1$ *and* $x + 1$ are both even. Since the difference between $x - 1$ *and* $x + 1 = 2$ and they are both even, one of them must be divisible by 4. Any multiple of 4 multiplied by another even number will result in a number that is divisible by 8.

Q9: If x is a prime number > 3 show that $x^2 - 1$ is divisible by 24.

$x^2 - 1 = (x - 1)(x + 1)$. Since x has to be odd, $x^2 - 1$ must be divisible by 8 (see *Q8* above). We now look at the remainder when we divide by 3, it is clear that we can't write x as $3n$, so either $x = 3n + 1$ or $x = 3n + 2$. Thus, either $x + 1$ or $x - 1$ is divisible by 3.

Q10: Can you define a prime number? Can you show every number is either prime or a product of prime numbers?

We proceed (surprisingly) by induction. We claim that every number above 1 is either prime, or is a product of primes. Suppose it is true for all $m < n$. Then either n is prime, in which case we are done, or there is some prime number p that divides n. So, consider $\frac{n}{p}$, which is strictly smaller than n. But then, by induction, we are done.

Q11: How many zeroes are there in 10! ? What about 100! ?

The number of zeroes is determined by the number of 5's, 10's and 25's in the factorial. Thus, 5! has one zero, 10! has two zeros etc…

25 can be expressed as 5 x 5 so contributes two zeroes. Similarly, all multiples of 25 contribute two zeroes. This can be extrapolated to give:

Number	Zeros	Number	Zeros
100	2	95	1
90	1	85	1
80	1	75	2
70	1	65	1
60	1	55	1
50	2	45	1
40	1	35	1
30	1	25	2
20	1	15	1
10	1	5	1
Total	12	Total	12

Thus, there are 24 zeroes in total.

Q12: If I have a square of paper that is 10 cm by 10 cm, I cut out squares from the corners and fold up the result to form a cuboid. What is the largest cuboid by volume I can form?

Denote the length that has been cut out by a. When we fold it up we get a cuboid of base length and width $10 - 2a$. It has height a. So the volume is $a(10 - 2a)^2$. Expand and differentiate, the volume is $4a^3 - 4a^2 + 100a$. Differentiating with respect to a, and setting equal to zero to find the maximum, we get $12a^2 - 80a + 100 = 0$, which we can factorize as $4(a - 5)(3a - 5) = 0$. $a = \frac{5}{3}$ is the solution we want, and thus the volume is $\frac{5}{3}\frac{400}{9} = \frac{2000}{27}$.

Q13: Suppose Alice, Bob and Charlie work together, digging standard sized holes. It is assumed that Alice, Bob and Charlie do not affect each other when they work. It is known that Alice and Bob can dig a hole in 10 minutes, Bob and Charlie can dig a hole in 15 minutes and Alice and Charlie take 20 minutes to dig a hole. How long does it take Alice, Bob and Charlie to dig a standard sized hole?

Suppose that digging a hole involves doing 60 units of work. Alice and Bob thus work at a rate of 6 units per minute, Bob and Charlie work at a rate of 4 units per minute, and Alice and Charlie work at a rate of 3 units per minute. So, if we denote the rate of work that someone does by the first letter of their name, $A + B = 6, B + C = 4$ and $A + C = 3$. Adding all of these together and dividing by 2 gives that $A + B + C = \frac{13}{2}$. So, it takes Alice Bob and Charlie 60/(13/2) = 120/13 ≈ 9 minutes 20 seconds.

Q14: Integrate $\cos^2 x$, $\cos^3 x$, $\cos^4 x$

$2\cos^2 x - 1 = \cos(2x)$, eg, $\cos^2 x = \frac{1}{2}(1 + \cos 2x)$. Thus, $\int \cos^2 x = \frac{1}{2}\left(x + \frac{1}{2}\sin(2x)\right) + C$. We have that $\cos^3 x = \cos^2 x \cos x = \frac{1}{2}(\cos x + \cos x \cos 2x)$. Then by the product to sum formula, $\cos x \cos 2x = \frac{1}{2}(\cos x + \cos 3x)$. Putting this in and integrating gives $\frac{1}{12}(9\sin x + \sin 3x)$. At this point it is quite likely that the interviewer would stop you as the principle is seemingly obvious at this point, $\int \cos^4 x \, dx = \int \frac{1}{4}(1 + \cos 2x)^2 = \frac{1}{4}\int 1 + 2\cos 2x + \cos^2(2x) \, dx$.

Expanding (again) gives $\frac{1}{4}\int(1 + 2\cos(2x) + \frac{1}{2}(1 + \cos 4x))dx$. Integrating we get $\frac{1}{32}(12x + 8\sin 2x + \sin 4x)$. There are a couple of other approaches to this question, De Moivre's theorem springs to mind, and we could also split and integrate by parts if we were looking for a general $\cos^n x$.

Q15: Integrate and differentiate x log x.

$\frac{d}{dx}(x \log x) = 1 + \log x.$ For $\int x \log x \, dx$ we integrate by parts,
$\int x \log x \, dx = \frac{x^2 \log x}{2} - \int \frac{x}{2} dx = \frac{x^2}{2}\left(\log x - \frac{1}{2}\right) + C.$

Q16: Integrate sin²x

The first key point to notice is that you cannot integrate this straight away and will need to manipulate sin²x in order to integrate this. A poor candidate will not notice this and will proceed to say that the answer is -1/3cos³x. When asked to differentiate this, they would hopefully realise that this is incorrect.

Knowledge of the trigonometric Identity $\sin^2 x + \cos^2 x = 1$ would be a good starting point. You could then use the double angular formula $[\cos(a + b) = \cos a \cos b - \sin a \sin b]$ as this can be used to remove cos²x.

As with all of these type of questions, it is essential that you talk through your working as much as possible. If the candidate seems stuck, then suggest formula you might get reminded of the trigonometric identities.

Once you've identified the identities, you can then substitute back in and solve by the following:

$\int \sin^2 x dx = \int \frac{1}{2} 1 - \cos 2x) dx$

$= \frac{1}{2} \int 1 - \cos 2x) dx$

$= \frac{1}{2}\left(x - \frac{1}{2} \sin 2x\right) + C$

$= \frac{x}{2} - \frac{1}{4} \sin 2x + C$

Whilst it is not mandatory to know how to do this straight away, the interviewer would expect you to be able to complete this once you're given the two identities.

Q17: As you may or may not know, $\sum_{i=1}^{k} i = \frac{i(i+1)}{2}$. As you may not know, $\sum_{i=1}^{k} i^2 = \frac{1}{6}i(i+1)(2i+1)$. As you may or may not know, $\sum_{i=1}^{k} i^3 = \frac{i^2(i+1)^2}{4}$. As one may guess there is a general rule lurking here, $\sum_{i=1}^{k} i^n$ is an $n + 1$ degree polynomial in k. Can you prove this?

(Hint: Consider $\sum_{i=1}^{k}[(i + 1)^{n+1} - i^{n+1}]$

We proceed by induction and use the hint. The question tells us that the answer is true in the case $n = 1$ (and 2 and 3) so we only need to show that the truth for all $n < p$ implies the truth for $n = p$. To see this $\sum_{i=1}^{k}[(i + 1)^{p+1} - i^{p+1}] = (k + 1)^{p+1}$, as every term apart from the last cancels identically. However, it is also equals $\sum_{i=1}^{k} \sum_{j=1}^{p} \binom{p+1}{j} i^j$ (by expanding the binomial series $(i + 1)^{p+1}$. If we write $S_j = \sum_{i=1}^{k} i^j$ we get that this equals $\sum_{j=1}^{p} \binom{p+1}{j} S_j = (k + 1)^{p+1}$. So, $S_p = (k + 1)^{p+1} - \sum_{j=1}^{p-1} \binom{p+1}{j}$. But now we're done, the right hand side is a polynomial of degree $p + 1$. This, in fact, gives an explicit expression for the polynomial, which was not required.

Maths Interview Questions

325. Do you know what a hyperbolic function is? [Gives definition of sinh or cosh].

326. Sketch sinh(x) or cosh(x).

327. Plot $\frac{x^2}{1-x}$

328. Plot ln x

329. Plot e^x

330. Plot $x^2 + x$

331. What is your favourite number?

332. Why do we approximate many functions in maths to be sine and cosine?

333. How would you prove that the square root of 3 is irrational?

334. $e^x = yx$. For what value of x is there only one solution?

335. How would you prove that e is irrational?

336. How would you derive Pi?

337. How would you prove that any integer can be expressed as prime factors or is itself a prime number?

338. I drove to this interview at 50 kmph and will drive back at 30 kmph because of the traffic. What is my average speed?

339. How would you write down 0.1 recurring as a fraction?

340. Estimate the fifth root of 1.2

341. There are 30 people in one room. What is the probability that exactly 2 of them have the same birthday?

342. Derive the formula for the volume of a sphere.

343. Integrate ysiny with respect to y.

344. Sketch y = sinx and y = $(sinx)^{-1}$

345. Prove pythagoras' theorem.

346. What is the significance of Euler's equations?

347. What do know about Fermat's last theorem?

348. What are modular functions?

349. Sketch the graph of $y = e^{x^x}$

350. Sketch the graph of $y = x^{e^e}$

351. Differentiate both of these curves – what do you notice?

THE ARTS

ECONOMICS

This interview will require you to demonstrate passion and a genuine desire to study your chosen subject. You can be asked to discuss a source extract, a diagram or a mathematical problem.

In E&M interviews, business-related questions will also feature, where applicants have to tackle basic problems related to the operation and management of a firm.

An economist may be asked economics-related questions or questions from a related subject, such as mathematics, business or even politics and history. An applicant for Economics and Management will be asked questions on both economics and business/management. (The **interviewers understand applicants may not have studied economics** before – be prepared to explain why you think you want to study economics and show through extra-curricular reading or activities how you've fostered your interest.) Before the interview it should be clear which subject will be the focus of any interview.

Candidates are not expected to have studied the subject they are applying for previously at A-level, but to have a good general knowledge, and to demonstrate interest in and enthusiasm for studying economics (and business in the case of E&M applicants), to demonstrate logic and critical thinking, and to communicate clearly and effectively.

Many of the questions asked in the interview will be a larger question, with many smaller sub-questions to guide the answer from the start to a conclusion. The main question may seem difficult, impossible or random at first, but take a breath and start discussing with your interviewer different ideas you have for breaking down the question into manageable pieces. Don't panic. **The questions are designed to be difficult** to give you the chance to show your full intellectual potential. They will help guide you to the right idea, if you provide ideas for them to guide.

This is your chance to show your creativity, analytical skills, intellectual flexibility, problem-solving skills and your go-getter attitude. Don't waste it on nervousness or a fear of messing up or looking stupid.

For economics, the questions will usually take one of a few possible forms based on highlighting skills necessary to 'think like an economist'. The six main question types are:

➢ Critical reasoning questions ("Tell me what your view on ... is").

➢ Normative questions ("Should the government do the following?").

➢ Practical questions ("How would you determine that...").

➢ Statistical questions ("Given this data...").

➢ Questions about proximate causes (mechanism; "How does...") and MultiMate causes (function; "Why does..."), usually both at once.

➢ Quantitative questions for example from game theory or economic principles.

The questions also have recurring themes because they are also prevalent topics for economic and management theory and research: markets, money, development economics, profit maximisation of a firm, game theory, unemployment and inflation, growth theory and international trade.

Worked Questions

Below are a few examples of how to start breaking down an interview question along with model answers.

Q1: I give you £100. You have to offer part of this £100 to someone. Unless they accept the offer, you get nothing. How much will you offer?

This is a mathematical question that will therefore require a numeric answer. The most important feature of a strong candidate is the ability to answer the question directly and from the analytical point of view the interviewer set through the phrasing of the question.

Applicant: So, I'm looking for a nominal value between 0 and £100 to be offered to the other person. This seems to be a question related to the field of game theory, the area that focuses on understanding optimal strategic decisions and their modelling. Unfortunately, I'm not familiar with the tools of this discipline, but I will try to tackle the question using my basic economic intuition and mathematics. I understand that economics primarily deals with incentives, and here the two participants have very different incentives. Let me consider both of them and then outline who will get their way or what kind of a compromise they will reach. Both me and the other person want to get as much money as possible, but we both can't get the £100, **there is a trade-off**.

We also have different ways of achieving our aims: I set the amount, the other person decides whether to accept or not. The other person can stop me from having any money whatsoever; this seems to be a strong tool against me. So I will have to make the other person happy otherwise we will both walk away without anything. Given this, how can I get the best outcome for myself, while navigating through my dual objective: getting money, but satisfying the other one? I have to give the person something, even though I don't want to. Anything I give should make the other happy, since the alternative is 0. Therefore mathematically, I should probably offer the least amount: £1. But would that be acceptable? At this point, I could consider other, alternative methods to understanding cooperation that can better deal with phenomena like envy, fairness, altruism, etc.

Assessment: The student immediately sets the context and frame of the question, which suggests a very strong candidate who is not trying different things but knows the direction of the answer. Identifying the relevant area in Economics for the question is a nice touch that doesn't require extensive prior knowledge of that particular field, but still shows that the student has a general understanding of what belongs to the subject.

The interviewers don't expect you to be an expert in a niche field. Instead they want you to apply your existing knowledge and experience to a new problem.

A good candidate will always **draw from multiple disciplines** and apply the seemingly most relevant knowledge they have. Structuring the answer is always key, most importantly to make it easier for the interviewer to help with the solution. If they know what the plan of attack is they can guide the applicant in the direction that leads to the correct answer most easily. An outstanding candidate goes beyond conventional wisdom and demonstrates real outside the box thinking, by having the ability to challenge seemingly fundamental assumptions. In this particular example, the candidate could point out that there are many people to whom getting the highest amount of monetary gain might not be a primary goal, hence making the simple mathematical analysis problematic.

Q2: What is globalisation? What does the average citizen gain from globalisation?

The main challenge in this question is clearly the broadness of the topic. This is a subject hundreds of academics and other pundits have written hefty books on. How does one answer this question in 2-3 minutes so the response has sufficient content but is still structured?

The important thing to keep in mind here is that sometimes the applicant's first response serves only as a discussion starter. There is no need to include everything you would want to talk about in excruciating details, the interviewers only want to hear a few points they can start from. Then they will drive the discussion in a direction they want to.

Applicant: Let me start by clarifying the concept of globalization. It's a household concept by now, but I'm not sure we have a universal agreement on what is meant by it. To me, globalization is the process through which national and regional borders become increasingly irrelevant, as a result of culture, business and general economic activity all become more homogeneous and are formed by actors unrelated to any single country. This definition allows me to capture the different aspects of globalization each of which require a different analytical perspective: sociology, economics, politics, international relations, etc.

From an economics point of view, **the average citizen gains in two main ways from globalization**. First, the citizen benefits from the diversification of products and services available for consumption at lower prices. Second, the broadening of opportunities allows citizens to have a better match between their skills and their occupation.

I will first consider the benefits of free trade. The emergence of transnational corporations and wider political movements supporting globalization have put increasing pressure on governments to allow for greater freedom in international trade. This has resulted in an unprecedented expansion of consumption goods and services available for all customers. Just think about all the exotic fruits, spices and craft goods one can buy even in their local Tesco. International competition, another benefit of globalization, has furthermore allowed all goods to be priced competitively on a global scale, leading to significant price drops. This process clearly benefits the average citizen.

My second point relates to the tendency that globalization comes with the **expansion of cross-border mobility** too. This happens for a range of reasons: better and more easily available information about opportunities abroad, the internationalization of communication (English as lingua franca) and the transnational HR procedures and multinational corporations. The average citizen benefits from being able to find a position more ideally suited for them than before globalization had emerged.

Having said that, I believe it's important to note the likely negative consequences of globalization too: the threat of dumping in developed countries, the threat of exploitation in developing countries or diminishing cultural diversity are just a few on the list.

Assessment: The interviewers most likely have already interrupted the interviewee by this time somewhere. They might be interested in a discussion on free trade, the applicant's thoughts on multinational corporations, etc. But by presenting a clearly outlined structure in the beginning, the applicant ensured that the interviewers know that a strong and well-argued presentation would follow had they not interrupted. It is also advisable with such a complex question to take some time before starting the answer, this allows any applicant to articulate any thoughts in a more organised manner. A focus on the economic arguments is also important, as this is an economics and not a sociology interview, and the points therefore need to be chosen accordingly.

Q3: Can you put a monetary value on this teapot?

An odd question clearly that is not interesting for the specific knowledge it requires, but much more because it pushes the applicant way out of their comfort zone. A question like this can easily appear on both an Economics and a Management interview, as it requires out-of-the-box thinking and independence to solve challenging, unfamiliar problems, crucial in both fields. Each student would answer this question differently; the only important point is to show confidence and originality in an answer.

Straight Economics Applicant:
I can certainly look for a suitable price for this teapot from my perspective. However, the valuation different individuals assign to the same product often vary significantly and also with changing circumstances too. Therefore, my monetary valuation is not going to be a universal one.

I would start from stating that the monetary value of the teapot will fundamentally be linked to the concept of a market. I am not looking for the intrinsic value (i.e the 'usefulness' of the teapot) but the ideal monetary amount it should be exchanged for. Thus I turn to the basic knowledge I have about the market and try to understand how those will determine the optimal exchange price of the teapot. There are two key factors on a market: supply and demand. I will consider both of them in relation to our example.

I know that if a good is supplied widely, its prices or monetary value will be lower than of goods in limited supply. Consider the example of water vs. diamonds. It's not that diamonds are more 'useful' than water, but that they are only available in a very limited amount; hence their supply is constrained. Whereas, water is essential for life, but is abundant in supply. Consequently diamonds have a much larger monetary value than water. In our case, a teapot can probably be bought in any large department store, however its cracks and tea marks on its side make it unique. Therefore one could argue that the supply of this teapot is extremely limited, indicating a high monetary price.

Equally, demand for the teapot is also probably fairly limited. While these qualities are visually pleasing, it is probably fair to assume that there aren't many who could appreciate its artistic beauty. Modest demand suggests a low monetary value, as people would not be willing to pay much for the item. This **concept of willingness-to-pay** is a central one for our analysis, and we would have to conduct a more thorough investigation into the existing demand for an artistically cracked teapot.

The two sides (supply and demand) put together suggest that **this teapot should be valued similarly to other niche products** with both small demand and supply. Such products include pieces of art, rarities or unique luxury products (e.g. custom made sports cars or watches).

Assessment: This is an economist's take on the question who tries to analyse the problem with the tools provided by the discipline. The question provides a great opportunity to enter a discussion on markets and prices, complemented by a basic summary of the forces present on a market. With such a question, a specific, numeric answer is not necessarily required, as the process of understanding the determinants of prices is much more important. A clear outline, clarification of definitions and real life examples all add to the answer and the image communicated to the interviewers. But once again, many alternative answers could be presented here the important point is that the applicant shouldn't feel intimidated by a seemingly unrealistic and unsolvable question.

Finally, if starting point of the question is already ridiculous, then the applicant is free to make unrealistic assumptions too, as long as those can be defended somehow (e.g. the artistic cracks on the teapot add extra monetary value to it).

Economics and Management Applicant:

From a firm's perspective it is crucial to understand the underlying processes that determine the monetary value of a product. In our situation, the monetary value is equivalent to finding the price of the teapot. I am going to consider three methods to establish that value:

➢ Pricing based on competition
➢ Pricing based on cost
➢ Psychological pricing

The first method seems to be the most obvious to me, as it simply builds on the competitive tendencies in a market. This would require us to look at any other seller of similar teapots and record their prices. Afterwards, we simply have to decide if we want to undercut them or simply price it according to their set monetary valuations. Online retailers and, in this particular case, used goods' resellers can both provide a starting point.

Secondly, I could simply figure out how much it costs me to produce it, if I'm a decision-maker in the company involved in the creation of the product. Then I would add some profit margin on my costs and that would give me the monetary valuation of the teapot. The **production costs** in this case could include: raw materials (porcelain, paint,etc.), labour costs, electricity, rent for the workplace and so on. A profit margin is required to make it worthwhile running the business and provide a payout to the company's owners.

Finally, I have read about behavioural economics before, for example in the book *Freakonomics* or in *Predictably Irrational*. These books showed me, how psychological factors play a crucial role in our perceptions of prices. The idea about the **relativity of prices explains the lack of a fundamental link between products and their monetary value**.

Therefore the **prices of this teapot could be anything in a wide range**, depending on the psychological connections I create, through procedures such as *anchoring*.

Assessment: The student always has to tailor the answer to the subject of the interview. One of the most important requirements on an interview is to show that the applicant is capable of analyzing problems from the perspective of the given discipline. Thus in this case the student had to demonstrate the ability to consider the firm's view, which can be done by collecting thoughts around basic concepts that an applicant might be familiar with: costs, competition, etc. The brightest candidates shine through their ability to complement the basic materials with extra reading and real life examples.

Q4: Has the Eurozone experiment worked?

A good response: "For me, the main objectives of the Eurozone were to improve trade between European nations and to provide more economic stability for those nations involved. I think the European Union has been successful in the first of these goals, however when addressing the latter it is clear that the last two decades have been rather turbulent for all Eurozone countries. Proponents of the Euro may argue that weak nations such as Greece would never have survived the economic crisis of 2008 without the presence of the Eurozone, but others may argue that a lack over control over individual countries' monetary policy contributed to the severity of the recession. One interesting aspect of the Eurozone process to me has been that it seems to have highlighted that there is quite high geographical mobility of labour in many European nations…"

Assessment: This is an extremely open-ended question, which provides the candidate with the opportunity to talk about a multitude of topics and issues. It is easy to get side tracked with such an unstructured question, but the applicant should make sure they answer the question. However, there is potential for them to talk about areas that interest them, and display their enthusiasm for the subject in doing so.

Candidates should however be wary about trying to suggest they have a substantial knowledge of areas that they don't, in reality, know much about.

This question may be followed up with further questioning by the interviewer on more specific aspects of the questions, and the least helpful thing a candidate can do when trying to impress a tutor is falsify knowledge of certain topics and then get "caught out" doing so.

It is worth bearing in mind that not only is the tutor looking for intelligence; **they are looking for someone that they are happy to teach for the next few years**. Personality can be a factor in determining their decision: arrogance or attempting to deceive a tutor may not be looked upon fondly.

Q5: What would you say if the prime minister were to take a report which shows that people who go to university earn more than those who do not, and then proclaim that going to university causes you to earn more?

This question invites the applicant to address a situation closest to what an economist is qualified for. Take a dataset and form a hypothesis. Then test the hypothesis using the dataset form a conclusion and thus, provide policy recommendations. In an interview a student might be asked to perform any part of the above process or to give an account of an understanding behind the approach in its entirety. In this case, an externally formed hypothesis and policy recommendation needs to be evaluated. The key, once again, is not to go into a detailed discussion about econometrics, but to demonstrate some basic aptitude for numerical analysis.

Assessment: In my answer I am going to focus on the plausible conclusions that can be drawn from a statistical result – in this case, that individuals who go to university have a higher average salary than those who don't –, while I am going to take the statistical result itself as given. We could and ideally should discuss the methods used to arrive at that result and of course their validity, but this would be too time consuming in the current circumstances.

We can illustrate the result on a graph that would look something like this. [Draws a simple x-y diagram with a 45-degree line from the origin and with scattered points around it The axes would be labeled: earnings and education]. More education is *correlated* with higher earnings.

This is an important result; making us wonder about the likely benefits of education towards people's wages and therefore living standards the improvement of which is one of the government's primary objectives.

However, as we know it well, ***correlation is not causation***. While the former simply means that two variables change their values similarly, the later means the changes in one variable lead to changes in the other variable. Basic statistical methods, such as a simple graphical illustration as seen before, are only able to show us *correlation;* we don't know why education and wages are high at the same points. More advanced statistical analysis would allow us to go into further details and hopefully enable to form statements about *causation* too. With the information given in the question it could well be that there is ***reverse causality***, a situation where causation actually runs reversely. Those who are richer might decide to go to university, as they can afford not to earn wages while studying. Equally, it could be that there is a third, unknown variable that affects both variables. For instance, the geographic area individuals live in: urban citizens can have both higher wages and better access to higher education, when compared to rural inhabitants.

In both of these cases, we would see correlation between education and wages, but that would not mean that education causes higher wages. Therefore, I would say, we need to **further investigate the data** to understand whether in this case, there is indeed a causal effect running from university education to higher earnings.

Assessment: This question allowed the applicant to demonstrate a number of vital skills. First of all, priorities needed to be set. The applicant had to understand that there is no time to address all aspects of the question, from data analysis to recommendations.

Second, the applicant could make use of graphs, the confident use of which is a fundamental skill any aspiring economist or management student should have. Third, the basic notion: ***correlation is not causation*** was required for the answer. This is a concept all applicants should feel comfortable about, as it's the basic principle of statistics.

The interviewee could also shine by bringing in originality in trying to come up with reasons other than education → wages. In an interview situation the interviewer would likely specifically ask about this, rather than expecting the applicant to feel the need to list examples, but the importance of original thoughts is evident nonetheless. Finally, the applicant needed not to forget that the question was: "What would you say?", therefore the answer needed to be specific. Had the applicant stopped before the last paragraph, some points would have been taken away for not directly answering the question.

Q6: Would you support the privatisation of the NHS?

This question provides an opportunity for the applicant to present their understanding of the issue, but they must be wary not to be drawn into giving a political argument. The focus should be placed on the economic impacts of privatisation, rather than personal opinions. The applicant has to formulate an argument about a topic that is both important and probably relatively unfamiliar for most A level students. As always, it is not the factual knowledge of healthcare economics which is required, but **good structure, and critical thinking**.

Applicant:
Privatisation is the act of transferring assets from public ownership (effectively state ownership) to private owners through the sale of the assets. Political parties from the left and the right have had a long standing debate over the desirable extent of public ownership of certain strategic companies and sectors e.g. schools, hospitals, utilities or public transportation operators. Out of these, the transfer of the healthcare provider, the NHS, has been one of the most controversial topics in UK politics, effectively since the creation of a universal healthcare provider shortly after WWII.

There are strong reasons for both supporting and opposing the transformation of the healthcare system into a market-driven system, but I still believe that the arguments against it are stronger, thus I would not support the privatization of the NHS. I have **three main reasons** to believe so: adverse effects on doctor-patient relationships, social injustice and insecurity of continuous provision.

Firstly, I have always thought that **doctors choose their profession very differently** from what economists assume about rational agents who only care about monetary reward. They are dedicated to helping the sick and doing everything they can to do their jobs best. If the NHS was privatized, there is a good chance business owners of hospitals would introduce measures to motivate doctors to think more business-mindedly. This would however, endanger the personal trust patients need to feel when they see their doctor about their health.

Secondly, allowing private owners to supply healthcare services would threaten with them **seeking profits above patient care**. They could increase prices of services, as demand for basic health services is inelastic (we are all willing to pay nearly anything for the health of our loved ones). While the well off could probably still pay for their healthcare, with higher prices many would not be able to purchase even basic services.

Finally, private owner might decide to continue the supply of profitable services and cut back on others or even shut down loss-making hospitals in less developed areas. This could mean that **healthcare is not universally available across the UK**, undermining citizens' inevitable right for equal treatment.

Of course, privatisation doesn't have to take such an extreme form and it can also be heavily regulated to improve some of the above-mentioned areas. Yet, the potential problems are so serious that **even if the NHS is not an economically viable business and costs the State a lot, it should remain in the public domain**.

Assessment: The applicant started with placing the question in a historical and political context, which is always a good idea with questions of this sort. It shows the interviewer that the applicant didn't just memorise arguments for topics, but actually understands how things come together. A clear structure and a strong stance are also qualities of a strong applicant. Of course, such a question is bound to lead to a discussion, where the interviewer challenges the applicant and comes up with strong counter arguments. The applicant is expected to respond to those challenges, but not to give up their stance unless factually proven wrong.

Another good response: "There are economic benefits and costs to privatisation, which would be particularly emphasised in the case of a large institution like the NHS. The benefits of privatisation may include the potential for improved competition in the healthcare provision industry. Improved competition has benefits for an economy, as it means that firms have an incentive to improve efficiency and innovate. This could mean lower costs for consumers, and improved service. However it could be argued that this is a welfare issue, and that healthcare would be underprovided to poorer citizens in a free market. It may also be reasoned that the high barriers to entry make healthcare provision a natural monopoly, and that privatisation would lead to one firm dominating the market, and exploiting its powers to overcharge. I would not support privatisation of the NHS, as I do not think healthcare is a good that should be made excludable based on price."

Q7: What is the biggest problem facing CEOs?

The applicant has to show the ability to 'think like a manager' and to analyse questions from their perspective. With such an open-ended question the challenge is not to find something to talk about, but to be able to make a proper case out of it, with valid reasons. There is no wrong answer, only insufficient reasoning.

Applicant: Chief Executive Officers are the people in charge of the overall business and with the final say on most daily issues, where the Board of Governors doesn't intervene. The pressure and responsibility on them is tremendous and finding a way to prioritise their tasks and problems is crucial. CEOs serve as the **ultimate link** between the company's employees, owners and customers. Therefore, rather than any individual task of theirs, I think it's the management of often opposing incentives and goals which is the biggest problem facing CEOs.

The workers in the company strain themselves to achieve better working conditions, higher wages and are often trying to minimize the work effort they exert. Shareholders seek a return on their investment. Therefore, they expect the CEO to deliver growth and most importantly profit, which is already in conflict with higher wages and less work. Customers care the most about price and quality.

The former needs to be low to attract customers, but high to have profits and pay wages. The later is costly to produce and requires stringent work effort. Finding the perfect middle ground is challenging and requires constant monitoring, re-evaluation from the CEO.

This is a big problem for CEOs because other challenges are one-dimensional e.g. developing future growth plans, creating more equality between workers, fighting competition, etc. Whilst these are all difficult areas, the desired outcomes are obvious. In the case of managing different interest groups, it's often **unclear what outcomes CEOs needs to achieve**.

Assessment: After demonstrating familiarity with the main stakeholders in a firm (CEO, Board, workers) the applicant took a clear stance and named a topic thought to be the most difficult. This was then analysed from the point of view of the CEO or any other business professional. The applicant didn't lose track of the question. And by mentioning other potentially important topics, a wider familiarity with the subject could be highlighted. After this intro the interviewer would likely invite the applicant to further discuss those other areas and compare their relative importance.

Q8: How does tightening monetary policy affect the prices of bonds in the bond market?

A good response: "I may be wrong, but I believe that restrictive monetary policy involves raising short term interest rates. I don't know if there is any formal relationship between interest rates and bond prices, but if I was investing in bonds at a time with high interest rates I would expect higher returns in order to stop me investing the money in a bank instead. Therefore, I would imagine that the **price of bonds would probably fall** in order to make them more attractive to investors who might otherwise save their money in a bank."

Assessment: The main point of this question is to identify an interviewee's ability to determine relationships between two ideas, and their understanding of how economic mechanisms allow policies to work. The candidate shows the interviewer that they are not completely certain on the topic, but this is perfectly acceptable – the tutor is attempting to test thinking skills and not knowledge. The logical, step by step approach shows that the candidate remains calm and methodical even when presented with unfamiliar information. Given the testing nature of the Oxbridge courses offered, it is important for tutors to establish the ability of potential students to work under pressure.

Q9: What, if any, is the value of studying counter-factual history?

➤ Counter-factual history is the history of *what if?* It challenges the historian to consider what would have happened had something else occurred. A common counter-factual includes: *What if Germany had won the First World War?*
➤ Consider the merits and limitations of this type of history.
➤ The advantages are that you can consider crucial tuning points – such as battles, political events or wars. An event is significant if the *What if* leads to a drastically different turn of events.
➤ They are an interesting and engaging way to deal with the past.

> However, some would argue that creating stories or ideas is not good history. We should be evaluating the evidence of what did happen, not following a distracting path of what might have happened.

> History is about the events, people and changes which occurred in the past. Arguably, counter-factual history is a subversion of that.

Q10: Compare and contrast Keynesian and Classical economic theories

Keynesian economists believe that the immense resources of the state should be deployed during periods of economic slowdown (recession). While, classical economists believe that the interference of the state distorts the working of the market to an extent that any well-intended policy will actually further hinder economic recovery and that, where possible, government spending should be limited and taxes cut.

It would be good to use a relevant example from current affairs. In 2008, Gordon Brown used a **fiscal stimulus** (Keynesian) to attempt to kick start the economy – he brought forward capital spending and cut VAT to boost consumption. While, in 2010 the Chancellor, George Osborne, began austerity to restore confidence in UK public finances and reduce the budget deficit, while supporting monetary expansion through the reduction of interest rates to facilitate business lending.

Who are classical economists? Friedrich Hayek *A road to serfdom*, Milton Freeman (negative income tax), Adam Smith *The Wealth of Nations*.

Who are Keynesian economists? Paul Krugman or Nicholas Kaldor.

Q11: Economists often model individual consumers as rational agents. Is addiction rational?

A good response: "To answer the question, we must first understand what rationality is. In my view, a rational decision is one that makes sense based on the facts or evidence presented to the decision maker. In the case of addiction, the facts available to the addict are the feeling which their addiction gives them – which may be seen as benefits, and the associated costs of the addiction.

If the benefits to the addict outweigh these costs, then it may be argued that addiction is rational. However it could be suggested that an addict has a distorted view on these costs and benefits, and therefore their ability to think rationally is compromised"

Assessment: This response is well structured, and focuses on attempting to answer the question at hand. By outlining a definition of rationality initially, the candidate displays that they fully understand the question, and are engaging with it critically. The response shows a consideration of both sides to the argument, without being side-tracked into irrelevant discussion. One area for potential improvement is the conclusion, where no definitive answer to the question is given. Tutors will be looking for students who can articulate their own opinions, and the lack of a conclusive response may suggest that an interviewee does not possess these skills.

Q12: Why do governments not seek 0% inflation?

A good response: "0% inflation may seem like a good idea, as lower prices provide consumers with the opportunity to get more for their money. Price increases are often poorly received by consumers, as they have to reduce what they buy. However, there is often a **trade-off between inflation and economic growth**, and aiming for zero inflation may lead to stagnation in an economy. Inflation only forces a reduction in consumption when prices are rising faster than wages, so a government may compromise on inflation – such as the Bank of England have done with their 2% target – in order to ensure that economic is being achieved."

Assessment: The candidate effectively pre-empts, and dispels, arguments in favour of 0% inflation goals. Given that this is probably a topic that the interviewee has never had to tackle before, it is advisable to ensure they can present a structured logical argument before attempting to answer. This may involve asking for a moment to think, and a good candidate should not be discouraged from doing this, in order to give themselves a moment to collect their thoughts.

This response is clearly well organised and thought through, which is clearly preferable to a rushed and illogical answer, even if it comes at the expense of a momentary pause. The candidate has the opportunity to show the extent of their understanding by referring to current policies or additional knowledge from further reading.

Q13: Why is economics seen as a social science?

A good response: "I would define a social science as any academic discipline that studies human interactions using scientific methods. Economics seems to fit this definition. Firstly, it is clearly the study of a human phenomenon; the core issue at the heart of the subject is how humans allocate resources. The methodology used is what provides the science part of the description in my view. Economics is based on quantitative analysis and modelling, and much of the theory is built upon scientific methods. Some people might disagree with the description of economics as a social science. They may argue that it has no real scientific grounding given that there is often very little irrefutable evidence to prove economic theory. However, I believe that this is inevitable in any study of humanity, because **human behaviour is so unpredictable** – and that if economics is not a social science then neither is any other field of study."

Assessment: A clear definition, even if it is one the candidate has concocted rather than one taken from a textbook, shows a real understanding of what the question is asking. This is a very difficult question to answer, given the vague nature of a "social science" and the difficulty in pigeon holing an entire subject such as economics. However, by considering how well certain criteria are met and assessing contradictory points of view, the interviewee is able to display their ability to grapple with testing problems and use logical reasoning to answer the question at hand. The answer may have been improved by suggesting alternatives to the description provided (e.g. "perhaps a better description of economics is as a series of 'fads and fashions'..."), and then assessing the credibility of those alternatives.

Q14: Are CEOs paid too much?

A good response: "I do not know a lot about current CEO pay levels, but it would seem to me that any **employee should be paid based on their contribution** to the firm. If the CEO has a serious positive impact on the business, for example if they are responsible for securing high levels of profits, then they deserve a large salary. However, if they have no greater impact than any other employee, then they should not be compensated any more generously. If the cost of paying a CEO outweighs the benefits they bring, they are being overpaid."

Assessment: The candidate is honest in their response, acknowledging the fact that this is a topic they know little about. However by applying more general economic intuition, they are able to provide a concise argument, and more importantly demonstrate their ability to engage with unfamiliar concepts. This is a very attractive skill to an Oxbridge tutor, and is preferable to an interviewee who attempts to deceive an interviewer into believing they know a lot about the subject.

Q15: Does OPEC show that a cartel can run a market efficiently?

A good response: "Am I right in the understanding that OPEC is the organisation that maintains oil prices?" [Interviewer: *"Yes, that's right."*] "In that case, I believe that OPEC has run the oil market relatively well. However, I do not believe that the market has even been close to efficiency, as many OPEC members have made large profits on the back of the cartel, and in a perfectly efficient market these profits would not occur. Large price fluctuations, particularly the fall in oil prices in the last 18 months, suggest to me that OPEC does not have as much control on the industry as it would like…"

Assessment: Asking for clarification on a question is not something a candidate should be afraid to do. It displays a willingness to fully understand the concepts that they are dealing with, and so would not be frowned upon in most scenarios.

If the topic in question was of a very basic level, there may be some questions raised, but tutors will not expect a candidate to know about every economic issue and will be expecting some gaps in their knowledge. In this case, the student was right to establish exactly what the question was before attempting to answer. Bringing in **knowledge of current affairs** regarding oil prices also displays interest in the subject, and this enthusiasm for the subject will be taken well by interviewers.

Q16: Diseconomies of scale exist when a firm's average costs rise as their output level increases. Do you think diseconomies of scale exist in the real world?

A good response: "If average costs are rising as an output increases, this suggests that it would be beneficial for firms to stay small. I think we can see plenty of examples of cases where it is beneficial for a firm to stay small. If a company would have to increase its spending on marketing greatly in order to sell any additional goods produced, then the average costs of those products may rise, and the company would be suffering from diseconomies of scale.

Assessment: Some applicants, particularly those who have previously studied economics, will have a good understanding of this topic, whilst others will have almost none. However, the interviewer is not using this question as a test of existing knowledge, but will be looking at the way in which it is approached. The ability to apply theory to real life is important, and this question may be designed to test that ability. The candidate excels by showing good real world knowledge.

Q17: What are the impacts upon an economy of using a pegged currency, as opposed a floating one?

A good response: "A pegged currency is when a country chooses to set its own currency as a direct proportion of that of another economy. It usually happens when a less developed economy aligns their currency with the exchange rate of a more established country.

This means that an economy has more stability in their exchange rate, which can lead to less volatility in balance of payments. However, it means a government cannot use economic policies to affect its exchange rate, so they are more susceptible to shocks from external factors – particularly from the nation they are pegged to. It also means that government policy elsewhere has an impact, so the pegged country need to ensure there is some congruence between the two nations' objectives."

Assessment: The candidate clearly shows great understanding of the topic, which may not have been covered in any real depth during A-Levels or equivalent. They are able to present a balanced argument even in a short answer, and draw on a variety of ideas. To improve, the applicant consider refer to real life examples, which shows that they have read around their subject and can be an indication of enthusiasm for the subject. However, in a situation where they don't know any examples then considering the types of nation that might use pegged currencies – "a less developed economy" – is a good alternative which still displays good understanding.

Q18: Do you think a government seeking economic growth should prioritise policies aimed at stimulating demand, or supply?

A good response: "Classical economists believe in a vertical long run average supply curve, and thus would argue that demand side policies are useless in stimulating growth. However, I feel like the Keynesian model is more realistic, and demand side policies can be effective when an economy is not at full employment. Despite this, I believe that supply side policies usually stimulate more long term sustainable growth, rather than one of boosts to economic performance. If a government is seeking growth, I think supply side policies would be preferable."

Assessment: This answer is good, and comes to a solid conclusion, but seems to lack the depth to impress an Oxbridge tutor. To improve, the candidate could spend more time analysing why a government may disagree with their viewpoint, and then providing evidence to support their own argument.

Another extension to the answer may be to consider the circumstances under which one approach is more suited than another. Questioning the context surrounding the question shows an inquisitive nature and shows that the candidate is analytical of information presented to them. In this case, a conclusion along the lines of "if a government is facing *situation x*, it should pursue *policy y...*" may add some substance to the arguments presented.

Economics Interview Questions

352. What would happen if there was no inflation?
353. Do economists rely too heavily on models?
354. Is sociology useful for studying economics?
355. Can we really measure GDP?
356. What influences a country's productive potential?
357. Should governments have debts?
358. Should inequality matter to economists?
359. Does a balance of trade deficit matter?
360. Should government intervene in the market?
361. Was the financial crisis of 2008 a failure of regulation?
362. The value of the US Dollar and Japanese Yen are swapped with each other overnight. What would happen to global markets?
363. What is the best way to win in monopoly? Is this possible in real life?
364. Why are diamonds so expensive? Why is steel so cheap?
365. Imagine you have just opened up a new airline that flies a unique route (London and Tokyo). How would you determine what price to set tickets at to ensure maximal profit?
366. What is the golden ratio? Why do banks and investments firms obsess over it?
367. How can we predict future economic recessions and avoid depressions?
368. Should we still be giving aid to countries that have international space programmes e.g. India?
369. What is the difference between capitalism and communism? Are they really that different?
370. Why are we privatising large services like Royal Mail and the NHS?

371. Why is there a starbucks or Costas every 100 meters or so in crowded cities?

372. What is the difference between a firm and a company?

373. How would you eliminate the national debt?

374. What is Gambler's Ruin? Why does it tell us about how casinos operate?

375. What drives immigration and emigration?

376. Why is Dubai expanding so rapidly given that it has no tax generated income?

377. You are the captain of a pirate ship and have found a treasure chest. Your crew gets to vote on how the treasure is shared. If fewer than half of the pirates agree with you, you die. How would you share the gold in such a way that you get a maximum share and survive?

378. Why do teachers become plumbers and who should pay for their training?

379. Would it be feasible to have an economy entirely based on the service sector?

380. Are there too many people in the world?

381. What is the point of using NHS money to keep old people alive?

382. What is the difference between buying and selling of slaves and the buying and selling of football players?

383. Why is a film actor wealthier than a theatre actor?

384. Why is deflation a scare to the UK?

385. If you and a business owner each have 10 loyal customers who will always buy from you unless you sell above £10, and there are an additional 80 who will choose who to buy from based on price alone, at what price does it become more profitable to stop undercutting your competitor and sell at £10 instead?

386. What is the difference between the chancellor and the governor of the bank of England?

387. What would be the implications of Scotland leaving the UK? What about Wales?

388. What will happen to oil prices in the next 10 years? What about 100 years?

389. Why is the American economy so strong?

390. What is point of the G8? What about the G20?

391. Compare and contrast the Indian and Chinese economy.

392. This graph shows salt prices for the last 200 years. They follow a very predictable and cyclical pattern. Given that there was a huge depression and two world wars, how is this possible?

393. What is the difference between management and leadership?

394. How would you calculate the return on investment of Christopher Columbus' voyages?

395. How would you calculate the return on investment for NASAs operations?

396. A new country is formed in Africa. They introduce a new currency. How does the international market value what it is worth?

397. Why don't we use Euros?

ENGLISH

The English interview will require you to demonstrate passion and a genuine desire to study English. Make sure you have thought, at least vaguely, about your answer to a wide question like: "Why English?", or "Why English at Cambridge"? You will usually be asked to discuss an unseen extract from a play, poem, or piece of prose; this will enable the interviewer to see whether you can think on your feet, both in terms of subject-related knowledge (of literary forms, techniques, and genres) and forming your own critical opinions on the spot ("Is this a good poem? Why?").

Apply the knowledge you have acquired at A-Level and from wider reading to unfamiliar scenarios. You may not recognise the text you have been asked to read, but that is probably deliberate: **embrace this chance to experiment**, make mistakes, and show off your imaginative readings of new texts. Indeed, the Cambridge English course places a strong emphasis upon Practical Criticism, which encourages you to explore unseen texts in isolation from their context (by erasing the writer's name or the date written) in order to understand how the form of a text influences themes and meanings.

If you are making an argument that is clearly wrong, that is, the interviewers are telling you it is clearly wrong, try to revise your viewpoint and expand your argument in light of this information. Remember, **making mistakes is no bad thing**; in fact, it can be very constructive to be wrong, since changing your argument shows real intellectual flexibility. The important point is that you address the mistake head on and attempt to revise your thinking, with the assistance of the tutors where necessary. For instance, perhaps a tutor has asked you to try and place a poem in its literary context – say, a sonnet by John Donne from the Renaissance – and you have given it the wrong date – perhaps thinking that it could be a Romantic sonnet instead.

This guesswork can be used as an exciting springboard for a fresh discussion. How did knowing the real date of this poem change the way you viewed the themes and message? You might find it interesting that enduring features of the sonnet form existed both in the Renaissance and in the eighteenth century –what subtle changes in genre might you notice, and are these conventions ever subverted? Try and think creatively and use this correction as the basis for a wider conversation about how the sonnet form has evolved over the centuries.

The tutors know what subjects you have studied at A-Level. They will try to theme your interview around the texts and periods that you have studied. However, they may ask you about certain literary periods that you have not studied in depth or detail. If so, be open-minded and respond to the information that you are given. If you are given Wilfred Owen's 'Anthem for Doomed Youth', and you have not studied any war poets before, you can still apply techniques and ideas you have learned. While you should discuss the poem with fresh eyes, analysing the form, the metre, and imagery as you would do with any unseen poem, feel free to make connections with other texts.

For example, you may have studied Tennyson's 'The Charge of the Light Brigade'; what can this earlier poem, which uses powerful rhetoric to valorise patriotism and male honour, illuminate about Owen's more nihilistic sonnet? Such **connections show that you are thinking actively** and enjoying the challenge of approaching new texts.

What Questions Might be asked?

Most of the questions asked in the interview will disguise a larger question within a network of smaller sub-questions to guide the answer from the start to a conclusion. The main question may seem difficult, weird, or random at first, but take a breath and start discussing with your interviewer different ideas you have for breaking down the question into manageable pieces. Don't panic.

The questions are designed to be difficult to give you the chance to show your full intellectual potential. They will help guide you to the right idea, if you provide ideas for them to guide. This is your chance to show your creativity, analytical skills, intellectual flexibility, problem-solving skills and your go-getter attitude. Don't waste it on nervousness or a fear of messing up or looking stupid: think aloud and work together with the interviewer.

An interviewer may question any decision you come to in response to a question, and it is possible that in the course of the ensuing conversation your original views will alter, as your thinking becomes more nuanced. Do not panic! This is perfectly okay, and shows an ability to adapt to new information and ideas and respond to them. Similarly, you should not feel the need to quickly agree with anything coming from an interviewer's mouth in order to appease them. An interview is a discussion, and a chance to show the interviewer how you think and respond to the thoughts of others.

To quote Robinson College's English admissions advice, you should show:

"A readiness to respond to challenges to your opinion, holding firm and arguing your case where appropriate, but also modifying your opinion in the light of contradictory evidence.'"

Worked Questions

Below are a few examples of how to start breaking down an interview question along with model answers.

Q1: Are these extracts written by a man or a woman? Why do you think this? Does it matter?

This seemingly complex question can be broken down first into a critical exercise in analysing an unseen text, followed by a wider discussion of whether biographical information is important in literary criticism: is the author "dead"?

Your starting point for this question might be your initial gut-reaction to the two contrasting texts: **do they seem more "masculine" or "feminine" to you**, and how would you define these adjectives? Since the interviewer is asking you to guess this information, without expecting you to know details about the authentic author, you might realise that they are interested in the assumptions that literary critics bring to bear upon texts seen out of context: *why* does this seem like a male writer wrote it?

For example, let's say you were given an extract from Ernest Hemingway's *The Old Man and the Sea*. Most obviously, the themes focus upon the traditionally male pursuit of fishing, or hunting, and centre upon nature in the vein of Romantic poets like Byron or Coleridge. You might describe the main stylistic features as abrupt punctuation and short, factual sentences, statements that seem almost scientific, in their logical structuring. Perhaps you notice the lack of flowery conceits or poetic set-pieces, the minimalist description and simplistic texture. Hemmingway tells it like it is, using efficient and controlled prose without stylistic excess or hyperbole. This realism and lack of explicit emotion might strike you as "masculine", reminding you of stereotypically reticent male discourse. Then, maybe the second extract is a piece from Virginia Woolf's *Mrs Dalloway*.

Initially, it may be clear that the text is centred around a female character, her emotions and feelings. Moving deeper, you might describe the prose as smooth and fluid, linked by flowing connectives, perhaps recognising this to be an experiment in stream of consciousness. Maybe you feel that Woolf prioritises chaotic human psychology and internal thoughts rather than linear events. The way she moves by association through clusters of images, impressions, and sensations in a way that reminds you of lyrical poetry more than realist prose, striking you as a more "feminine" way of writing.

However, you may argue none of the above, and analyse these two texts in a completely opposite way, arguing for the femininity of the Hemingway piece and showing the masculinity of Woolf's prose (which is even more interesting). In a way, it doesn't matter: the interviewers just want to see you **argue your case for the author's gender with a detailed, analytical piece of prose analysis.**

Once this starting point is established, they might ask you to reassess your answers, pushing you to define these gendered observations and defend your argument. Is there – as Woolf discusses – a specifically 'feminine', or feminist, style? Can a text ever have a neutral, or androgynous style, mixing both genders?

Finally, the interviews are likely to steer this discussion towards a final twist: **does the gender of the author matter?** (See question 8). Should we celebrate anonymity? Does biographical information restrict or generate meaning? The interviewers are inviting you to think broadly about texts and contexts. You might have come across theories like Roland Barthe's "death of the Author", or be aware of New Criticism, which argue for texts as self-contained units of meaning liberated from biographical constraints. Maybe you have touched upon the "intentional fallacy", a phrase coined by critics Wimsatt and Beardsley, and recognise the difficulties involved in interpreting a text solely in terms of what the author meant. Even if you have not formally studied any of these theories, it is likely you will voice some of these central ideas as you debate, aloud, whether biographical knowledge in literary criticism is useful, limiting, or both. As you can see, from these two short extracts, you have covered an enormous amount of ground, both technical, in terms of analysing prose, and theoretical, asking huge questions about the author and the text.

A **Poor Applicant** may take a number of approaches unlikely to impress the interviewer. The first and most obvious of these is to say "I don't know who wrote these texts", or similarly uncooperative responses. In fact, the whole task assumes you won't know who wrote the texts, but rather invites you to speculate about unseen extracts in order to investigate your assumptions about the relevance of gender or biographical information when studying literature. Another approach which is unhelpful in this interview situation is the 'brain dump', where instead of engaging with the question, the applicant attempts to impress or distract with an assortment of related facts. For instance, you might offer a fantastic stand-alone stylistic analysis of these prose extracts, listing the different ways in which Hemingway uses punctuation, or how Woolf uses connectives in her languid sentences.

However, unless this is used to strengthen your final argument about the gender of each author, and why you think that, then this is irrelevant information. Instead, listen and respond to your interviewers as they prompt you further, continually asking you to extend and defend your analysis by asking: "why?", or "so why do these connectives make the prose seem feminine to you?" These **observations should be pieces of evidence in a reasoned argument for authorial gender**, which will provide a basis for productive discussion of whether this biographical information is important or irrelevant in the task of literary criticism.

Q2: Is Fifty Shades of Grey literature? Why, and if not why not?

This question invites you to think about the sets of criteria used to evaluate what is 'literature', what is a 'classic', 'literature', or the 'canon'. Does popularity diminish the cultural prestige of art? Does the audience matter? Can *Eastenders* ever be 'literature' in the same way as works by Samuel Beckett or James Joyce? Begin to criticize and reevaluate these throwaway terms that you use everyday, imagining how a dictionary might define them: what do we really mean when we categorise texts as 'canonical' or 'literature' and what (or whose) criteria are we using? Can a contemporary novel ever be a classic? Think about the rise of English Literature as a respected academic pursuit and your own A-Level syllabus, and the influence of criticism like F.R.Leavis's *The Great Tradition*: what has been included, and, more significantly, what is excluded, marginal, and devalued? Ask questions and probe your own answers in what will become a lively two-way discussion.

This is a playful, provocative question which introduces the theme of popular culture, of "high" and "low" art, asking you to analyse shifting or enduring artistic standards and tastes, of 'art' or 'entertainment'. What about the way in which Shakespeare meshes 'high' tragic art and 'low' comedic clowns? You might want to approach this in terms of obscene or taboo subject matter across the ages. Why do institutions study John Donne's most erotic poetry – 'To His Mistress Going to Bed' – or obscene Elizabethan pamphlets, but neglect this exceedingly popular novel?

You could explore the idea of censorship, linking *Fifty Shades* to D.H.Lawrence's *Lady Chatterley's Lover*: perhaps the book deserves to be seen as a historically-interesting celebration of artistic freedom and liberated female sexuality?

Q3: What makes a tragedy?

The interviewers are pushing you to explore one of the **most famous literary genres in an imaginative fashion**.

Perhaps you might start with the classical formulation of 'Tragedy' that you might have come across in your A-Level studies, including Aristotle's tragic precepts (hamartia, hubris, *peripeteia*, anagnorisis, catharsis etc.). However, use Aristotle's definitions as a starting point, a springboard, not the answer. What does it really mean to have a tragic 'catharsis'? Can you think about any modern examples that reinforce or subvert these ideas – what about Arthur Miller's *The Crucible*, or *Death of a Salesman*? Think about plays you have studied that illustrate or undermine this term in practice. You could then move on to how these precepts manifested themselves in later literary movements, discussing Shakespearean tragedy and the moments that you think illuminate these aspects.

There is no 'correct' answer: this is an exercise in probing the boundaries of a 'genre'. What about women? Does Shakespearean tragedy prioritise the aristocratic male at the expense of the poor or female characters? What about class? What about other media – can cinema, comic books, paintings, television soap operas, news programmes, or Twitter statuses ever be tragic? Your interviewer might ask similar questions, maybe discussing iconoclastic critics like Raymond Williams, who argued for a more egalitarian view of the tragic. Perhaps you might agree with George Steiner, who famously argued for the 'death of tragedy' – is tragedy dead, or is it still alive and kicking? You don't have to recognise or have read these critics, but respond and be interested when their ideas are mentioned – do you agree, or not? If not, why? Use examples that spring to mind from your reading and be as varied as you like.

Q4: Do you think the ending of [Novel] is poor?

This question invites an explanation of your verdict and a consideration of what makes a "good ending". **What is the point of a conclusion?** Is it to provide a final commentary on the preceding themes, to tie up any loose ends of the plot, to introduce a parting thought for the reader to mull over? Do different genres demand different things of their endings? Should endings have certain qualities to help the overall structure of a novel?

For example, if you were asked to comment on the conclusion of 'Mill on the Floss', you may answer that it *is* a poor ending, as the sudden destruction of two characters both jars and frustrates the reader. The flood incident was unprecedented and random, and in a way gimmicky. The preceding novel focussed so much on character development and the effect of human actions, that the sudden 'act of God' disrupted the style of the book. Moreover, having invested time and energy into the heroine's struggles, the reader may well feel frustrated and betrayed at receiving such an unsatisfactory resolution for Maggie. One could argue that the ending felt lazy, and that the final note that follows the drowning is sentimental. George Eliot could stand accused of having not provided a proper conclusion to her work, and opting for an easy way out of dealing with the mess Maggie's life was now in. The sudden flood could be compared to the often mocked "and it was all a dream" ending.

Alternatively, one could argue "no", as the unexpected flood was a representation of the cruelty of the world, of the ultimate futility of human struggle. Our frustrated expectations and shock could be argued as a testimony to the strength of the ending: the power it has to compel the audience to react makes it not "poor", but great. **An ending does not have to satisfy**, one may argue, if it is able to teach us something new. Or perhaps the horror of this incident justifies the work as something tragic, and in its way is true to its genre.

There is also room to discuss **what constitutes an ending?** The discussion includes the flood in understanding George Eliot's conclusion, but another person may argue the final epilogue is the ending, or demands more attention than the deadly incident. Moreover, one can explore the idea of endings and link it with the idea of literature itself: if literature is meant to please, provoke, or has different purposes in different situations, what does this mean for endings?

Q5: What makes a short story different from a novel?

This question asks you to consider the nature of form and the impact it has on a piece of literature. A weaker answer will state the obvious: "a short story is shorter than a novel". A stronger answer will take this into account and then consider how length will affect the treatment of a story's content. For example, one may consider if the significance of individual words is affected by the total word count within a work. Or they may discuss how characterization is affected by having fewer words to explore a person within a narrative, and argue that short stories must establish protagonists and antagonists in ways novels are not necessarily constricted by. The answer could contrast the characters of Edgar Allen Poe to those of Jane Austen, and note the differences in the way they present individuals in the plot.

One may also talk about how **structure differs between a longer and a shorter work** and how the latter needs a clearer, more concise plot, whereas the former has more space to meander and add multiple episodes within the narrative. Again, this idea could then be corroborated through examples provided by the candidate's reading. A candidate could also consider the difference between a novel and a collection of short stories, and consider how the overarching theme of a novel is explicit, whereas a theme across the group of stories is more implicit.

Q6: Tell me about a novel you've read recently.

A **weaker candidate** will simply summarize a text, whereas a stronger one will analyze it. For example, if a candidate has recently read 'Oliver Twist', they could discuss it within a context: for example, how does this book differ to other Dickensian novels, or Victorian novels, or even modern novels the candidate has read? What do they think of the story's use of comedy, or perhaps the characterization of Nancy or Oliver himself? Why do they think this is considered a 'classic'? How do they think the structure affects the story, and does a consideration of the novel's roots – as a serial printed in installments in a magazine – affect the way the candidate reads the novel as a whole? Does the movement from segments to a single volume improve the work, or do they think something has been lost in the translation?

A candidate is invited here to show the **thoughts that have arisen through their reading**, and to make a judgment. They can explain what they find interesting, or enjoyable, or why they disliked a work, or found it uncomfortable. Beyond simply having a reaction to the text, a stronger candidate will also explore their reaction to the text: if they felt frustrated with a certain character, why do they think this was? Was it the author's intention, or a limitation in their skill? Does the context of a work affect its reception – do Dickens' idealised characters charm a certain audience and not another, and is this due to different time periods, or social, economic or religious contexts? Whatever time or location a text originates from, consider it on its own, in comparison with other things you've read, within its context, and consider why and how it elicits a reaction from you, as a reader.

The answer does not necessarily have to mention all these different aspects, but it should mention the title and then an analysis of the text, showing what the interviewee finds interesting about the piece of literature, whether he or she likes it or not.

Q7: What's the difference between poetry and prose?

An applicant may wish to begin with the difference between the two by thinking about their **respective formal qualities**: poetry and its use of metre, for example. They may then wish to think if this alone is the simple distinction, and discuss prose-poetry, and explain whether they believe it belongs either to prose, or poetry, or is a separate category in itself, and crucially *why* this is so. One may also want to discuss other elements associated with either poetry or prose specifically, and see if these elements define them (or why they do not).

For example, "poetic devices" such as metaphor and alliteration can be found in prose. Any given subject matter, one may go on to explain, can be explored through both: love can be discussed in *Tess of the d'Urbervilles* or in Robert Burns's 'My Love is like a Red, Red Rose.' If they then dismiss other possible differences, they could again reaffirm their original thoughts on the definition that separates poetry from prose. If in the process they then wish to add to their original statement, they can do this. The movement from the original idea to a discussion of it, backed with examples, and a consideration of the answers other people may provide to this question will lead to a nuanced response to the interviewer.

Q8: Is a protagonist's gender important?

An applicant may first wish to **define gender** – e.g. "the state of being male or female – normally used to in a social or cultural context as opposed to a biological one."

An applicant may then say "yes" and describe the manifest ways gender affects a text: either by informing character or influencing the plot. They may go on to use many examples to explain this: for example, Jane Eyre would not have a romantic attachment with Rochester if she was a man, and so all the events relating to their relationship would not have happened, and the plot of *Jane Eyre* would be non-existent. If she was a man, and she and Rochester shared a homosexual love, it would be an entirely different book.

Moreover, one's relationship to the world can be seen as partially defined by their gender. Cathy (the elder) in *Wuthering Heights* believes her way of achieving a greater rank is through marriage to a wealthy man, whereas if she were herself male she might have gone the way of Heathcliff, who found his fortune through mysterious enterprises. One cannot simply dismiss her gender as irrelevant: her identity is bound in the societal expectations and legal status of women of her time, and this limits her expectations of what she could achieve, and forces her to retreat into the status of desired marital object in order to pursue her worldly ambitions. The treatment of women/men in different periods and places will be read in a work, as it will inform the *writer's* viewpoint and so inform the book. As there is still a perceived difference between men and women, **gender identity is still important to recognise**, and modern books still see the importance of gender in defining a character's history, relationship to others and awareness of their place in the world. One may then go on to question how different *Harry Potter* would have been if Harry were a girl.

Of course, one may argue that men and women are equally capable of feeling and acting, and that a female protagonist for a novel like *Harry Potter* is entirely possible. It could be argued that, believing in the equal rights of men and women, gender should cease to be a definitive aspect of character. However, "should" is very different than "is", and though feminism has come a long way in changing attitudes towards women's rights, society is not ignorant of the individual's gender. There remain preconceptions, and arguments, relating to notions of a female or male identity. If a girl was fighting Voldemort, different associations would arise in the reader's mind than they would when reading a boy battling the Dark Lord.

One may also argue that **certain characters within plays are considered quite gender neutral**, and can be performed by either male or female cast (for example, though Ariel is a man in *The Tempest*, he is often played by a woman). The counter-argument to this is that, though this ambiguity exists, once the neutral body is gendered through the performer, it again elicits a reaction specific to that gender.

One could argue that, on the page, a character could be considered gender-neutral, but then **this absence of gender may be of importance**, the "neutrality" becoming a third gender to consider, and eliciting a different reaction than the other two.

The answer could also go on to discuss the idea of a transgender protagonist.

Q9: Is there a book you think you should not have studied?

The question invites an exploration of what the purpose of literary study is. An applicant will look at the books they have read for schoolwork and consider and answer truthfully if they think they were all valid choices, or if one was not. Having clarified this, the candidate may then explain what he or she thinks is a requirement for a book to be worthy of "study" – what merits does a text require to validate its place in education? Having clarified what these qualities are – or indeed if there *are* any requirements for a book to be worth studying – they can then compare the works he or she has read for class against these requirements. If they decided that everything is worth study, the applicant can then discuss the idea of this further, and explain **the value of any text within a classroom**, providing examples to corroborate their argument. This discussion may then lead to a greater analysis of the purpose of literature: is what makes a text worth studying what makes it worth reading, or is there a difference between books that should be pursued in leisure time as opposed to academic time?

Q10: Should every piece of literature have a moral in it?

If the applicant answered "no", he or she may go on to explain that though literature *can* be a source of moral edification, it should not be unified by an ethical cause, because there are a variety of purposes that can inform a text. It could be written simply to be beautiful (and the candidate may then talk about aesthetic criticism of literature) or perhaps to hold "a mirror up to nature" and capture something of reality or the human condition – whether this is through naturalism, or through another expression of an emotional state.

One may argue, for example, that *Waiting for Godot* would be rendered absurd if a moral was added: it's purpose it not to provide ethical education, and the complexity of the piece would be crudely simplified. It would be turned from a challenging work to a didactic one, simple to understand but with all its original intention and meaning deleted. One could question if literature "should" ever be or do anything.

One may, however, question whether literature that can be considered immoral can also be considered harmful. The relationship depicted in the *50 Shades* series is often considered abusive, and one may wonder if this sets a bad example for impressionable readers who will go on to idealise this couple.

The candidate may then argue that **responsibility lies in the reader**, and the censoring of work is in itself troubling. He or she could go on to name any number of banned books, and then demonstrate their value as opposed to their potential to damage.

Q11: I'm having trouble with the meaning of three words: Lie, Deceive, Mislead. They seem to mean something a bit similar, but not exactly the same. Help me to sort them out from each other.

An applicant should begin with explaining one of these on their own: for example, to "lie" is to deliberately say something the speaker knows to be contrary to the truth, such as "trees are made of purple cheese". To "deceive" is not, however, necessarily to lie: it is to lead someone to believe in something that is not true. The word is **more to do with intent**, the desire to make another believe in something false, than the action of simply stating something that is not true. There are also other uses of the word – one can "deceive oneself" or an object may give a mistaken impression – which gives it different meanings, and one may wish to consider these. However, one should ensure the differentiation between "deceive" and "lie" is clearly stated. To "lie" describes an action; to "deceive" describes an action coupled with intent.

Having established the meanings of these two words, the candidate may then compare these to the definition of "mislead".

Often "mislead" is treated as a synonym of "deceive", with dictionaries using one to define the other. However, the subtle difference may be that **one can "mislead" unknowingly**. If we take "mislead" to "cause someone to have the wrong idea or impression" or to "lead astray", we can see that someone might "mislead" *without* intent, but purely by error. For example, if one believes he or she knows the quickest way to a location, but is mistaken, that person may have misled a group of friends without meaning to at all. One *can* definitely mislead with intent, but one does not *necessarily* have to.

This is a question that **demands careful attention to the nuances of words**, so it is good to constantly compare the differences between these three terms. For example, one can say you might "mislead" without lying. One may even deceive without lying, by refraining from revealing crucial information that would lead to a fuller understanding of the scene. For example, if someone wanted to make you believe Mr. X killed Mrs. Y, he or she might say "Mr. X went to Mrs. Y's house an hour before the crime", and then neglect to mention that he left the same house two minutes later and went across town. One might then discuss whether one can "lie by omission", and how this would again affect the relationship between "to lie" and "to deceive."

Q12: Do you think there is any point to reading criticism?

If one was to answer "yes", they could argue there is a dual purpose to criticism. Firstly, it can introduce new ideas to the reader, ones they may not have considered alone. Perhaps the critic has a **novel interpretation** of the words that inspires a new train of thought. For example, WH Auden's description of *Twelfth Night* as a "nasty" play may encourage his reader to reconsider the nature of the comedy within the drama, and potentially find darkness where previously they saw only light humour. The second purpose of criticism could be seen as *confirming* the reader's thoughts.

If the critic offers an idea that reaffirms their previous views, or that the candidate is annoyed by / disagrees with, it helps them to **solidify their own views on literature**. For example, Oscar Wilde's comment that "All art is quite useless" may be so infuriating that it provokes a strong reaction, and this reaction allows the reader to clarify his or her own understanding of the purpose of a text.

One may argue that **analysis does not necessarily require a critic**. For example, a look at the historical context of a work can inspire thought. One may also refer to the use of Practical Criticism, which asks the reader to simply respond to an unseen text, and discuss the potential merit of this exercise. It is useful to respond to a text without your mind being coloured by another's critique. However, once one has gained this perspective, it can be argued that considering another interpretation can further deepen his or her analysis. Using several approaches to a text ensures a more nuanced understanding of it.

Q13: Hamlet speaks to the Ghost, what significance does this have?

Firstly, one may want to unpack the phrase "speaks to the Ghost". Another character has attempted to engage the Ghost in conversation, but significantly the spectre did not respond. Should we make a distinction between being "spoken to" and "spoken at"? Are we looking at the fact that Hamlet is speaking, or at the fact there is a communication between the two figures?

If we are looking at the fact that they have a conversation, there are several ways to look at this significance, depending on how one interprets the figure of the Ghost. Hamlet himself is unsure at first whether this is truly the spirit of his father, or some demonic being tempting him to sin. If the latter, this conversation means potential damnation, and implies peril for Hamlet's soul. If the former, we may see this dialogue as an insight into the familial relationship between father and son.

As Shakespeare shows the father calling on the living for revenge, he portrays a character who foists the burden of vendetta onto his offspring, potentially risking Hamlet's chance of reaching Heaven, potentially dooming Hamlet to Hell. This conversation can be used to define the characters via their relationship with one another.

One may look at this conversation as a manifestation of madness: though others spot the ghost at first, he is crucially neither seen nor heard by Gertrude in the bedroom scene. Perhaps we can then dismiss the earlier sightings as a sort of group hysteria by a bunch of men on watch, not really there at all. Or maybe we can divide the Ghost into two: one which can be seen by others, and one that solely haunts the guilty, addled mind of Hamlet. Again, the fact that only Hamlet can communicate with the spectre of his father may suggest madness, a reality which is solely his and inaccessible to any other.

How "real" the ghost is can be debated because of these two very different impressions - a spectre that is seen by some, but utterly invisible to the dead man's wife. One may then go on to say that the Ghost does not wish to be seen by Gertrude, only by his son, and this in itself is significant. One may also wish to speak about how the audience can see the ghost, and wonder if this implies Gertrude alone is in the dark about his presence, or whether we are being granted access to Hamlet's vision, and so his mind, something other characters cannot access.

If we decide that the phrase "speaks to" is simply the action of Hamlet trying to initiate contact, one might say the significance here is of a son who desperately wants contact with his father, who overcomes his fear of the potentially dangerous spectre due to his great need to speak to his dad. Hamlet remarks that he does not set his life at a "pin's fee", so does his conversation with the deathly spirit also suggest a desire to join it in death, a rejection of the living? As Hamlet speaks to the Ghost alone, on stage, we see a living man forming a relationship with a dead one. This image is worth analysing.

Renaissance ideas on ghosts, damnation and superstition differ to the predominate beliefs in 21st Century London (superstition is now mocked by many, though some may cling to their beliefs in spirits), and this may also be taken into context and used to describe how a Shakespearian audience's understanding of ghosts would affect how one would witness a scene.

Tests, Essays & Personal Statements

Written Tests

It is crucial to have a tool-kit, or checklist, of techniques at your fingertips for analysing poetry, prose, and drama effectively in order to compare, contrast, and comment upon different extracts. You should always be thinking about how to explore form and structure (syntax, metre, versification, scansion) as well as language (imagery, motifs, similes, metaphors). **Try and practice your timed essay technique** and find ways to use your observations as evidence for a powerful argument, noticing what links are apparent, rather than just a list of random feature-spotting. Remember, these selected texts will be set because the examiners want you to notice distinctive features, make connections and interesting arguments: look for overlapping themes or juxtaposing techniques, keeping an eye out for examples of the traditional and the subversive. You could pick up an anthology of poetry, prose, or drama and pick interlinked texts at random to practice: what is similar or different about them?

Essay + Personal Statement Discussions

Read and reread your personal statement and make sure you have interesting things to say about your ideas and chosen texts. Try to pre-empt off-kilter interview questions, which will be designed to steer you away from pre-packaged speeches learned before the day itself. **Make sure you have a deep awareness of different periods** and prepare by using anthologies to gain a rough sweep of chronological developments. For instance, if you mention liking T.S.Eliot's poetry, you might be asked which other modernist poets you have read, and how these have deepened your understanding of what it really means to be a 'modernist poet'. Is this a useful categorisation or not?

Expect the interviewers to undermine your arguments and to push you into defending, or adapting, your beliefs. Go back over texts you might not have studied for a long time and try and develop, or argue against, your ideas, which might have changed over time if you have read more widely.

Be Inventive

The interviewers may have heard forty interviewees discuss revenge in *Hamlet*, or the radicalness of Jack Kerouac's *On the Road*. Why not talk about *Pericles*, or *Timon of Athens*, or Shakespeare's poetry – *The Rape of Lucrece* is an excellent accompaniment to *Titus Andronicus* – instead? If you are fascinated by the Beat Generation, look further than the obvious texts: make an effort to explore the writing of other ground-breaking writers like Hunter S. Thompson or William Burroughs, comparing and contrasting how their formal techniques can be used to investigate similar themes. Follow your natural interests to the furthest extreme, and you will be surprised at how enjoyable the interview can be.

Branch out from your set texts and you will show off your own drive to read and study. Talk about different mediums if you feel they illuminate your discussion, from films, to plays, to song lyrics. For example, you could talk about how a certain set-design or production aesthetic changed your understanding of a play, such as the recent all-female *Julius Caesar* at the Donmar Warehouse.

English Interview Questions

398. What is the point of studying English?
399. What do you want to get out of this course?
400. What is 'literature'?
401. What's the difference between poetry and prose?
402. Tell me about something you've read recently.
403. Should politicians study English?
404. Why do we bother studying literature that is hundreds of years old?
405. Is a protagonist's gender important?
406. Don't you think Hamlet is a bit long? How would you shorten it?
407. Do we have the right to interpret the story of the birth of christ as a comment on Tony Blair's current political situation?
408. Have you read Macbeth / King Lear / Hamlet? If yes- what makes that play a 'tragedy'?
409. The first two years of the Cambridge English course is structured around period papers: 1350-1550, 1500-1700, etc. Do you think it is important to study literature in chronological order?
410. Have you ever visited an author's birthplace, or home, or a place that a text is about? If yes- did this change the way you read the text? Is it a valuable thing to do?
411. Did Shakespeare write Shakespeare's plays?
412. What Elizabeth Bishop poems have you read?
413. What is haiku? Why are they so different in structure to a sonnet?
414. If you could design the Cambridge English course, what would you change?
415. Define tragedy?
416. Is the Bible a fictional work? Why?
417. Should every piece of literature have a moral to it?
418. What do you mean by words not being trusted in Elizabeth Bishop's poetry?
419. Is poetry a particularly good medium for expressing doubt over words?
420. What do you think about Malcolm Lowry's references of other writers in Under the Volcano?
421. Compare and contrast Harry potter and lord of the rings.

422. To what extent is Romeo a rebel? What about Shakespeare?
423. Do you think there is any point to reading criticism?
424. Who is your favourite character? Why?
425. Can a carrot be considered a theatrical fruit, if it is used as a prop during a play?
426. Do you think the ending of 'The Mill On The Floss' is poor?
427. What is your favourite book of all time?
428. Does Malcolm Lowry overwrite his prose?
429. Tell me about your coursework.
430. What's significant about family relations in Hamlet?
431. What does the Ghost in Hamlet have to do with madness?
432. Hamlet speaks to the Ghost, what significance does this have?
433. Do you think Hamlet knows he is being listened to when he says 'To be, or not to be'?
434. Have a look at this poem (by Yeats, but I wasn't told so at the time). What do you think about it?
435. What makes a short story different from a novel?
436. Is poetry meant to be difficult to understand?
437. Is literature a different language to speech?
438. Coronation street has been running for 50 years – why is that interesting from an English viewpoint?
439. Why is English a formal subject?
440. How is poetry linked to music and media?
441. What is your opinion on ambiguity?
442. If you could make up a word, what would it be?
443. How would you describe a cucumber to an alien?
444. What type of literature is bad for you?
445. Why is a classic novel a classic? Can a modern novel be a classic?
446. Is an understanding of rhythm important when writing poetry? What about prose?
447. Is an author's life important when looking at their work?
448. Would you rather be a novel or a poem?
449. Is there such a thing as an immoral story?
450. What is your favourite word?

GEOGRAPHY & EARTH SCIENCES

If you're applying to Geography it is important that you prepare for both human and physical geography questions since you could be asked questions on either sub-field. If you're applying for Natural Sciences at Cambridge (with the aim of studying Earth Sciences) or Earth Sciences at Oxford, you are also likely to have a course-work related interview.

➤ This interview will require you to demonstrate passion and a genuine desire to study your chosen subject. You will be asked to discuss a source extract, a diagram or even an object depending on the subject you are applying for. You may not recognise the text you have been asked to read, but that is probably deliberate.

➤ The tutors know what subjects you have studied at A-Level. They will not ask you for detailed knowledge about areas of your subject that you are not familiar with. Nobody knows every aspect of their subject.

➤ **Apply the knowledge you have acquired at A-Level** and from your wider reading to unfamiliar scenarios. Feel confident to make references to academics whose works you have read, this shows that not only did you read widely but you can also pin-point specific researchers and apply this to questions they ask.

➤ If you begin by answering and you realise that you actually want to take a different direction, ask to start again. It's ok to change your mind. In order to help you avoid making any unnecessary comments, always take a few seconds to think about your response before saying it out loud. This will give you time to formulate your thoughts and arrange them in a logical order that you can then present before the interviewers.

➤ Remember, **making mistakes is no bad thing**. The important point is that you address the mistake head on and attempt to revise the statement, perhaps with the assistance of the tutors where necessary.

➢ The interviewers want to see students are willing and able to elaborate on their answers, so if you have something crucial to add when responding to a question, make sure to include it. At the same time, make sure not to keep on rambling when you have noted all the crucial points that directly address the question asked.

Being accepted into Oxbridge is not determined by how much you know, but by how well you think and how analytical your thought-processes and responses are.

What Questions Might be asked?

Most of the questions asked in the interview will begin with a larger question, followed by many smaller sub-questions to guide the answer from start to end. The main question may seem difficult, impossible or random at first, but take a breath and start discussing with your interviewer different ideas you have for breaking down the question into manageable pieces. Don't panic. **The questions are designed to be difficult** to give you the chance to show your full intellectual potential. They will help guide you to the right idea, if you provide ideas for them to guide.

This is your chance to show your creativity, analytical skills, intellectual flexibility, problem-solving skills and your go-getter attitude. Don't waste it on nervousness or a fear of messing up or looking stupid. It is also important to remember that especially for a subject like Geography, **answers are often more complex and multifaceted than a simple yes or no.** This should give you some reassurance during the interview process that your responses can take one direction but also refer to anomalies or include instances where the response would be different. If this is the case, make sure to elaborate on why a response could be both yes and no and under which circumstances.

Geography

For Geography, at some point in the interview **questions will likely draw on data** (for example graphs, diagrams or photographs). These types of questions are used to test whether you are able to analyse trends, make sense of the information and therefore apply it to a real world context. It is worthwhile using a two-step process to answer data-related questions which will give you time to think of a response if you are unsure of what to say, as well as allowing you to provide a really clear and well-formulated answer. The first part of your response should describe what you see, for example; 'this graph demonstrates an X trend with a greater clustering of points towards a certain axis'. The second part of your response should comment on why the graph looks that why; for example, why does one trend rise as the other falls?

In particular for geography, **questions have recurring themes** because they pose critical issues for geographical research and for policy makers too: climate change, glacial melt, and also questions exploring the overlap between human and physical geography for example conservation and ecosystem loss. The interviewers want to see that you can think analytically (meaning how well you can unpack a given question and how you think of varying possibilities and topics relevant to the response) and how you can think critically (meaning whether you can identify the flaws in certain arguments or data sets and what reasons could be provided for these).

Earth Sciences

No previous subject knowledge is necessary although you'll be expected to be comfortable with the core sciences i.e. have studied at least 2 of Physics, Chemistry and Biology to A2 level.

It is important to keep in mind that the aim is to understand **how the earth functions in the manner that it does**, what led to its processes, how different processes can be interlinked, and what their influences are on the physical formations and natural landscapes we see around us. The subject also touches on pressing concerns including the urgent problem of climate change, as well as sourcing water, coal, oil and minerals.

Course-Work Interviews

When applying to do Geography or Earth Sciences/ Natural Sciences at Cambridge, an applicant may be asked to submit course-work and called for a course-work interview. Usually in the morning on the day of the interview, this work is submitted and read by the interviewer. The work is used as a basis for discussion of research and experimental methods and analysis.

The interviewer may open by asking for a summary of the piece of work, they might open a discussion about certain ideas that you mention or they might want to understand how you reached your conclusions. They may then ask some follow-up questions related to the work, or the subject matter. This part of the interview will be very individual and depends on the nature and subject of the work submitted.

After the discussion of the work, the interviewer will probably guide the conversation toward some questions about a related topic to test the applicant's ability to think like a Geographer/Earth Scientist.

Worked Questions

Below are a few examples of how to start breaking down an interview question, complete with model answers.

Q1: This map displays a distribution relating to a natural hazard event. What do you think the natural hazard is and what do you think the map is showing in relation to it?

50 and above

22 to 49

10 to 21

6 to 9

3 to 5

2

1 and below

[Extremely clear-headed] **Applicant**: Well, I can tell that this is a map of North America. At a purely descriptive level it is evident from the map that there is a higher concentration of the natural event on the west coast than on the east coast. There is also a notable hotspot located on the continent's south-western region. It could be that **darker shades represent a higher incidence of events** in particular areas, for example in the California region. On the other hand, darker colours could also refer to places in which the effects of the hazard are more pronounced.

Before suggesting what the natural hazard could be, I want to first provide a definition of the term. The definition of natural hazards on the World Meteorological Organisation website is useful for an overall definition, refers to 'events that occur naturally in all parts of the world, with some regions being more vulnerable to certain hazards than others'.

From my knowledge of common natural hazards in California, I would say this map shows the **distribution of earthquake events**. Darker zones probably point to areas where earthquake are more common. A different distribution which the colours may represent could be the regions most affected by ground shaking following an earthquake, and those that are less affected.

The details are unimportant, but the general idea of breaking down the question into manageable parts is important. Notice how a better applicant begins by describing what he sees in order to provide directions for his upcoming explanation and to guide his interviewer through his thought process. The interviewer is not looking for a natural hazard expert, but someone who can problem-solve in the face of new ideas. Note that even though the question begins with 'What', it is actually expecting you to consider '**Why**' certain distributions look the way they do. The point of these questions is to suggest different ideas, and to show an ability to use data usefully.

A **Poor Applicant** may take a number of approaches unlikely to impress the interviewer. The first and most obvious of these is to say "We were not taught about natural hazards in America at school" and make no attempt to move forward anyway. It is worth providing some sort of logical response rather than giving up completely, the **interviewer is likely to help you by asking follow-up questions**. This is especially if they see you showing a genuine interest and if you make obvious your attempt at some sort of response that is at least headed in the right direction (for example, even just providing a description of what you see will be better than giving up altogether).

Another approach which is unhelpful in the interview is the 'brain dump', where instead of engaging with the question, the applicant attempts to impress or distract with an assortment of related facts: "Natural hazards are geographical events that occur naturally across the world. These become natural disasters when there is a chance for populations to be affected/at risk". This isn't as impressive as a more reasoned response.

Nevertheless, the interview could be salvaged by taking feedback from the interviewer. This would depend on the applicant's attentiveness and ability to take hints and suggestions from the interviewer.

Q2: How do human and physical geography overlap?

A question such as this is a classic way of integrating the two main streams found in Geography, and to test whether you can provide a concise response to a very broad question.

You could begin by speaking about how **each stream is integral to the other**, resulting in them both being inherently intertwined.

While human geography strives to understand how societies organise and why they organise in certain ways, physical geography strives to understand how natural systems operate and why they function in certain ways. To understand topics more cohesively, such as conservation and climate change, you need an appreciation of how physical and environmental systems function, as well as how these understandings can be applied to societies in social, political and economic terms.

At the same time, it is important to consider the manner in which human societies affect their environments and what the short, medium and long-term implications are of these social activities.

It would be useful to note the real-life instances in which these two streams overlap, for example when policy makers use scientific information to implement policies that affect our lives (i.e. encouraging use of public transport rather than personal vehicles to reduce CO_2 emissions).

A more advanced response may touch on the gap that exists between both streams as social and natural scientists often fail to communicate effectively with one another. One example of this may be evident in the plethora of research on **climate change** existing today and the lack of ability to communicate this to much of the population in ways that makes them understand the implications of their actions. You could then briefly discuss what other implications this gap may pose for societies.

Q3: Why is the concept of 'space' important in Geography?

This is an example of a more theoretical/philosophical question that could be asked in an interview situation, and certainly during your undergraduate career. Start with more simple and basic concepts and build from there.

First address the concept of space. The more obvious notion of the term implies a **physical or rooted place/location**. This is important in Geography in terms of pin-pointing certain locations and analysing their physical facets.

At a closer look, we can say that the concept of space in Geography is important for understanding how humans interact with the physical features of the land. For example, one place can be used differently by different people and for various purposes. Therefore, understanding space is vital in order to understand the meaning of why certain relations arise between people, arise in specific locales and how they impact on economic and political institutions.

Q4: Why is it that in some developing countries slum settlements have sprung up near wealthier neighbourhoods?

Before answering this question it is useful to consider **what the term 'developing countries' refers to**. Today many developing countries are those located in the Global South which are typically less economically and socially advanced than Western countries. However it is also important to keep in mind that the development trajectory of each region and nation varies significantly.

That said, there are certain patterns evident across most developing countries. The emergence of slums in these countries largely refers to informal settlements in urban areas characterized by substandard housing and squalor including unreliable sanitation services and electricity. Often, the people living in slums have arrived from rural regions of the country in search of better employment and other opportunities. The only places they can afford to live in are the ones they create themselves.

By positioning themselves near wealthy hubs, poorer settlements are able to benefit from access to various established services such as electricity and water, which they could even tap into illegally. They also have **easier access** to employment, healthcare and educational opportunities than they would if they were in say, poorer neighbourhoods.

Q5: Estimate the mass of the oceans.

You can state at the beginning that calculating this accurately depends on the data you have to work with. Since this is an estimation question, you don't need to worry about being precise – rounding numbers is perfectly acceptable. An interviewer wants to see what your thought process is - they are less concerned with receiving a specific number. **It's the journey- not the destination that matters.**

The key part to providing a coherent response is knowing which key factors you need to identify for the calculation to be made. Start by breaking down the question:

Firstly recall that Mass = Density x Volume
You should know that the density of water is 1,000 kg/m^3.

The Volume of the oceans is trickier. The easiest way is to make a series of assumptions:
The Surface Area of a sphere $= 4\pi r^2$
You could then ask the interviewer for the Earth's radius (6,000 km) or use a sensible estimate.
Approximate $\pi = 3$ to give:
$Area = 4 \times 3 \times (6 \times 10^6)^2$
$Area = 12 \times 36 \times 10^{12}$
$= 432 \times 10^{12} \approx 4 \times 10^{14} \ m^2$

Approximately 75% of the Earth's Surface Area is covered by the Oceans so the surface area of the ocean's $= 4 \times 10^{14} \times 75\% = 3 \times 10^{14} \ m^2$

Finally, you need to convert the area into a volume by multiplying it via an average depth of the oceans. Again, any sensible estimate would be fine here (100 m – 10,000m).

Volume of Oceans = $3 \times 10^{14} \times 1,000 = 3 \times 10^{17} m^3$
Thus, Mass of Oceans = $3 \times 10^{17} \times 1,000 = \mathbf{3 \times 10^{20} kg}$
Real Answer: $1.4 \times 10^{21} \ kg$

Q6: How do mountains originate?

Geography Applicant: It is important to note at the outset that mountain formation is a phenomenon unique to the specific geography and previous conditions of a given location. That said, there are specific processes that in general lead to the formation of mountains.

One example is mountains originating from **fault-line movements**. For example, if a fault exists where both sections push against each other and one rock mass is moving up while the other is moving down, then the upward moving rock mass may form a mountain as it gets pushed up.
Mountains can also originate from volcanic eruptions. This can occur as rock builds up from an explosion, as magma solidifies and thirdly as the earth's crust heaves upwards (due to the pressure of the explosion), eventually forming a mountain. Triggers for fault line movements and volcanic eruptions are often unknown and may be the result of several processes occurring within deeper layers of the earth's structure.

In all cases it is important to note that for mountains to form there needs to be an external trigger that allows for sufficient matter and mass to mobilise in order to create such a phenomenon. Also, while in most cases the process is rather gradual (fault-mountains), in some the process can be more sudden (volcanic eruptions).

Q7: How do mountains originate?

Earth Sciences Applicant: Answering this question would involve suggesting possible scenarios and important parameters. For example, a candidate could begin by explaining that mountain formation is associated with large-scale movements of the earth's crust (making a distinction at the onset between the layers of the earth which could result in such formations). Then one could discuss the various factors that lead to mountain formation, for example volcanic eruptions and tectonic movements, perhaps providing a brief description/example of how these processes result in mountain formation.

It would then be useful to comment on timescale and explain how mountains tend to organise over a very long time scale (e.g. due to gradual tectonic movements) or can be formed more suddenly (e.g. during volcanic eruptions). The point of these questions is to **suggest different ideas**, and to show an understanding of their strengths and weakness and an ability to use data usefully.

Crucially, the point of these types of questions is for you to address the key terms (notably volcanoes, **global** climate) first by defining and describing them, and later by explaining their influences in a logical manner.

Q8: What is the point of conservation?

Before considering the aim of conservation it is important first to understand that it is a loaded term. As such, it could be argued that a loose definition is most appropriate to explain the term. Many definitions include a normative judgment about how the world should be, in other words what nature should be like given human relations to natural environments. Perhaps one of the most all-encompassing definition is the one provided by Adams in his 2013 publication. This definition refers to conservation as a "social practice that reflects choices about relations between people and nature".

Given this preliminary understanding, we can see that **the 'point' of conservation is very context specific**. Therefore, its aim very much depends on the people carrying out conservationist activities and the ecosystem in question. Given this, conservation aims will include various parameters such as: the economic betterment of involved actors, or the environmental preservation of local species or perhaps the social inclusiveness of local people in environmental programmes.

To summarise, I would say that the point of conservation encompasses the enhancement of relations between nature and people, and the maintenance of this interaction. That said, this heavily depends on the motives of players involved in conservationist activities and the environment in question.

Q9: What effect does an increase in sea level have on coastal morphology, and why does this impact vary geographically?

The area that will see the greatest **morphological impact from sea level** rise is the shore and beach area since it is subject to wave action. Sea level rise is caused, to the greatest extent, by ocean thermal expansion and glacial melt. Since characteristics of coastal zones vary considerably worldwide, due to: a) the rate of relative sea level rise, b) the type of coastline and c) human stresses, the geographical impact of sea level rise on coastal morphology varies.

Coastal landforms are extremely sensitive to changes in sea level. The likely outcome of increased sea level rise will be that submerging coastlines will become more extensive and erosion rates will increase along most coastal areas. However other coastlines, mainly around previously glaciated regions, may see a fall in sea level and as a result may see coastlines growing rather than retreating. In turn we see that **different types of coastline respond differently** to increasing sea level rise, depending on the sensitivity and resilience of the coastline, as well as the human interference implemented. Furthermore, since sea level rise is not uniform across the globe, the response of coastal areas will change depending on the region in question.

It is also essential to consider that existing models of costal morphology are inadequate in determining responses to sea level rise as they do not take into account the variety of responses and interconnectedness of different processes. As a result, fully determining the extent of geographical variation in coastal geomorphology as a result of sea level rise remains difficult, making it subject to continuing research.

Q10: Define risk.

The field of risk is influenced by two major streams: **positivist and normative**. The former stream sees risks as real events or dangers that can be approached objectively and calculated using probabilities. Meanwhile, the second streams sees risks as being socially constructed. In this sense, the notion of risk becomes a way of dealing with hazards and insecurities. Such variation in opinions make it difficult to define what a general 'understanding' of risk really is.

Today, in particular among policy makers, emphasis within risk still relies on it being something calculable, with science remaining at the basis of attempts to reduce the vulnerability of certain populations in the face of hazards. However, this idea that science can provide an understanding of future risk through mathematical predictions is being increasingly challenged, particularly by academics of the social sciences and particularly within the geographic discipline. This is especially because quantitative analysis tends to overlook the short and long term influence of communities likely to be affected by various risks.

According to one of the most prominent risk theorists, known as Beck, risk can be defined as '**the anticipation of catastrophe**'. Alongside other social scientists, Beck has played a key role in advancing a social understanding of risk so that the term can be easily understood by the societies it influences. Therefore it is becoming increasing clear that with time, the definition of risk is changing at its core to incorporate the social aspects of the term.

Q11: What is sustainable development?

The definition which I think best encompasses the idea of sustainable development is the one provided by the Brundtland Commission in 1987. It refers to the term as "development which meets the needs of current generations without compromising the ability of future generations to meet their own needs". This definition foregrounds **careful management of resources** in order to facilitate a high quality of life for current and future generations as well.

It is important to remember that sustainable development does not oppose the idea of humans' use of resources and manipulation of natural environments. Sustainable development in fact supports such activities though in a manner which ensures that the integrity of nature's processes are preserved. The preservation of such processes is important since it allows the reproduction of key biological resources and cycles on which humans depend for sustenance.

Furthermore, it is necessary to consider that sustainable development can be divided into separate, yet intricately connected, subdivisions. For example, development may be economically sustainable though socially unsustainable. Therefore for development to be considered truly sustainable it must encompass the following pillars; social, economic, political and environmental.

Q12: How do cities act as sources of resilience in an era of heightened risk?

Before providing a response, you need to address two key aspects of the question: the **definition of resilience** and an understanding of what an 'era of heightened risk' refers to. Martin and Sunley (2006) define resilience as the capacity to bounce back to some previous state following a disruption to the system. Resilience is also about a system being able to withstand total collapse, during which some parts will inevitably become damaged and others will remain intact. Resilience is not just about the ability to recover to a previous state, it is also about reaching a new state that is arguably more robust than the previous by learning from previous catastrophes and incorporating solutions into the urban environment through infrastructures and by educating citizens. Crucially, redundancy and slack are a key aspect of resilience, referring to the idea of leaving space for the unexpected, having spare capacity. Furthermore, questions of resilience have gained new prominence in our era of heightened risk. This new era of global risks is largely the product of human activities and is worsened by the nature of the interconnected global economy in which we live.

I think the main way in which cities act as sources of resilience in today's world is by combining three central factors: resilient communities, smart infrastructures and intelligent governance. The first makes references to societies that are characterised by solidarity and altruism in the face of a crisis. The second refers to the hardware, and software, that underpins the functioning of our cities for example sewage systems and electricity grids. Intelligent governance is the factor that brings the first two characteristics together, including city leaders, academic communities and researchers. Resilience then becomes the product of a combination of sophisticated modelling, information based governance and strong, clear and intelligent urban leadership that creates a sense of community.

In conclusion, we can see that **resilience is the product of humans and non-humans coming together**. Though the relative balance of each factor varies from city to city and in turn creates different forms of resilience in each urban community.

Q13: What are the limitations of hazard mapping?

Hazard mapping displays the distribution of hazards according to their geographical location. Such maps are typically created for natural hazards, such as earthquakes, volcanoes, landslides, flooding and tsunamis.

Even so, hazard mapping has several limitations. I will discuss two specific issues. Firstly, and perhaps most importantly, these maps often make no reference to hazards' **potential social impact**; either in terms of human life or economic loss.

At times this renders hazard maps less useful or understandable for local communities. Another issue is attributable to the uncertainty inherent within natural hazards themselves, in turn compromising the accuracy of hazard maps. For example, we are still **unable to predict the timescale** of certain hazards, such as volcanic eruptions, given that we cannot always identify which forces trigger their manifestation. Furthermore, inaccuracies in modelling tools create uncertainties in mapping, again limiting the applicability of such maps for use in warning communities.

Q14: Does cost-benefit analysis (CBA) helps us make difficult decisions with regards to the environment?

This isn't a simple yes/no question – it requires that you to address both sides of the argument.

A cost-benefit analysis is a useful tool for making difficult decisions with regards to the environment since it breaks down issues into separate factors. These can then be quantified, with the numerical values of each benefit and cost being used to consider the overall soundness of the project in question. This type of analysis is also good for identifying which players are involved in decision-making and who will lose or win from the proposed project. While this type of analysis is helpful for making difficult decisions, it has its downfalls which must be considered if such a tool is adopted for decision-making. Perhaps the core issue of CBA is that some issues with regards to the environment cannot be quantified. For example, it may be difficult to quantify the aesthetic and spiritual value of environments to their indigenous populations. Furthermore, the outcome of the CBA will largely depend on the player that is carrying out such analysis, with an economic developer likely to place greater positive weighting on the economic benefits of a project rather than the need for environmental preservation.

Overall, we can see that **CBA is a useful tool for helping us make difficult decisions** with regards to the environment. Even so, it may be necessary to adopt supplementary tools for analysing environmental questions in order to make up for CBA's shortfalls.

Q15: Do you think that access to education lies at the heart of development?

Development loosely refers to processes of social change or class that aim to transform national economies, particularly in formerly colonised countries or countries situated in the global south. Access to education is an important part of a country's development, though given the complexity of the subject **it's not possible to isolate one factor** that will on its own assist a country to improve economically, politically and socially. Furthermore, since each country begins at a different stage of development, its educational needs will vary. For example, in certain countries, the state of healthcare may be so dire that economic productivity may suffer significantly. In this case, healthcare would be a more urgent factor for targeting development. Therefore, education doesn't lie alone at the core of development because the process itself is multifaceted and because it is dependent on the country.

That said, and as also stated by the Campaign for Global Education in 2010, **education remains a focal point for development initiatives** since it is an important catalyst for national economic and social growth. For example, national expenditure on education can be seen to promote development if the investment results in improvements in the quality of labour which in turn raises GDP over the long term. The importance of education is reiterated by its status as a millennium development goal and it being one of the dimensions for measuring the Human Development Index (HDI). Furthermore, access to education has the capability of acting as an important force for social change and even political transformation (you may wish to reference specific case studies here).

In summary, since development cannot be distilled to one factor alone, it may be more useful to consider in what ways access to education can be used to propel development rather than trying to weigh its relative importance within the development field.

Q16: When it comes to climate change, does the past help us predict the future?

If we look at current publications regarding climate change, there is no doubt that the data collected about past climate trends has been instrumental in making future projections. This is because **paleo-climactic evidence** from the past sheds light onto the emergence and functioning of the Earth's climate system, and what changes it has experienced. This in turn suggests what path it might follow in future. In his writings on Paleo-climatology, Bruckner states that past climate reconstructions can then be 'integrated with observations of the Earth's current climate and placed into a computer model to deduce the past and predict future climate'. Additionally, in a social context, using past records is important for identifying what exposes certain physical and human vulnerabilities; which is crucial for climate change forecasting.

While the past is useful in predicting the future, it is important to keep in mind that reasons for changes in climate can be attributable to various sources. In the case of climate change, we must very **carefully analyse the impacts of humans in creating new, unusual climatic patterns**, and the potential consequences of these for society. Following from this, it is important that we are aware that the past will not provide a precise analogue of the future given inherent uncertainties in nature and inaccuracies in our modelling tools. Thus, uncertainties in measurements and forecasting must be acknowledged to ensure that inappropriate actions aren't taken by policy makers.

In sum, while the past is crucial in helping us understand the potential future trajectory of climate change, various social factors and discrepancies in data need to be accounted for to ensure that projections about climate change's trajectory are more accurate and relevant to today's societies.

Q17: How can volcanic eruptions change global climate?

Answering this question can begin with recognition of the meaning of global climate. Since our planet's climate is comprised of a complex mixture of processes and elements, any significant influence to this system has the potential to change the climate.

You should then address how volcanic eruptions, given their nature and force, are able to influence global climate. First you must note the **types of elements ejected** by volcanoes during an eruption, including the release of vast amounts of ash and gases into the atmosphere, as well as flows of lava and ash covering the ground. You could suggest that lava cover on the ground can have some effect on regional (though perhaps not global) climate, and how the most important influence on climate comes from volcanic gases released into the atmosphere e.g. sulphur dioxide. The cloud formed by the gases and ash can **reduce the amount of solar radiation** reaching the earth. This can result in the Earth's surface temperature decreasing significantly.

Changes in one region's climate can result in climate changes in other regions. You can also launch a discussion of how the deep earth and bio-sphere are linked through the carbon cycle. For example, erupting magma releases CO_2 into the atmosphere. Years of weathering remove most of this gas – causing to end up in the oceans as calcium carbonate sediment. Therefore, an excess of this from eruptions can offset the balance of CO_2 in the system.

The idea of **timescale is also important** here. Ash cover created by volcanic eruptions can have an immediate impact on a region's climate. Contrastingly, changes in the carbon cycle can result in long-term impacts.

Q18: Are humans ethically obligated to stop global warming and environmental change?

This is a question about Ethics. To answer a question like this, the important thing is not to have a strong opinion that you defend to the death, but to be able to discuss the different viewpoints based on different understandings of right and wrong, and always with a sound understanding of the underlying issues- both scientific and humanitarian.

One way to break down this question would be to **consider whether an ethical obligation extends only to other humans or to other organisms** as well, and whether it applies in any situation or only when contributing to a situation that wouldn't occur naturally. Similarly, one could also discuss whether humans as a whole are obliged to halt global warming or just a select few members of the human race. Showing an ability to think flexibly about abstract concepts is always good, but don't forget to then argue for the different cases using knowledge of past and present climate and environment, as this is the subject-relevant part of the question.

For instance, don't waste time discussing if climate change is a reality – the scientific community has already reached a consensus. However, if you would like to argue against an ethical obligation instead, discuss the natural climate variations which have occurred on Earth in the past. Use probable climate-change driven events, like the Permo-Triassic extinction when 96% of species died out 250 million years ago, to argue that humans have no ethical obligation to save other species from anthropogenic extinction, because **even without human presence there are climate-driven extinctions**. Or argue the opposite, that despite past extreme environmental change being a reality, humanity is pushing the Earth further than it has ever sustained humans, and that we are obligated to do our part to leave a habitable Earth for people in other parts of the world and the future.

Alternatively, you could argue the complete opposite - that there can be no ethical obligation because everyone **contributes to the problem in their own way**, and everyone will face the consequences. Or that only those who contribute more than they suffer are in the wrong for dumping their consequences onto others. Whichever argument you put forward, be sure to include scientific examples so that your discussion doesn't veer away from the question.

Remember that climate change is not the same as global warming, and your discussion could include pollution (trash, toxins, chemicals, light and sound pollution, etc.), agriculture and monoculture, invasive species, hunting and fishing, deforestation and habitat fragmentation, or any of the other issues beyond the Greenhouse Effect which effect the environment.

Similarly, global warming is not just about fossil fuel use and carbon dioxide, but a range of gases and their effects on weather, ocean acidity, desertification, pathogen spread, etc. Show that you have a deeper understanding of these issues than you could get from skimming the headlines of the Daily Mail.

Geography Interview Questions

451. Why are temperatures rising more in polar regions than in tropical regions?
452. What is culture?
453. Why are glacier melting rates non-linear?
454. What is the relationship between global population and atmospheric CO_2?
455. Plot the graph of CO2 emissions vs. time starting from the 10th century.
456. Why did India progress more quickly through the DTM than the countries it was based on originally?
457. How do human and physical geography overlap?
458. What are natural hazards?
459. Define risk.
460. What is the role of maps in modern day society?
461. Why is it that in some developing countries slum settlements have sprung up near high-rise buildings/wealthier neighborhoods?
462. What is the point of conservation?
463. Why do you think some people don't take global warming seriously?
464. How can ICT help geographers understand physical process and natural hazard events?
465. Can we consider nature as natural in today's world?
466. How can volcanic eruptions change global climate, and at what timescales?
467. Given a graph showing the number of years that people have been driving on one axis and the amount of accidents they experience on the other axis. Asked to describe and expla
468. What is Malthus's 'principle of population'?
469. Why is biodiversity not evenly distributed around the world?
470. Why is it important to know the number of living species on Earth?
471. What are the challenges in trying to assess this number?
472. Why is place important in geography?
473. What is the impact of the economy/policy on social inequality?
474. Do you think that access to education lies at the heart of development?
475. What are the limitations of hazard mapping?

476. What percentage of the world's water is contained in one watermelon?
477. The atmospheric pressure is 10,000 Pa. Calculate the mass of Earth's atmosphere.
478. What is the difference between a volcano and a mountain?
479. What would happen if a 10 km wide asteroid smashed into the Pacific Ocean?
480. Would you rather conserve Antarctica or the Amazon?
481. How do we know what the Earth's core consists of?
482. How did the ancient Greeks know that the earth wasn't flat?
483. How do we know that Pangaea existed?
484. How does carbon dating work?
485. What would happen if the Earth had two Moons of equal size?
486. Where would you survive longer- in the arctic or Sahara?
487. Would it matter if pandas became extinct?
488. How do we measure sea levels? Why is this a poor method?
489. How do we know that dinosaurs once existed?
490. How would you definitively prove that global warming was man made?
491. What is the impact of globalization and multi-national corporations?
492. Could the great biblical flood have ever happened?
493. Why is Antarctica so much colder than the Arctic?
494. Compare and contrast Venus and Mars.
495. Why do we know so little about the depths of the Ocean? How could this be rectified?
496. Why do rainforests contain so much biodiversity compared to the Sahara desert?
497. Give me an example of a geological phenomenon that has had a significant impact on humans.

HISTORY

The subject interview for History can take several different formats, as each college has their own way of conducting interviews. The Admissions Office for your college will let you know what format your interview will take in good time. If you have any questions about it, it is best to contact them directly.

It may be the case that you have prepared extensively for one aspect of your interview, but aren't given a chance to draw on that preparation. For example, they might not ask you about anything on your personal statement, even if you are very keen to talk about it. If this happens, try not to let it rattle you. The interview process can be unpredictable, so try to remain as calm and flexible as you can.

In a standard history interview, the interviewers will ask you a **series of questions pertaining to your subject**. Some of these will be related to topics you have studied before. Others will be related to certain areas of historical methodology.

The interviewers know what subjects and what areas of history you have studied at school from your application. For example they will know if you have studied modern history or ancient history. They will **not** ask you for detailed knowledge about areas of your subject that you are not familiar with. However, questions on topics you've studied are fair game.

Draw on the work you have done at school to answer these questions, but be prepared that the conversation might go beyond your syllabus. Avoid saying things like 'we haven't covered this in school yet' – just try your best to answer each question.

The interviewers will also have read your personal statement (and your SAQ form, if you applied to Cambridge). They are likely to ask you questions about the academic sections of it.

For example, if you have mentioned that you furthered your understanding of historical practice by reading Richard Evans' *In Defence of History*, then they may ask you to summarise an aspect of the book, or ask whether you agree with the author on a certain issue. If you have mentioned work experience in a museum, they might ask you about the work you did there.

Worked Questions

Below are a few examples of how to start breaking down an interview question, complete with model answers.

Q1: Does the study of history serve any practical purpose?

Applicant: This question covers quite a lot of potential areas, so I will start by looking at the study of history in the context of university/higher education, as that seems most relevant. Firstly I will evaluate a few potential arguments. Studying history at university serves many practical purposes, both for the student and society as a whole. The student gains many skills, such as research and formulating an argument. Society gets to benefit from these skills when they graduate. But these benefits are not unique to history alone, as this description could also cover other humanities subjects such as Classics, or Sociology.

The other argument that is that **history teaches lessons**, without which history would simply repeat itself, and humanity would go on making the same 'mistakes'. This is also not a particularly convincing view in my opinion. Though there can be similarities between different historical events, all historical events are unique, which I believe undermines the idea that history constantly repeats itself. I think this idea is based too much on hindsight, as it is easy to see similarities between events after they have happened.

Instead, I think that historical causation (what makes events happen) depends above all on the context in which those events take place. This means that we cannot necessarily learn specific practical 'lessons' from history to apply in the future, because the context of the future will be completely different.

However, this does not mean that history does not serve any practical purpose. Even though I don't think one can learn concrete 'lessons' from history, being able to understand how a certain problem came about can make it easier to find a solution. This means that the **skills gained by studying history can have a positive practical impact** on policy-making. Aside from that, the study of history also serves to educate and entertain the public. Most historical works are written by historians at universities, and TV documentaries are usually made with the input of historians.

Analysis: You will not be expected to answer questions as fully as this. This answer is an indication of some of the things you might be expected to talk about in response to a question like this, but the interviewer will help you along the way with additional questions and comments. The merit of the answer is that it **breaks down the question** into manageable chunks, and proceeds through an answer while signposting this process to the interviewer. These are good skills for you to try to develop, but remember that the interviewer is there to help get the best out of you.

Poor applicant: A poor applicant could begin by saying 'we haven't studied this in class', and make no effort to further the conversation. He or she might then, if pressed, express a vague opinion that history serves a practical purpose, in that it teaches people lessons for the future. (As discussed, this is not a very strong interpretation, because historical events depend on a specific configuration of circumstances. It would be difficult to gain a concrete and specific 'lesson' from one historical situation that could be applied in another historical situation, as no two historical situations are the same.)

A **poor applicant** may also respond to this question by saying that there is no practical purpose to history at all. Unless you have a very good argument to back this up, this would be a bad answer to this question, because it would overlook the practical benefits that a historical perspective can bring to various areas of public life. It would also be a bad answer, because it would imply that there is no practical purpose to the career to which your interviewers have dedicated their lives, as well as the degree to which you are applying.

Q2: Is it ever possible to find out 'what really happened' in the past?

A **good applicant** will recognise the complexity of this question. Throughout school, one is encouraged to assume that every statement written in a history book is a statement of fact. But at university level, it becomes clear that sources are subjective, historical interpretations are subjective, and the idea that history is just a series of events and facts seems a little simplistic. With a question like this, a good way to break it down is to focus first on one side of the argument and then on the other, before coming to a conclusion. If you do this, you might choose to say to the interviewer 'first I will look at the idea that it is not possible to find out 'what really happened' in the past', so they know the approach you are taking.

Then you might choose to discuss the fact that you can never really know whether a source is telling the truth, because **historical sources are inherently subjective**. A diary entry or letter about a certain event is only written from one person's perspective, and they might not have had a full understanding of events, or may be recording them in hindsight, having forgotten some of what happened. Even official documents are subjective; they might have an agenda behind them, or be subject to censorship. When it comes to more distant historical events, the source material is necessarily subjective, because it depends to a large extent on what documents have survived.

So in many ways, it may be impossible to find out 'what really happened' in the past – there are too many obstacles in the way, and history is only ever an interpretation of past events, rather than an objective statement of fact.

On the other hand, however, it would be unfair to say that this means all interpretations are equally invalid. While historical sources are subjective, it is possible to come to a reasonable interpretation of past events by using a wide variety of sources that corroborate each other. If all available sources say the same thing about a certain event, we can be reasonably sure that this is correct. This is how we can ascertain certain facts that are beyond interpretation. For example, the French Revolution occurred in 1789. Therefore, it is possible to find out some aspects of what really happened. Even though sources and interpretations are subjective, **history is not fiction**.

Q3: Is history moving away from the study of great men to that of ordinary people?

In many ways the answer to this would be quite straightforward. Yes, history does seem to be moving away from the study of great men to that of ordinary people – whereas in the early 20th century, for example, 'history' was almost synonymous with '**political history**' and focused largely on politicians and generals, history seems to have democratised in recent decades. Scholarship in recent years appears to have focused more than ever on people who had not been represented by historical studies before, such as women, ethnic minorities, the working classes, etc.

A good answer may therefore, challenge this obvious response in a few ways. While all of the above is true, it would be worth mentioning that some **parts of history still focus disproportionately on 'great men'** rather than 'ordinary people'. Political history still occupies a big part of university history curricula, while 'popular history' such as TV documentaries and historical bestsellers are more often than not focused on 'great men' (or great events or, occasionally, great women such as Elizabeth I) rather than 'ordinary people'.

A good answer would also recognise the secondary question implicit in this question – **Why** *is history moving away from the study of great men to that of ordinary people?* Answers to this would perhaps include a discussion of how minority rights movements (eg African-American civil rights, or second-wave feminism) often initiate new historical interest in minorities, or a discussion of the democratisation of education in recent decades.

Q4: How would a biography of a major political figure written during their lifetime differ from one written after they had died? Which would be more accurate?

This type of question is great one to get, as it gives you a lot of scope to be creative, and to bring in your own knowledge. The interviewers may ask this in response to a political biography you have listed in your personal statement, for example, which would allow you to speak about a topic you are familiar with and passionate about.

However, assuming you are asked this question hypothetically without a specific biography in mind, there are **several ways** to approach it- even if you are not familiar with any biography of a major political figure yourself.

First, it would be sensible to tackle the first part of this question in isolation, and leave the additional question (*'which would be more accurate?'*) for later in the discussion. A biography of a major political figure written during their lifetime would be likely to differ significantly from one written after their death.

The biographer may have had **access to meetings with the political figure**, or the biography may even have been written with the input of the political figure. This may make the text richer in its detail, but may also mean that it is coloured by the politician's political agenda and desire to manage his image and reputation. A biography written after the politician's death may have access to **newly released sources** not available during the figure's lifetime. There are many possible answers to this question.

In response to the second part of the question, a **weak candidate** may have a strong opinion on this, saying something like 'a biography written during their lifetime would be more accurate because the biographer would know the politician, so they would tell the truth', or alternatively, 'a biography written after their lifetime would be more accurate because the biographer would have the benefit of hindsight'. Both of these answers fail to take the complexity of the situation into account.

A **stronger candidate** would investigate both options more fully, and would not take too dogmatic a view on what is a complicated question without a clear answer. After considering the merits and weaknesses of each type of source, a stronger candidate may conclude that one cannot deem either type of source more accurate than the other, because this would depend entirely on the specific biography and biographers in question, or may conclude that it would be best to draw upon both sources to get the most accurate depiction of the politician in question.

Text/Source-Based Interview

If your college decides to give you a text or source based interview, you will be given a piece of **academic text to look at before the interview**. You may also need to write a summary or commentary; the Admissions Office will tell you if this is the case. It is likely that the text you are given will be unfamiliar to you, on a topic or area of history you have not studied before. Do not be daunted by this – you are not expected to have any detailed factual knowledge related to the text.

The interview will then be based on the contents of the extract, and issues surrounding it. Things to keep in mind:

➢   When reading the text in advance, **pay attention to the author, the date of publication, and the nature of the work**. It may be an historical source, or an extract from a work of historiography by a theorist such as E.H. Carr or Richard Evans. It may be an introduction from a history book on a topic you have never encountered before.

➢ Try to pick up on aspects of the publication that are unusual or revealing (e.g. was it written anonymously? Is it a revision of an earlier text? Is it clearly written in response to another text or another writer's view? Who is the intended audience?)

➢ When reading the text, pay attention to the argument it is making. Is it a strong argument or a weak argument, and why? Can you think of any counter-arguments?

➢ Does the text relate in any way to any other area of history and historiography with which you are familiar, that you might be able to draw on in the interview?

What Questions Might be asked?

For this type of interview setting, the interviewers will ask questions about the text, and about the broader historical issues that the text raises. Questions about the text directly will range from content comprehension (what is the author arguing? What does the author mean by X?) to interpretation (do you agree with the author's characterisation of X?) to questions of historical methodology (why has the author approached this subject in this way? Is the author's method valid?)

The thing to remember when answering these questions is not to panic! **The questions are designed to be difficult** to give you the chance to show your full intellectual potential. The interviewers will help guide you to the right idea, if you provide ideas for them to guide. This is your chance to show your creativity, analytical skills, intellectual flexibility, problem-solving skills and your go-getter attitude. Don't waste it on nervousness or a fear of messing up or looking stupid.

Q5: You are given an extract from an introduction to a historical work that is based entirely on oral sources, such as Robert Fraser's Blood of Spain.

Can one ever understand a historical event from oral history sources alone?

This question is asking you to evaluate a particular type of source. A good way to approach a question like this would be to look firstly at the ways in which this type of source can help to understand an event, then to look at the **weaknesses of this type of source**, and then to come to a conclusion. There are lots of aspects of a historical event that could be understood through oral history sources alone. Using the example of the Spanish Civil War, oral history allows one to understand what the war was like in terms of lived experience, as in a fairly decentralised state with low levels of literacy and high levels of censorship, oral history can bring a perspective to the war that is lacking in other types of sources and official documents.

Furthermore, seeing as oral histories are generally collected in interviews after the event in question, this type of source allows the historian to understand not only the event itself, but also its aftermath and long-term effects on those who lived through it.

However, there are several drawbacks to oral history. While it is a useful way to understand what it was like to live through an event, it only shows what it was like for those individuals interviewed to live through that event, and this experience may not be representative of the people of Spain as a whole. It also would not take into account political, economic, or international factors influencing the course of events, which can only be illuminated by other types of sources. Oral history is also fallible, in that people are interviewed about events that happened years or even decades earlier. Therefore, **recollections of events may not be entirely reliable**.

A good conclusion to this question would be that, while certain aspects of historical events could be understood from oral sources alone, no one type of source is comprehensive enough to encapsulate every aspect of an event. For the best understanding of the Spanish Civil War, it would be necessary to use as wide a variety of sources as possible, including oral history.

Q6: You may be given an extract from an introduction to a history book on a very specific topic about which you know very little, and asked to comment on the historian's proposed method. For example, it may be an extract from a work that looks at Georgian England from a woman's perspective, such as Vickery's Behind Closed Doors: At Home in Georgian England.

This work looks at Georgian England from a feminist perspective. Do you think it is acceptable to analyse a period through the lens of a concept that didn't exist during the period under study (ie. feminism)?

This would be a difficult question to be presented with in an interview. It is important to stay calm and be open-minded, and **the interviewers will help guide you to an answer**. It would be useful to analyse both sides of such a question before coming to a conclusion. You might start by looking at the drawbacks of analysing a certain period through the lens of a concept that was not contemporary to the period you are looking at.

There are several problems with analysing Georgian England through a feminist framework (for example). Many historians argue that it is better to analyse the past through terminology that was in use in the period under discussion.

By looking at Georgian England through a feminism perspective, you may be imposing ideas onto the past that are incompatible with the period under study. You could argue that **this is not so much history as sociology**, as it is putting more of an emphasis on the modern concept (feminism) than on the period you are supposed to be studying (Georgian England).

However, there are also benefits to this type of historiography. Part of the purpose of history is to look at the past through a new perspective. Even if this perspective would not have been understood by the people who lived in the period under discussion, it may still illuminate aspects of the period that have not yet been covered by scholarship.

Q7: You may be given an extract from a work about a certain aspect of historical theory, such as Niall Ferguson's Virtual History or Richard Evans' Altered Pasts, both of which deal with counter-factual history.

What, if any, is the value of studying counter-factual history?

Counter-factual history is the history of *what if?* It challenges the historian to consider what would have happened had something else occurred. A common counter-factual investigated by Ferguson is *'what if Great Britain had never entered the First World War?'*

A good answer to this question would **reflect on the merits and limitations of this type of history** and the basis of the information given in the source.

There are several merits to studying counter-factual history. It allows one to focus on crucial turning points in historical events. You may only really be able to understand the consequences of a certain event (such as Britain entering the First World War) if you have gone through the process of imagining how things might have turned out if this one event had gone differently. It may also help in thinking about causation in history. You may come to the realisation that a certain factor was a key cause in a certain event only by considering whether the event would have gone ahead without the factor. *What If?* history can also be entertaining and engaging, and may be a good way of inspiring interest in history.

However, there are also problems associated with studying counter-factual history. Many counter-factual hypotheses (such as *'what if Britain had not entered the First World War?'*) can be taken too far. It is one thing to reflect on such a question in order to analyse the importance of what did happen, and the consequences of Britain's entry into the war. It is another thing to imagine a complete parallel universe in which a hypothetical scenario (Britain staying out of the war) is extrapolated into a completely different historical narrative. Perhaps **counter-factual speculation** is a useful historical tool when used in moderation, but can easily slide into fiction.

Essay-Based Interview

Some colleges at Oxford and Cambridge will ask you to submit one or two essays with your application. The details for this will be made clear in the application process. One of your interviews may therefore be based in part on the contents of your essay. This is a chance for you to **demonstrate your detailed factual knowledge** about an area of history you are familiar with, as well as to show your passion for the subject.

The interviewer may open by asking for a summary of the piece of work, of the methodology behind it, and the conclusion reached. They may then ask some follow-up questions related to the work, or the subject matter. This part of the interview will be very individual and depend on the nature and subject of the work submitted. Here are some things to keep in mind if you are submitting essays as part of your application.

➤ Ensure that any work you are submitting is your own. You will not be able to justify an argument you make in an interview if that argument was written by your tutor or teacher. The interviewers will be able to tell if this is the case.

➤ Ensure that any work you are submitting is on topics that you feel comfortable talking about in detail (e.g., something you have studied at AS-level, rather than something you have only just started studying)

➤ Of course, ensure that the work you submit is of a high standard that you believe reflects your academic abilities. If it is a piece of work you are proud of, you will better be able to defend it in your interview.

➤ Re-read the essays you have submitted before the interview, so they are fresh in your mind.

➤ While it is good to remain flexible and open to revising your arguments, **try not to disagree with your own essay**! If the interviewer asks about a certain aspect of the essay and you respond by saying 'I wrote this ages ago, I don't think it's very good', that won't come across well. (On the other hand, if you have a very solid reason for revising your argument, this is something you can bring up in your interview.)

Example Questions
These questions are likely to be **tailored to the individual essay you've submitted**, so it is likely that the answers given are not relevant to the topics covered in your own essay. However, it is useful to read them anyway, and think about the *types* of questions you might be asked.

Q8: The questions are likely to build on the essay you have written, or investigate an aspect of the topic that your essay has not covered fully. A candidate who has written an essay on the topic 'Did Napoleon bring an end to the French Revolution' in which he/she has argued in the affirmative could be asked the question when did Napoleon bring an end to the French Revolution?

A good answer to a question such as this should firstly **acknowledge the complexity of the question**. In this case, this would require recognising that there are many potential answers to the question. One could argue that Napoleon ended the French Revolution in 1799, when he became First Consul, or in 1802 when he declared himself Consul for life, or in 1804, when he made himself Emperor. You may have a strong opinion in favour of one of these interpretations, but before making your case it would be good to show that you are aware that there are many possible arguments that could be made.

If you believe that the French Revolution ended when Napoleon made himself Emperor in 1804, you would need to explain why. In this type of question, factual detail and a command of the material is crucial, as the topic on which you have written an essay should be one with which you are very familiar. You may, for instance, talk about this event from a constitutional perspective, and argue that this is the point at which leadership of France technically returns to the type of monarchical system the Revolution had aimed to overthrow. You may mention that the Pope takes part in Napoleon's coronation ceremony, showing that the anti-Catholic nature of the Revolution has been reversed. Whatever you decide to argue, you must show clear factual evidence to back up your interpretation.

A **poor candidate** may respond to this question in a number of ways. The most obvious mistakes to be avoided would be to reply 'I don't know', or to say '1804' and refuse to explain your answer. It would also be unwise to reverse the argument you originally made in your essay by saying 'Napoleon didn't bring an end to the French Revolution' (unless you have very good reason, for example new research, to back up this revision).

Q9: A candidate who has written an essay on the Enlightenment could be asked a question such as Why do you write the Enlightenment (with a definite article and capital letter) in your essay, rather than enlightenment?

A **good answer** will recognise the complexity of the question. It is not a question about grammar and formatting at all. Instead, it highlights the issue of whether the Enlightenment (or enlightenment) can be seen as a movement that was clear and homogeneous enough to warrant being labelled with a proper noun (The Enlightenment) rather than a more vague descriptive term (enlightenment).

A good answer would then talk this through with the interviewers, with reference to factual evidence you are familiar with. You could talk about how the Enlightenment was a very diverse movement, encompassing ideas as varied as Rousseau's *The Social Contract* to enlightened absolutism in the Habsburg monarchy, and might therefore be better characterised through a descriptive term rather than a proper noun, as The Enlightenment makes these ideas seem more uniform than they were in reality. However, you might on balance argue that it should still be categorised as The Enlightenment, if only because many of its thinkers referred to themselves in these terms.

A **weaker candidate** may simply say 'my teacher said it was The Enlightenment' or 'my textbook says The Enlightenment' and refuse to engage with the topic. A weak candidate may also say 'I had never really thought about it' and leave it at that. If you have genuinely never considered an idea with that you are presented in the interview (which is very likely to happen), it is fine to say so. But then do go on to engage with the idea critically e.g. 'I had considered that, but it's a very interesting point'.

History Interview Questions

498. What are the problems that come up when analysing colonial societies from a postcolonial context?
499. What is the role of student uprisings in historical progress?
500. Do you think eras such as Progressive, Romantic, etc should be written with a capital letter?
501. Why do you want to study history?
502. How can we justify public funding of the study of history to the taxpayer?
503. Do you think history can have any practical purpose?
504. Is there any justification to the argument that we can learn 'lessons' from history?
505. Do you think that Ancient History should be seen as a different subject from Modern History?
506. What are the main differences between Modern and classical sources?
507. Can we take anything written in a classical source at face value?
508. Is race a useful concept for historians?
509. Does history repeat itself?
510. Is medieval history relevant to us today?
511. What is a Revolution?
512. Is there such thing as ideology?
513. How do we know what people in the past really though?
514. Is class a useful concept for historians?
515. Should we study contemporary history?
516. Should we simply narrate the past?
517. Is religion important for modern historians?
518. Assess the role of dance in history?
519. Is Marxist history still worth studying?
520. Are verbal sources more useful than written sources?
521. Compare the French Revolution with a modern event.
522. Did 9/11 change the way we write history?
523. Do we ever learn from the past?
524. Does Keynes still influence economic policy today?
525. How should we remember World War One?

526. Do you think all history is the history of great men?

527. What do you need to consider when evaluating the reliability of a source?

528. Would history be worth studying if it didn't repeat?

529. What do shoes tell us about the past?

530. What is the difference between a terrorist and a patriot?

531. If you could have dinner with anyone who's ever lived, who would it be and why?

532. How is the Arab Spring similar to the Russian Revolution?

533. Compare and contrast the rule of Hitler and Stalin

534. Do you consider history a science?

535. To what extent can a historian remain impartial?

536. When was the British Empire at its strongest?

537. All historical records in the world are lost to a natural disaster. All that remains is historical records on sport. How much of the past could we relearn?

538. How would you have stopped Hitler?

539. Where does history end?

540. Compare and contrast the French and Russian revolutions.

541. Compare and contrast WWI and WWII.

542. Can losers ever write history? How?

543. Why is there a United States of America but not a United States of Europe?

544. Who was a better leader – Alexander the great or Napoleon?

545. Can we still learn lessons from 18th century warfare?

PPE & HSPS

A politics applicant may be asked a question relating to politics or questions from a related subject, such as sociology. Despite stating a previous knowledge in one particular area of HSPS or PPE on your application, you may be asked a question on any of these subject areas. However, you will not be expected to demonstrate specific detailed knowledge in an area not studied previously, you will simply be expected to apply your own point of view and understanding to the topics.

HSPS & PPE interviews generally consist of a large question with many smaller sub-questions to guide the answer from the start to a conclusion. The main question may seem difficult, impossible or random at first, but take a breath and start discussing with your interviewer different ideas you have for breaking down the question into manageable pieces. Don't panic.

The questions are designed to be difficult to give you the chance to show your full intellectual potential. They will help guide you to the right idea, if you provide ideas for them to guide. This is your chance to show your creativity, analytical skills, intellectual flexibility, problem-solving skills and your go-getter attitude. Don't waste it on nervousness or a fear of messing up or looking stupid.

The interviewer wants to see what you know and what you are capable of, not what you don't know – "positive interview".

When answering a question you should be responsive to the interviewer and take on board their prompts and suggestions. If you are making an argument that is clearly wrong, then concede your mistake and try to revise your viewpoint – it is ok to say 'I didn't think of that' when taking on board a different viewpoint. Do not stubbornly carry on arguing a point that they are saying is wrong. **Making mistakes is not a bad thing** – if you can show that you have addressed a mistake and attempted to revise your argument upon the realisation of more information you are showing a skill crucial to getting through essays and supervisions at an Oxbridge university.

Due to the amount of subjects available under the HSPS and PPE courses **there are no set patterns to the questions you can get asked**. Most questions however, will focus on a topic for which it is possible for any individual to have an opinion without previous knowledge of the area. This is to test the way you think about a topic and to test whether you are able to apply your own experiences and knowledge to an unknown subject area. These skills are important when studying HSPS/PPE as the courses are essay-based and rely strongly upon the ability to construct an argument based on the information provided. Many questions are related to society today and may require the individual to be familiar with current affairs and big events in the news.

A sociologist may be asked sociology questions or questions from a related subject, such as politics. An archaeologist will likely be asked questions on archaeology, history and anthropology. Given the very broad nature of the course, candidates are required to have a general interest in all aspects of the course, but it should be clear before the interview which subject will be the main focus of any interview.

The questions will usually take one of a few possible forms based on highlighting skills necessary to 'think like a social scientist. **Five main questions types** are:

➤ Why do we need.... (borders, welfare state, international institutions, museums etc.)?

➤ Compare X to Y...... (normally based on your essay or personal statement, so something you are familiar with)

➤ Distinguish between...(state and nation, race and ethnicity, liberalism and libertarianism etc.)

➤ What do you think about...(the current British school system, nature vs. nurture debate etc.)?

➤ Why is there...(gender inequality in the workplace, poverty etc.)? How would you solve it?

Questions also have recurring themes that appear because they are important for social sciences: legitimacy and role of government, human rights, poverty, feminism, international institutions, purpose of education and different educational systems, voting systems, inequality and social classes.

Worked Questions

Below are a few examples of how to start breaking down an interview question, complete with model answers.

Q1: Can a violent protest ever be justified?

[Extremely clear-headed] **Applicant**: Well, I know that the law states that violence against other people or property is not acceptable, and yet I also know that violent protests still occur and this makes me wonder why. There must be a reason that people feel the need to turn to violence. This might be because of their personality or it may be something deeper such as the feeling of having no choice. If a point is important and the protest is for a serious reason, such as fighting for human rights, and all other forms of protest have been avoided then maybe the only way to be heard is through violence. However, I don't think a violent protest can ever be justified.. For example, take the 2011 UK Riots – violence didn't solve anything – it is a way of being seen and heard, but a horrific one. I don't think being heard for doing something that is wrong is the right way to be recognised.

This shows that **the question can be broken down into smaller-parts**, which can be dealt with in turn. At this point the interviewer can give feedback if this seems like a good start and help make any modifications necessary. In this particular case, the applicant might be asked to expand on the reasons a person might resort to violence in protests and to give an example if possible. They may also be asked to provide a suggestion as to a better way to be heard than a violent protest. The details are unimportant, but the general idea of breaking down the question into manageable parts is important. The interviewer is not looking for an expert, but someone who can problem-solve in the face of new ideas.

A **Poor Applicant** may take a number of approaches unlikely to impress the interviewer. The first and most obvious of these is to simple answer 'yes' or 'no' with little justification or reference to an alternative point of view and with no attempt made to move forward. The applicants who have done this only make it worse for themselves by resisting prodding as the interviewer attempts to pull an answer from them, saying "fine, but I'm not going to be able to expand because I don't know anything about this", or equally unenthusiastic and uncooperative responses.

Another approach which is unhelpful in the interview is the '**brain dump**', where instead of engaging with the question, the applicant attempts to impress or distract with an assortment of related facts or events: In this case reeling off the law on violence or a list of historical riots and their outcomes. Having gotten off to this start isn't as impressive as a more reasoned response, but the interview can be salvaged by taking feedback from the interviewer.

Many of these facts could start a productive discussion which leads to the answer if the applicant listens and takes hints and suggestions from the interviewer.

Q2: How do you know the moon isn't made out of cheese?

[Extremely clear-headed] **Applicant**: What I am first going to think about is what needs to be considered when deciding whether or not something is true. This is things like 'is it patently absurd?', 'Is it backed up by evidence?', and 'What types of evidence do we require'. Next I consider whether it is reasonably possible that this statement fits with other associated and established pieces of knowledge e.g. the formation of the planets, stars and satellites. If the claim is at odds with established knowledge then I may be more inclined to believe it untrue. However, this does not necessarily prove anything. For example, in this case what is meant by cheese? If we are talking poetically, or aesthetically then it may be considered reasonable to make the above claim.

Moreover, whose reality are we talking about, and indeed does the result vary depending on this? I mean, is it really possible to 'know' anything, or are we just making educated guesses based on a set of assumptions married with some data – and does this count as I 'real'? Essentially, when I first looked at the statement I thought it was completely absurd and previously proven otherwise. However, after consideration of perspective, definition, reality and knowledge I am now not so convinced.

Just like the previous example questions this is a step by step answer. The applicant has broken down their thoughts and provided the interviewer with a stream of their own workings of their mind. This allows the interviewer to understand how the individual is breaking down the question and gives opportunity for the interviewer to intervene with further questions if required.

A **Poor Applicant** may state something like 'well because it obviously isn't' – without any further justification. The point of a question like this is to consider the many different ways in which we experience reality and develop our understanding therein. If the applicant fails to address more than the superficial then they are unlikely to show an understanding for the point of the question.

Q3: Despite knowing the health implications of smoking, why does it remain legal in the UK?

Good Applicant: I'd like to think about what other areas are considered by the **legislators of the UK** when they allocate legal status to things as it can't just be health implications. With regards to smoking there are a number of vested parties including tobacco companies and smokers themselves. Tobacco companies rely on smoking being legal in the UK for their income. If smoking were made illegal then these companies would lose 100% of their UK revenue which in turn may impact the economy as a whole (these sales are far from insubstantial. Secondly, when thinking about smokers who are 20% of the UK's adult population (equating to around 10 million people) they represent a large fraction of the potential electorate.

Therefore, banning smoking would have significant implications for political intervention due to unpopularity, loss of freedoms etc.

As another point, smokers may claim that they have an addiction which is difficult to stop. They may also argue that smoking was legal when they first started to smoke. Thus, the government may face a legal battle if they were to suddenly make the product illegal. This may make a total ban on smoking impractical and a breach of an individual's right to choose. However, banning smoker on a more gradual basis may be feasible and is happening today; for example it is now against the law to smoke in cars, in the workplace and in public areas. Maybe **phasing out smoking** is more realistic and is therefore what is being attempted in the UK. This would imply that it is not the case that legislators are unaware or uncaring of the health implications of smoking but that they are attempting to reduce smoking in a less disruptive manner.

A **poor applicant** might fail to address the reasons why smoking has not been made illegal. It is not simply a case of saying 'smoking is bad, therefore the government should ban it'. The question of whether it should be banned impacts many people and showing an understanding of different perspectives and potential arguments is important for answering this question sufficiently.

Q4: If all countries have nuclear weapons, would there still be wars?

A **Good Applicant**: We all have learnt how dangerous nuclear weapons can be when **Hiroshima and Nagasaki** were destroyed at the end of World War 2. The threat to the environment, human lives and even future generations is known, and the risk is too high. Nuclear weapons should not be used at all. On the other hand, it is true that there was no direct war between the USA and USSR during the Cold War and both had nuclear weapons. It seems possible that countries with nuclear weapons do not engage in war with one another as the high risk of a catastrophe deters them from using nuclear weapons, and hence the proliferation of nuclear weapons may prevent wars.

This shows that the candidate understands the question and is able to draw on some examples from A-level History. A **better candidate** would then engage in a discussion with the interviewer about the moral aspect of the topic or may choose to draw on a broader range of examples and realize that although proliferation of nuclear weapons may deter another world war it could lead to more frequent small-scale wars. Examples of wars in Iraq, Vietnam, Afghanistan and Korea during the Cold War demonstrate that there were, in fact, "real wars", and the USSR and USA backed smaller countries in war. So, the proliferation of nuclear weapons may have led to small-scale wars yet prevented another world war. Making a moral case against any use of nuclear weapons, for instance referring to the experience from Hiroshima and Nagasaki, shows sensitivity about the topic.

A **Poor Applicant** may make a moral argument against the use of nuclear weapons before providing any insightful analysis and attempting an answer to the question. Another approach which is unhelpful is focusing too much on providing a Yes/No answer to the question, and hence missing the point that the proliferation of nuclear weapons is a gradual process with various political, moral and economic difficulties and it is not plausible that all countries could get nuclear weapons overnight. The question is very broad and raises many interesting arguments for discussion but 'brain dump' is note helpful here.

Q5: When we make contact with an extra-terrestrial civilization, what should we tell them is humanity's greatest achievement?

[Extremely clear-headed] Applicant: The concept of humanity's greatest achievement is very subjective. It can either be measured in terms of effort needed to accomplish it, or in terms of impact. In the first case, humanity's greatest achievement could be for instance the pyramids, since they required a tremendous amount of work with little technology, and are still standing today after thousands of years. In terms of impact, humanity's greatest achievement could be for example the discovery of penicillin. I think that it makes more sense to focus on a ground-breaking achievement from the past, rather than the most recent accomplishment of humanity.

If I were to tell an extra-terrestrial civilization about penicillin, however, I would also have to provide an explanation on humanity's problems which it solved. Finally, I would have to take into account the aim of my message: am I trying to impress, intimidate, or simply inform?

A good applicant will understand the true aim of the question: creating an abstract situation in which he is encouraged to problematise the subjective concept of 'greatest achievement' and make an argument.

A poor applicant could misinterpret the question, and focus on the extra-terrestrial civilization, talking about space technology and means of communication. Alternatively, he could choose an accomplishment and fail to justify his answer, or provide a lot of facts on the subject without problematising the concept of 'greatest achievement'.

Q6: In a democracy, can the majority impose its will on the minority?

[Extremely clear-headed] Applicant: First, I am going to think from the practical point of view: if by 'minority' we mean 'the ruling elites', does the majority have the actual ability to impose its will? The population only gets to take decisions on rare occasions: elections and referenda. Most of the time, decisions are taken by a small group of people: the government. In 2002-2003 there were mass protests against war in Iraq, but this did not stop Tony Blair from sending troops. It seems that once a government is in power, there is little that the majority of the population can do before the next elections. Secondly, we could think about the question from a normative point of view: should the majority be able to take most decisions in a democratic system? There is a difference between democracy and populism, where power is held by the masses. The latter could be problematic. If by minority we understand things such as small ethnic or religious groups, in a populist system they would have no say, and could end up being oppressed. In a democratic system, minorities are protected by laws. However, we can see that the system is sometimes flawed. For example, in the US there are only two major political parties: people with different agendas than Republicans or Democrats are pushed away from power.

This question can be answered in a number of ways, but a good candidate will show his capacity to deconstruct it, and think for a moment before replying. He will support his points with examples.

A poor applicant will rush into an answer without thinking, and might end up getting confused between the different aspects of the question. He will either make generalizations without giving examples, or focus exclusively on a single real-life case, giving a lot of facts but without any argument or acknowledgment of a different point of view.

Q7: Why is there social inequality in the world? How would you resolve this issue?

[Extremely clear-headed] Applicant: I do not think that there is a single reason for social inequality in the world. Of course, it is not normal that 1% of the population controls almost 50% of its wealth. Greed and self-centredness seem to be inherent flaws of humanity. However, I also think that there are other, underlying factors behind social inequality. I cannot imagine a society in which everybody would have the same proportion of wealth and the same professional opportunities. People live in different places, speak different languages, and simply have different talents and skills. Thus, I do not think that social inequality can ever be fully resolved. Experiments such as communism in the USSR have attempted to artificially suppress inequality. This has not only entailed terrible crimes such as extermination of entire groups in the society, but has also proved economically unsustainable in the long term, with the Soviet economy eventually collapsing. Nevertheless, perhaps some form of **efficient taxation and governments granting more funds** to international organisations and NGOs could help reduce inequality.

A good applicant can have a different opinion on the subject, but will take into account other points of view, and will identify the difficulties associated with resolving such a complex problem, supporting his argument with solid A-level type factual knowledge.

A poor applicant could focus on only one of the two questions. He might give a 'trendy' answer such as 'it's all because of the rich' or 'humans are bad so there is nothing you can do', without giving any real explanation or evidence, and refuse to engage fully with the questions.

Q8: To what extent is taxing the rich likely to lead to greater equality in society?

[Extremely clear-headed] Applicant: There is a big disproportion in terms of wealth between a small group of the 'rich' and the 'poor' majority. Therefore, it would seem logical to find a way of redistributing that wealth. As we can see, altruism does not suffice, since the problem persists despite a few notable examples of rich people giving big proportions of their fortune to charity, for instance Bill Gates. Taxation does seem like a good solution. However, it needs to be designed efficiently. For instance, we must make sure that such a tax does not affect the economy negatively, for example by dissuading the wealthy from opening new businesses and sources of income. Secondly, there have been cases where large funds were not used efficiently, but rather usurped by local warlords and criminal organisations, for instance in Somalia in the 1990s. It might be necessary to establish an international body of experts to design and monitor the implementation of projects funded by this tax.

A good applicant will be able to **identify both the positive and the negative sides of such a policy**. Regardless of whether he has any knowledge on the subject, he will provide a well-structured, logical answer.

A poor applicant might be intimidated by the question, and refuse to answer by saying something like 'I don't know anything about taxes'. Alternatively, he might provide an answer which focuses only on one side of the coin, making it very vulnerable to counterarguments.

Q9: Is alcohol addiction always a result of the social environment, peer pressure, and negative role models?

[Extremely clear-headed] **Applicant:** Alcohol addiction is more widespread in certain social environments or countries: for instance, it is a much bigger problem in Russia than in the UK. I don't think that it would be appropriate to argue that nationality or ethnicity inherently determines the likelihood of alcohol addiction.

This is why explanations such as **peer pressure and negative role models** are very useful. Indeed, peer pressure can become integrated into culture. For example drinking alcohol in large quantities on a teenage trip abroad, or on an American Spring Break, has become almost a ritual. In some cultures drinking vast amounts of alcohol can be considered as a mark of virility, or politeness, which is conducive to alcohol addiction. However, we should not generalise. It is possible for someone to develop an alcohol addiction in an environment where drinking is frowned upon or rare, just as it is possible to remain abstinent while being surrounded by alcoholics. If an individual's parents and friends do not drink, and yet he becomes an alcohol addict, citing a musician with questionable habits as his role model, it seems reasonable to assume that other factors, perhaps psychological, were at play. Thus, while the social environment is a very potent explanation for alcohol addiction, ignoring the possibility of other factors could have negative consequences, such as failing to properly address the issue.

A good applicant will **note the use of the word 'always'**, and attempt to come up with a counter-example.

A poor candidate might fall into the trap of agreeing with the statement without thinking of other points of view. He could refuse to reply stating his lack of knowledge on the topic, or give anecdotal evidence from his experience or environment, without constructing an argument.

Q10: Imagine you are a historian a hundred years in the future, looking back on today. What aspects of society would you focus on?

[Extremely clear-headed] **Applicant:** I do not think that any aspect of history should be discarded as unimportant. However, I am most interested by politics and geopolitics. It is basically impossible to predict the future, and very hard to fully understand the present and its implications. A hundred years from now, we will have a much better understanding of some of today's unanswered questions. For instance, how successful are international organisations in fostering cooperation and preventing conflict? After all, the UN and the EU are relatively recent constructs, and did not fully exploit their potential until the end of the Cold War.

Determining whether international institutions have any real influence or whether they are just tools in the hands of self-centred states is one of the big debates in the study of international relations. Secondly, it would be interesting to see whether in the **age of mass information** and communication, humanity is able to learn from its previous mistakes. Parties of the extreme right are currently gaining a lot of votes in Europe, due among others to economic hardship. Will European countries suffer a fate similar to the Weimar Republic?

A good candidate will demonstrate a certain degree of knowledge on the current topic of his choice, and will be able to identify the way in which it might be perceived by a historian.

A poor candidate might avoid the question by saying something like 'I think that humanity will destroy itself within a hundred years so there will be no historians left'. He could also lose track of his argument by trying to impress the interviewer with his factual knowledge on a current topic, or attempt to make unjustified predictions of future developments.

Q12: What are the main reasons for persistent unemployment in the UK?

Extremely clear-headed] Applicant: I think that people are often tempted to look for simple explanations behind complicated issues. This is why extreme political parties are so successful: they provide the population with easily identifiable scapegoats such as 'the current government', 'immigrants', or 'the EU', and blame them for every economic and social problem. In reality, issues such as unemployment have many reasons. One of them could be the discrepancy between supply and demand: what type of jobs people are prepared for at schools and universities, and what type of jobs are offered on the market. For instance in Scandinavian countries, when an unemployed individual cannot find work for a certain period of time, he is offered courses which allow him to perform a different type of work, where there is more demand.

Another reason could indeed be **globalisation**, with the **international economic crisis**, and many companies moving abroad to reduce costs. This however does not justify oversimplifying the issue by blaming solely external factors such as foreigners or international organisations. Instead, efforts should be made to better adapt the national system to the realities of the globalised world.

A good candidate will try to provide a balanced and well-argued answer, regardless of his political or moral stance. He will stay away from generalisations and normative statements based on little or no evidence.

A poor applicant might refuse to engage with a question on which he has little previous knowledge. Alternatively, he may make sweeping generalisations or provide an exhaustive list of factors without really explaining any of them.

Q13: Should prisoners have the right to vote?

[Extremely clear-headed] Applicant: I think that in a democracy, voting is one of the **citizen's basic rights**. The question is: should prisoners still be considered as citizens? It could be said that when they break the social contract of norms governing the society, their rights are also revoked. However, if a prisoner is deprived of all his rights, his eventual reintegration into society will be even harder. In my opinion, the right to vote should be granted to those prisoners who have not committed the most grave of crimes, such as murder or rape.

Moreover, in some countries the issue of 'political prisoners' is still prominent, for instance in China or Ukraine. If someone is imprisoned for disagreeing with the regime, and has no right to vote for a different party or candidate, then there is little chance of change and the system moves one step further towards authoritarianism.

A poor applicant could focus too much on providing a yes/no answer based on personal beliefs or anecdotal evidence, without trying to engage with alternative perspectives on the question.

See Question 10 in the Law Chapter for a more legal perspective.

Q14: Is there such a thing as national identity in the world of globalization?

[Extremely clear-headed] Applicant: In my opinion, while borders are becoming more and more permeable and people can communicate and travel from one part of the world to the other, national identity is not necessarily losing its potency. Already according to Marxist theory, national identity was supposed to disappear, giving way to an international movement of workers. This was not really accomplished, and the communist countries which survived the longest such as the Soviet and Chinese systems, were those which mixed communism with nationalism. While from our 'Western' perspective it might seem that national identity is dying, this might be related to the fact that we live in relatively peaceful times: there has been no war on the current territory of the EU for decades.

However, in times of conflict, national identity becomes very powerful. We can see this on current examples such as Ukraine and Russia, but also in post 9/11 USA. I think that in times of external threat, people tend to unite under a symbol which differences them from the 'other'. Since the nation state remains the main actor in international relations, most conflicts are likely to oppose one nation against another, thus reinforcing the sense of national identity.

A **good candidate** can argue either way, but should be able to acknowledge both sides of the coin. He should be able to support his ideas with some factual A-level type knowledge.

A **poor applicant** might fail to engage properly with the question, instead trying to impress the interviewer by dumping facts. Alternatively, he could make broad generalizations without supporting his argument without any real evidence.

Q15: What areas of Philosophy are you interested in?

[Extremely clear-headed] Applicant: I am interested in theories of the state. Many thinkers have attempted to tackle this issue throughout history, ranging from Plato, through Hobbes and Rousseau, to Marx. They all have very different visions of what an efficient political system should look like, whether the human being is inherently good or bad, and who should have the right to rule. What is interesting in this area of Philosophy is that the thinkers have often actually affected the reality.

The writings of Marx are the best example of this phenomenon, since they have been used and abused by activists in many countries, leading to the October Revolution in 1917 and the establishment of the USSR, one of two systems dominating the international system for decades. I think that there are many interesting questions in this area of Philosophy. Is it possible to design a system which would be applicable to any setting and society? Do philosophers have a responsibility over how their writings are understood and used?

A good candidate will show both a certain degree of knowledge and of genuine interest in the topic of his choice. He will identify some of the big questions related to the field.

A poor candidate might give an exhaustive list of areas of Philosophy without going into depth on any of them. Alternatively, he could try to demonstrate his extensive factual knowledge of the writings of a single author, without engaging with the wider question on the area of Philosophy.

Q16: Tell me about some political texts that you have read.

[Extremely clear-headed] **Applicant:** I have looked at some political theory texts, such as Plato's Republic. In this text, the author is describing a perfect political system, an ideal city led by a philosopher-king. He also talks about other, flawed political systems, such as tyranny or democracy. I think that this text is very interesting and useful for understanding political systems from the past, and has also inspired other, more recent authors. However, it is important to note that Plato writes from the perspective of Ancient Greece, and many of his concepts are outdated. I think that the term 'political text' could also apply to other types of documents, for example party programmes, but even literary fiction. I recently read Bulgakov's Master and Margarita, a novel with fantasy themes such as the devil and witchcraft, written in the Soviet Union. Its focus on religion and the occult was also a hidden critique of the atheistic Soviet society. Similar things could be said about the Animal Farm or 1984.

A **good candidate** will try to go beyond simply giving factual knowledge on a text studied in class. He will try to come up with a critical approach towards the text showing a certain degree of independent thought, or problematize the term 'political texts'.

A poor candidate might panic if he has not studied texts of political theory in school, instead of making the best of it by trying to come up with different types of political texts. Alternatively, he might opt for dumping a lot of factual information on a text, instead of showing his understanding of it, or demonstrating a critical perspective.

HSPS Interview Questions

546. What is the difference between race and ethnicity?
547. What is the difference between state and society?
548. What are the similarities between the Roman empire and the UN?
549. Some neoliberals say that poor people are poor because they are lazy to work, what do you think?
550. Why is it that nationalism has strengthened in Europe over the last few years?
551. How are national boarders drawn?
552. What is free will and how does that relate to the concept of the state of nature?
553. Should a chimpanzee have human rights..?
554. What is something you find interesting about the place you're from and why?
555. How would you begin to decipher these cave paintings?
556. What do you think constitutes love?
557. Which area of the world would you want to learn more about and why?
558. What is current affair at the moment that you find particularly indicative of a world issue?
559. Give me an example of material culture in contemporary society.
560. Do you think perception of colour is culturally specific?
561. What do you first look for when deciphering a symbol?
562. What makes us human?

PPE Interview Questions

563. How many people are in this room?
564. Can we be said to 'know' anything?
565. If you and a business owner each have 10 loyal customers who will always buy from you unless you sell above £10, and there are an additional 80 who will choose who to buy from based on price alone, at what price does it become more profitable to stop undercutting your competitor and sell at £10 instead?
566. Tell me about some philosophical works you've read.

567. What would happen if there was no inflation?

568. Do economists rely too heavily on models?

569. Is sociology useful for studying economics?

570. Can we really measure GDP?

571. What influences a country's productive potential?

572. Should governments have debts?

573. Should inequality matter to economists?

574. Does a balance of trade deficit matter?

575. Should government intervene in the market?

576. Was the financial crisis of 2008 a failure of regulation?

577. The value of the US Dollar and Japanese Yen are swapped with each other overnight. What would happen to global markets?

578. What is the best way to win in monopoly? Is this possible in real life?

579. Why are diamonds so expensive? Why is steel so cheap?

580. Is outsourcing a good thing?

581. Imagine you have just opened up a new airline that flies a unique route (London and Tokyo). How would you determine what price to set tickets at to ensure maximal profit?

582. What is the golden ratio? Why do banks and investments firms obsess over it?

583. How can we predict future economic recessions and avoid depressions?

584. Should we still be giving aid to countries that have international space programmes e.g. India?

585. What is the difference between capitalism and communism? Are they really that different?

586. What 3 simple things could you recommend to a shopkeeper to increase their sales? They only have £25 to spend.

587. What causes some brands to go global whilst others to fail?

588. What caused the great American depression in the early 20th century? What can we learn from it?

CLASSICS

Classics applicants will typically be asked **questions about the Classical world**, but usually not about things they have studied in detail at A-Level. This is to avoid some candidates gaining an advantage by simply having studied the topic in question, since *interviews are designed to assess how you think and how you adapt to new information, not what you know*.

The interview will usually consist of a large question with many smaller sub-questions that the interviewer will ask in order to guide the applicant to an answer. The main question may seem difficult, impossible or random at first, but take a breath and start discussing with your interviewer different ideas you have for breaking down the question into manageable pieces. Don't panic. **The questions are designed to be difficult** to give you the chance to show your full intellectual potential. They will help guide you to the right idea, if you provide ideas for them to guide. This is your chance to show your creativity, analytical skills, intellectual flexibility, problem-solving skills and your go-getter attitude. Don't waste it on nervousness or a fear of messing up or looking stupid.

Often questions will pick up on a theme from your written work or your personal statement and take it in an unexpected direction. For example, if you mentioned visiting the Parthenon in your personal statement, an interviewer may well ask you to talk about a particular frieze from the building and what you consider its significance to be, what its purpose might be and who might have commissioned it. In this scenario they would not expect you to know anything about the frieze in question, but simply to **make sensible suggestions based on the given information** and talk the interviewer through your thinking process.

The only other main section of the interview process is the language test, for Cambridge candidates with Latin, Greek or both, conducted in one interview. The interviewer will allow you to study a Latin or Greek text for a few minutes and then ask you to translate it aloud, giving you assistance with vocabulary and grammar as appropriate.

This will usually be a difficult and obscure piece to ensure that no candidates are better prepared than others. Again, the emphasis is on showing a good working method for working out the meaning of a sentence, rather than knowing lots about grammar or vocabulary - remember to think aloud and ask about any vocabulary you don't know.

Worked Questions

Below are a few examples of how to start breaking down an interview question, complete with model answers.

Q1: Why might it be more useful to study ancient texts in their original languages, as opposed to in translation?

A **good applicant** might begin by acknowledging the benefits of texts in translation, i.e. that they are more accessible and retain most of the content, but then go on to examine how translations can present difficulties. For example, discuss that some ways of thinking and figures of speech simply do not translate into English and, hence can only be understood in the original language. A very good candidate might then broaden this into a discussion of how far it is necessary to study ancient texts in their original context and how far they can be considered to be stand-alone works, and what the merits of these different approaches might be for a scholar.

It is often useful to **break the question down into sub-parts**, which can be dealt with in turn. At this point the interviewer can give feedback if this seems like a good start and help make any modifications necessary. In this particular case, the interviewer may well begin to ask further questions to direct the discussion once the candidate has made an initial survey of the issues; you would seldom be expected to talk about a topic unguided for a lengthy period as interviewers will always be keen to challenge your thinking and see how you react to new information.

A **poor applicant** may take a number of approaches unlikely to impress the interviewer. The first and most obvious of these is to say "We never learned about that in school" and make no attempt to move forward with the discussion. In this event the interviewer will likely try and prod the candidate to make an inroad by asking subsequent questions, in which case the important thing to do is make an effort to make sensible conjectures and not worry about whether you know any facts. Another typical tactic of poor applicants to avoid is the 'brain dump', where a candidate simply spouts all of the knowledge they have on the question topic, without considering whether it is relevant. It is important to remember *that interviews are about giving thoughtful answers to questions which demonstrate your thinking process, not about demonstrating knowledge.*

Q2: What can we learn about Roman emperors from the depictions of them on statues and coins?

A **good applicant** will likely begin by narrowing the question to a manageable dimension, for example talking about a specific depiction(s) or a specific emperor(s) (it is also likely that the interviewer will provide some visual stimuli to help you).

One might then explore what these items could tell us about how the emperors wanted to be seen (e.g. how widespread they are, how the emperor is depicted upon them, what the inscriptions say), how the emperors were seen by people in a given area (e.g. statues were often commissioned by local dignitaries in the provinces, what message did they want to send by putting up a statue of, say, Augustus?) and how this might be compared with other sources, such as the written accounts of Tacitus and Suetonius. The interviewer would be likely to offer the candidate information and examples to help them test their theories, as well as asking further questions.

Outlining the concepts in this way would provide a good starting point to mention any relevant reading you have done. For example, if you have read Suetonius' biography of Claudius you might be able to contrast his depiction in that work with his depiction in a statue or coin you have seen and suggest why that might be and what we could usefully learn from it. This type of **proactive and thoughtful approach** to the question is likely to impress the interviewer, but it is still important to listen to their directions and interjections carefully so as to ensure that you answer their question fully.

A **poor applicant** would be more likely to protest that they don't know anything about statues or coins, or attempt to offer a shallow and relatively pedestrian statement of the obvious. For example, they might hypothesise that such artefacts can tell us what the emperors looked like and then struggle to conjecture anything any further when asked for more suggestions by the interviewer. The worst thing to do in these situations is to seem unreceptive and attempt to derail the interviewer. Seeming interested in the topic and being seen to make an effort to consider your answers to the questions carefully is often half the battle.

Q3: What is literature? Why do we value it?

This is a very open-ended question, and one to which there are no wrong answers, the key is to cut a sensible path through the material.

A **good applicant** would quickly seek to address the broadness of the question and state their angle of approach. The most useful tactic would be to try and develop a theory of literature which differentiates it from other types of written material. Such a theory might try to establish how far authorial intent and how far audience reception determine what is literature, as well as addressing the role of form (e.g. poetry or prose) and the question of whether anything can be said to be entirely literature, or entirely not literature. Other peripheral questions may be posed by the interviewer such as 'Does literature have to be written down, or can it be an oral culture?' - you should attempt to address these and incorporate them into your theory to provide nuance to your answer.

The good applicant might then tackle the question of why we value literature with reference to their theory of what constitutes literature, since how we define literature likely tells us about why we prize it. Such an answer is likely to make reference to a variety of ideas, possibly focusing on the allegorical and didactic powers of literature, i.e. its potential benefits to society, versus its more intrinsic goods, e.g. beauty, the human condition and so forth. The interviewer will be looking for candidates to make a **lively, intellectual and sensible approach to the question** but will be no means expect revolutionary or fully-formed analyses of such large concepts.

A **poor candidate** is therefore likely to try and be dismissive of the question with a brief answer such as 'books and poems' or 'I don't know' and fail to engage with the scope of the topic. They may also attempt to avoid making useful analyses by simply listing things which are and aren't literature, or erring from the main point of the question by talking about their love for literature and/or its value to them. Some of these points may complement a good answer but they are highly unlikely to form the cornerstone of a good response.

Q4: Who wrote the Iliad and the Odyssey?

This question is looking to see how applicants analyse what might, superficially, seem to be a very simple question and tease out its hidden complexities and potential difficulties.

A **good applicant** would likely begin by acknowledging that these works are attributed to the poet we know as 'Homer' but that in reality the situation is more complex. An interesting avenue to start with would be what we mean by 'wrote', since we know that the works in question were an unwritten oral tradition for the first 400 or so years of their lives, which were eventually written down in Athens around the fifth century BC.

Building on this, we might suggest that to posit a single author for works with a long oral tradition is inherently problematic since a work which is purely performed as an unwritten tale must be subject to constant change and reimagining by those performing it - even if the core of the works originate from 'Homer' himself.

Very well-read applicants may even be able to go further and discuss scholarly theories that the origins of the *Odyssey* are different from those of the *Iliad*, or the aspersions cast on the Homeric authenticity of some later books of the Odyssey - but this would only serve as the icing on the cake.

A **poor applicant** would be one who attempts to give a very short and overly factual answer to the question, which fails to be analytical. For example, to reply simply 'Homer' would hardly impress the interviewer since this basic factual knowledge would be expected.

The interviewer is looking for evidence of analytical abilities in terms of how we think about texts, and hence would be more than likely to provide the candidate with additional information about the provenance of the works in the event that this is not something the candidate has previously encountered. If you find that you know very little about a topic on which you are questioned, feel free to admit this and ask specific questions, but be sure to do so in such a way that it shows an analytical method rather than resignation to failure. A good question to ask would be something like: *'Is there any historical evidence about the origins of the works?'*

Q5: Did the Romans or the Greeks leave a more notable impression on the culture of today? How?

This question is another broad one and is looking for candidates to demonstrate an ability to analyse the Classical world within its wider context, and also in a way which will be less similar to the way in which they are taught at school.

A **good applicant** could take any number of successful approaches, though useful topics to cover will be language, politics, art (including literature and architecture) and possibly something more nebulous such as 'identity'. In light of this it may also be useful to make a distinction about what you take 'culture of today' to mean: Britain? Europe? The world? - feel free to define it as you wish, but it may be prudent to restrict yourself according to your knowledge.

Linguistically one could make a number of points about more words in English being Latin derived than Greek, but also that Latin developed largely from Greek origins. This might tie in with a discussion of how strictly we can define Greece and Rome as civilisations, given the great deal of influence Classical Greece had on Classical Rome and the Roman rule of Hellenistic Greece.

You might also like to speculate on what effects Roman rule in Britain until c. 400AD has had on modern Britain, from the law to roads and our sense of national identity - is the Roman past a matter of pride for Britons?

Literature is an extremely broad topic and could take any number of directions but you could usefully begin by listing some widely read works of ancient literature and why you think they are culturally significant (or not), perhaps with reference to the influence they may have had on more modern literature - e.g. could we have Milton without Homer or Vergil?

The key thing with this question is simply to demonstrate some sort of analytical route through the vast material which resembles an argument. The interviewer will probably question your hypotheses and responding to these with your own examples and arguments will serve you well. A **poor applicant** would be more likely to give a short answer about how we were never ruled by the Greeks and so the Romans were probably more influential. Such an answer, whilst making one useful point, demonstrates a lack of engagement with the breadth of the question and a pedestrian mode of thinking which is unlikely to impress the interviewer.

Q6: Are history and myth compatible?

This question is a little more specific in scope than some of the previous but still leaves substantial scope for interpretation. A **good applicant** would likely begin by defining terms that pertain to the central issue of the question, i.e. what do we mean when we say myth or history and how neatly can we divide the two concepts from one another.

The key issue to tackle in the question is how we **interpret the idea of 'compatible'**, since myth and history might be of very similar significance or hardly differentiated between in the ancient world, e.g. the Roman foundation myths were notionally regarded as 'historical' in ancient Rome and certainly had the cultural significance of real historical events, though they were known to be largely fictitious.

In Greece, one might argue that the question is even more vexed given that the line between myth and history is so blurred, e.g. the question of the extent to which the Trojan war is historical fact and the extent to which it is myth. Further, one might question whether such a distinction is relevant to the Trojan war, since it's significance to Greek literature and culture is unchanged in either case. Moreover, one might also discuss whether all history is myth. For example, if 'all history is written by the victor', how far can we be sure that any 'historical' account of events is not, in fact, a biased mythologisation?

The most important thing with a question like this is to attempt to **pull the question apart** and ask to what extent its premises are valid by dissecting what we mean by the various terms and how far these terms can truly be said to be distinct from one another. This demonstrates an ability to think in a critical and original way and is likely to impress the interviewer.

A **poor applicant** would likely make some more pedestrian distinctions about history and myth being incompatible because history is about things which really happened, whereas myths are simply fairy tales and fictions, without digging much into the wider significance of the question.

Classics

589. Can you speak German, French or other languages?
590. Can you justify a classics degree when it is subsidised by the taxpayer?
591. Would you say Sulla was a tyrant? Why not a dictator?
592. Compare and contrast ancient Greece and Rome.
593. What was the difference between Roman and Greek gods?
594. When did the roman republic end? Why?
595. Was Alexander the great, actually great?
596. What can we learn about Roman foreign relations from *Jugertha*?
597. How is the study of classics useful to the modern world?
598. How do we separate fact from fiction given that myth and reality are so intertwined?
599. How would you have ended the siege in troy more quickly?
600. To what extent is the film '300' historically true?
601. What is the significance of Stonehenge?
602. What is the significance of the change in artistic style between the republic and mid empire?
603. Was Triumvirate a success?
604. Was Alexander the great gay? Is this unusual for the time period?
605. Romans watched gladiators fight in large arenas. What can we learn about them from this?
606. How civilised was the Persian Empire?
607. What makes a book a 'classic'?
608. What is a neoteric?
609. Is the ending to the Iliad really necessary?
610. What is Turnus' role in the *Aeneid*?
611. Is Aeneas an ancient hero or a modern one?
612. Compare and contrast Ovid and Catullus.
613. What rhetorical devices does Cicero use?
614. What is Catullus' sparrow really about?
615. Do you think Ovid is a good love poet?
616. If you were making a movie about the odyssey, would you include Poseidon?
617. Name Heracles' twelve labours – what can we learn from them?

LAW

A law applicant may be asked legal questions or questions from a related subject, including history, politics or current affairs with a legal slant. None of the questions asked of you will assume any previous legal knowledge, as the interviewers understand that applicants will likely not have studied law before. Be prepared to explain why you want to study law and show through extra-curricular reading or activities how you've fostered this interest.

The interview will usually consist of a large question with many smaller sub-questions that the interviewer will ask in order to guide the applicant to an answer. The main question may seem difficult, impossible or random at first, but take a breath and start discussing with your interviewer different ideas you have for breaking down the question into manageable pieces.

The questions are designed to be difficult to give you the chance to show your full intellectual potential.

For law, the questions will usually take one of a few possible forms based on highlighting skills necessary to 'think like a lawyer'. Five main question types are:

➢ Observation-based questions ("tell me about...")
➢ Practical questions ("how would you decide if...")
➢ Statistical questions ("given this data...")
➢ Ethical questions ("are humans obligated to...")
➢ Questions about proximate causes (mechanism; "how does…") and ultimate causes (function; "why does…"), usually both at once.

Questions also have recurring themes which appear in many questions because they are central to jurisprudential thinking: the workings of the English legal system, problems of access to justice, the centrality of morality in legal development, the future of the legal profession, the impact of international treaties and legal institutions, looking carefully at words and drawing fine distinctions, building up an argument and applying that to examples.

Worked Questions

Below are a few examples of how to start breaking down an interview question, complete with model answers.

Q1: In a society of angels, is the law necessary?

Applicant: Well, an angel could be defined as someone who is always inclined to do what is good, just and moral in any situation. If I thought that the sole purpose of the law was always to achieve what is good, just and moral, I might conclude that in a society of such creatures, law would not be necessary as angels would already be achieving this goal on their own. Why don't I continue by giving my own definition of the purpose of the law in society, taking account of law's function as a social coordinator and as an international arbitrator? Perhaps I should also add a brief of what it means for something to be necessary and apply that definition to my discussion at hand. I may even expand this discussion further and think about what a society without any laws would look like, or indeed, if such a society would be at all possible.

This shows that **the question can be broken down into sub-parts**, which can be dealt with in turn. At this point the interviewer can give feedback and help make any modifications necessary. In the case of the above interview, the applicant will realise that the function of the law is not just to promote what is good, just and moral, but also to act as a method of social cohesion. The details are unimportant, but the general idea of breaking down the question into manageable parts is important. The interviewer is not looking for an expert of legal philosophy, but someone who can problem-solve in the face of new ideas.

A **Poor Applicant** may take a number of approaches unlikely to impress the interviewer. The first and most obvious of these is to say "I don't know anything about societies of angels" and make no attempt to move forward.

The applicants who have done this only make it worse for themselves by resisting prodding as the interviewer attempts to pull an answer from them, saying "fine, but I'm not going to know the answer because I don't know anything about this", or equally unenthusiastic and uncooperative responses. Another approach which is unhelpful in the interview is the 'brain dump', where instead of engaging with the question, the applicant attempts to impress or distract with an assortment of related facts: "angles would not murder each other.

Murder is a crime which can be split into two constituent parts of *mens rea* and *actus reus*, both of which are necessary for the commission of the crime. The terms *actus reus* and *mens rea* developed in English Law are derived from the principle stated by Edward Coke, namely, '*actus non facit reum nisi mens sit rea*'. This is not nearly as impressive as a more reasoned response, but the interview could be salvaged by taking feedback from the interviewer. Many of these facts could start a productive discussion which leads to the answer if the applicant listens carefully.

Q2: What is best: a written or non-written constitution?

This question is looking to see if you understand something of the nature of the **British constitution** and whether you can lay down pros and cons of an argument, with a conclusion that comes down on one side or the other of the debate.

Perhaps begin by defining what is meant by a written and a non-written constitution and perhaps give examples of countries with each (e.g. UK and USA). A constitution could be defined as a legal contract which states the terms and conditions under which a society agrees to govern itself, outlining the functions, powers and duties of the various institutions of government, regulates the relationship between them, and defines the relationship between the state and the public.

Problems of a non-written or uncodified constitution – firstly, it is difficult to know what the state of the constitution actually is and secondly, it suggests that it is easier to make changes to the UK constitution than in countries with written constitutions, because the latter have documents with a 'higher law' status against which ordinary statute law and government action can be tested. Is the problem then more with the perception of our constitution than the legal status of the constitution itself?

Are they really so different? The American constitution may be elegantly written and succinct but it can be amended or reinterpreted or even broken as the times demand, in the same way that the UK's unwritten constitution can be. Furthermore, even a written constitution is supplemented by unwritten conventions and most countries' constitutions embody a mixture of the two. This line of argument could lead you to conclude that the issue here is really only with semantics as **there isn't any real difference in governance**.

This question could lead to a discussion of the ways the UK constitution allows for laws to be made – e.g. "should judges have a legislative role?"

A poor applicant would not attempt to address both written and non-written constitutions, instead sticking staunchly to whatever they have read on either subject.

Q3: What is the difference between intention and foresight?

The question is looking for your ability to give **accurate definitions of two principals central to criminal law**. Intention could be defined as an aim or a plan, whilst foresight could be defined as the ability to predict what will happen. Thinking about the way these subtly different definitions might be applied in a legal context we see that one might foresee that doing X will lead to the death of B but that consequence was not necessarily intended.

This intuitive distinction is mirrored in **criminal law in the UK** - there are two different types of intention: direct intent which exists where the defendant embarks upon a course of conduct to bring about a result which in fact occurs, and oblique intent which exists where the defendant embarks on a course of conduct to bring about a desired result, knowing that the consequence of his actions will also bring about another result.

A particularly topical example of the application of this distinction in practice can be seen discussing **"the doctrine of double effect"**. This doctrine is only really applied in medical cases. Consider this example – a doctor who administers a lethal dose of painkillers to their terminally ill patient in order to relieve their suffering also foresees that such a dose will kill the patient. Should this doctor be guilty of the murder of her patient? Ultimately, the doctrine says that if doing something morally good has a morally bad side-effect it's ethically OK to do it providing the bad side-effect wasn't intended. This is true even if you foresaw that the bad effect would probably happen.

A **poor applicant** would fail to distinguish the two and would fail to see how these definitions are applied in modern criminal law.

Q5: Does a computer have a conscience?

Intuitively, we want to answer this question with a resounding "no" as it seems obvious that only living things can have consciences. Computers are creations of man and therefore merely act according to our needs, having little or no agency of their own. A poor applicant would be able only to articulate this very basic intuitive response and would be incapable of digging further.

In fact, **the answer depends entirely upon which definitions you choose to give to the key terms** in the question. Conscience could be defined as a moral sense of right and wrong which is viewed as acting to a guide to one's behaviour.

A computer is an electronic device which is capable of receiving information and performing a sequence of operations in accordance with a predetermined set of variable. Given these two definitions, it could be possible to program a computer with a conscience.

You could discuss the **distinction between having a conscience and being 'sentient'**-the former being a form of moral compass, whilst the latter is merely the ability to perceive or feel external stimulus. Do you think "artificial intelligence" is possible? Is it dangerous? If a computer does have a conscience what might this mean for data protection laws? Freedom of expression? Ownership? Would this mean that computers should have rules protecting them from abuse e.g. Computer Rights?

Q6: What is justice?

It might be good to begin with a succinct **definition of 'justice'** like 'behaviour or treatment which are just' with just meaning 'equitable, fair and even-handed'.

You might then want to expand on this initial definition. Perhaps an exploration of what justice means in the context of criminal law which might go as follows:

Firstly, custodial sentences are used for their deterrent effect. Secondly, decisions on the form and duration of the sentence focus upon the crime itself rather than looking at how the punishment will best rehabilitate the offender, appease the victim and benefit society as a whole. This judicial inflexibility which we see in the sentencing of criminals reflects a right-wing conception of justice based upon the maxim 'an eye for an eye'.

You might put forward that an alternative conception of justice might achieve fairer results - perhaps one which takes a **utilitarian approach** to punishment. Such a conception would necessitate finding the best possible outcome for the largest number of people.

However, the counter argument to this would be that this approach would not allow for the idea of **'moral forfeiture'**, the principle that in committing a crime you give up some of your rights. This contextual approach gives us a taste of just how difficult it really is to define justice, even in such a narrow context.

We often hear the term **'social justice'** which is another context in which the term is applied. The concept in this context is very difficult to reconcile with justice as vengeance in the criminal context. Social justice too has several definitions; one might be socioeconomic equality amongst all members of any given society, whilst another might be more meritocratic and insist upon greater social mobility and fairness in general. We see that, upon examining this wider application of the idea of justice to non-criminal contexts that the conception of justice itself is made even more difficult to define.

To conclude, we have proven that our initial definition of justice was not sufficient. The concept seems to defy any coherent definition as it is so broad and subjective.

Q 7: Should the aim of the law be to make people happy?

One might argue that the aim of the law is to generally make everyone's lives better. Indeed, improving the quality of citizens' lives is the explicit focus of much of the policymaking and regulatory work done by many governments around the world. If we accept this, the next question would be 'what does better really mean?' One account could be that to make someone's life "better" we should render that person more able to get what they want. Another account might be that the quality of someone's life depends on the extent to which they do well at the things that it is characteristically human to do. This difficulty in defining what it might be to make any one person's life better and therefore making them happy is one difficulty with placing this as the law's overarching aim – happiness is internal – how can we accurately know what anyone is feeling, and therefore truly know how well the law is working?

Perhaps one way to combat this problem could be to develop a **method of measuring subjective happiness** – a type of well-being analysis – how might we do this? Well, we could introduce a system of weekly online surveys which would be answered by a representative portion of society on how happy they were able particular administrative decisions. Over time, such large masses of data would allow us to accurately pin-point just what really makes people happier and just how the law can shape itself to better achieve this.

Q8: Which laws are broken most frequently? Are they still laws?

Millions of people who declare themselves law-abiding citizens actually commit on average seven crimes per week. The most common offences are things like speeding, texting while driving, dropping litter, downloading music illegally or riding bicycles on the pavement. Many of these more common 'minor crimes' are committed so regularly that they have almost become legal, which might be the reason so many people aren't fazed when they do break these laws.

Are these 'minor laws' still laws? You might argue that a law is a law even if it's not followed, as the definition of a law, as a law, lies in the process by which it is enacted i.e. the legislative process. This line of argument would lead you to believe that all laws are of the same importance because they become law by the same process.

However, you might not necessarily think that is the case. For instance, most people would think that killing someone would be much worse than accidentally dropping your train ticket and therefore littering. That this is the case would suggest that there is a hierarchy of laws and therefore that some laws are more important or that some laws are more immoral. This would lead you to conclude that 'minor laws' are still laws but merely a lower class of laws, perhaps because the repercussions of infringement in these cases is lesser or the infringement is seen as less immoral and therefore these laws are less thoroughly enforced.

Q9: After you have been to the hairdressers and had all of your hair cut off, do you still own your hair?

Intuitively, we believe that when our hair is attached to our heads, we do own it. The law supports this and if someone were to cut off your hair without your consent you would be entitled to compensation.

However, where you have **consented to your hair being cut** off the situation is very different and there is very little precedent to go on. You might argue that if you hadn't expressed an interest in maintaining your ownership of your hair once it had been cut off, it would be for the hairdresser to dispose of as he saw fit, in line with common practice in a hairdressers. You might think that the hairdresser's use of your hair would be of no consequence to you but what if he sold it on eBay? What if it was used in an art exhibition to make a political point with which you disagreed? Would you then have a claim to your hair in these cases?

This question might lead on to a discussion about whether or not we own our own bodies. Surprisingly perhaps, we **have no legal right to decide what happens to us when we die** – instead, we can only express preferences and there are some things that the law will not let us do (e.g. leave your body to be used as meat for the dogs in Battersea Dogs' Home). We may contrast this with the approach the law takes to our other possessions after we die – in the case of all other property your wishes are absolute. This contrast would suggest that we do not have the same legal relationship with our bodies as we do with our toasters, our cars, or our pocket-watches- but the really interesting question is – *should we?*

Q10: Should prisoners have the right to vote?

The **European Court of Human Rights** has ruled that Britain's blanket ban on voting for all convicted prisoners is a breach of their human rights. Allowing only some prisoners to vote would be ok, states the Court; but refusing the vote to all convicted prisoners is unacceptable.

Prison is generally considered to serve three key purposes; 1) to protect the public, 2) to serve as a deterrent, 3) to rehabilitate. Most prisoners have not committed crimes that warrant a life sentence. Most will eventually be released from prison. It's in everyone's interests that once out of prison, they do not commit any further crimes, but instead become useful members of society. That involves reform whilst still in prison, and rehabilitating offenders to think - and act - more positively about their civic duties and responsibilities. One of the most important contribution a citizen can make to society is to take part in democracy and vote – removing a prisoner's civic duty does not therefore seem to accord with the aims of putting them in prison in the first place.

Alternatively, one might argue that all citizens of a country have implicitly agreed on a set of rules that gives them, and those around them, certain rights. It is the duty of every citizen to protect this framework, and to respect the rights of others. If a person is in prison, it is because he/she broke the rules, and hence, in a way, forfeited his/her rights. The citizenship of prisoners can be seen as temporarily suspended along with all their rights.

Human rights do not mean that someone cannot be suitably punished or imprisoned for a crime once fairly tried and convicted. Human rights mean that all humans deserve that society, and the State, protect them from abuse of their basic civil rights. If the State can be allowed to abuse humans – any humans, for any reasons or excuses – then how can we justify laws against humans abusing other humans? How the State behaves must be reflective on how we want all humans to behave.

Human rights are meant to be universal, which means the rights apply to all humans without exception; to you and to me; even to criminals and foreigners, and even to those humans we do not like. Once we take basic rights away from one human, we start to erode the basic protections for all humans.

Q11: Should 'immoral' or 'evil' laws be obeyed?

Note: if candidates are unsure of what the question means, interviewers can share Victorian jurist Dicey's famous example: should Parliament legislate for all blue-eyed babies to be killed, the law would still be valid law but citizens would be 'mad' to obey it.

This question requires candidates to take a step back and consider the purpose and basis of the law. A good candidate would be able to make some comment about **legal normativism versus legal positivism** but this is not essential. It is more important that they can engage with concepts and ideas, not get bogged down in technical terms.

A sensible place to start would be a discussion on why people obey the law -- out of a sense of moral obligation independent of the law (e.g. if I think stealing is wrong, I will not steal regardless what the relevant statute precisely says) versus wishing to adhere to social norms (i.e. not being "looked down upon" or shunned by one's peers for being involved with illegal activities) versus actually fearing legal sanctions (e.g. avoiding recreational drugs while travelling in the Far East because I fear the death penalty being applied to me as a 'trafficker'). This should lead to strong candidates taking a step back and addressing to what extent morality should be the basis of law in a liberal society.

Candidates are free to proceed in a number of ways. It is only essential that they show that they have thought about the topic and have read some appropriate material. However, they must highlight that such 'immoral' laws would attract political criticism, and be conscious of the fact that political and legal mechanisms must work in tandem to **protect basic constitutional values and civil liberties**.

Q12: Given that juries consist of untrained people who do not have to give reasons for their decisions, are juries inherently inefficient and unreliable?

Candidates may not be aware of precisely what role juries play in the British justice system. It may be necessary to simply state that juries decide questions of fact but not law, only are used in certain more serious criminal trials, and jury members are picked at random from **all adults on the electoral role** (except for members of certain professions, such as solicitors or MPs).

Candidates must be aware of the fundamental constitutional significance of trial by jury, an institution dating back to the time of the Magna Carta: being tried in front of a body of one's peers is purported to be central to democracy as they are held to be fairer and more objective than a single judge as the jury is drawn from members of all strata of society, and thus better able to understand the lifestyle of the ordinary man (as opposed to the white, middle-aged, male and upper middle class views of most judges). Juries can also play a role in repudiating repugnant, undemocratic laws. Not having to give reasons, the jury may refuse to convict if they believe the law was enacted to be overly harsh.

Candidates should also be aware that jury trials are expensive and inefficient. A balancing between these two competing factors is necessary, and being able to provide sensible reasons for their preference is all that is needed.

However, **strong candidates** should question whether unelected juries ought to have a de facto power to ignore the legislation of the elected parliament if they think the law is repugnant. They should also consider whether or not jury decisions are even reliable.

Q13: Is the British monarchy antiquated and undemocratic? What reasons are there for either keeping or abolishing this institution?

This question is general and superficially familiar to any British applicant. However, it is one which hints at the complex, **uncodified nature of the British constitution**.

Candidates should know that a large range of powers are vested in the Monarch nominally. However, the Monarch does not exercise these powers independently as a matter of convention: there is no legal requirement that the Monarch must take the advice of the Prime Minister in, for example, giving Royal Ascent to any Act duty passed by the elected Parliament. However, it would be unthinkable that she would refuse such advice, and, if she were to exercise such powers arbitrarily, it is likely that legal sanctions would be enacted to severely curtail the Monarch's power or to abolish the Monarchy altogether. There must be awareness that what is right and wrong in law is not what is right or wrong generally, and that the law is not the sole control of behaviour in society.

It would not be wrong for candidates to discuss the advantages or disadvantages of constitutional monarchy vs. republicanism in general, but they should not waste time discussing something not strictly pertinent to the question asked.

Strong candidates must frame their answer with reference to the tension between the theoretical anachronisms and empirical modernity which exist in the British constitution. A balanced approach is crucial, or, minimally, one which at least acknowledges the popularity (and therefore quasi-democratic mandate) of the Monarchy, and the importance of the Monarch as **uniting numerous Commonwealth countries** (eg Australia, New Zealand, Canada and the Bahamas), and how the removal of the Monarch in the UK would force citizens of many other counties to change their constitutional arrangements, possibly against their will.

Q14: Should publications like Charlie Hebdo be free to circulate uncontrolled? What kinds of restrictions on the media are compatible with freedom of speech?

If candidates are unfamiliar with the Charlie Hebdo killings, they would be told that Charlie Hebdo is an 'irreverent' French magazine which published inflammatory cartoons of the Prophet Mohammed. Outraged by these 'blasphemous' cartoons, Muslim extremists stormed the Charlie Hebdo office and killed a number of cartoonists. Many reacted with horror and immediately highlighted the importance of the freedom of speech. However, a smaller number of voices, while decrying what had happened, also highlighted the importance of responsible journalism.

Obviously, this is connected to ideas about **Freedom of Speech**. More generally, this raises fundamental questions about the nature of rights, and how rights are balanced against one another, and how the rights of the individual needs to be balanced against the rights of the community.

A sensitive, nuanced approach would take into account the overtones of Islamophobia which have tainted discourse on this episode. When the actor Benedict Cumberbatch used the word 'coloured' to refer to 'people of colour' in an interview, he was lampooned and severely criticised and essentially compelled to apologise. In contrast, many simply spoken about 'the right to offend' and the 'terror of extremism' with reference to this case.

A candidate who is able to think laterally may talk about how, in the UK, one's personal reputation is strongly protected by the **UK's vigorous defamation laws**. In contrast, offending or defaming an entire religion does not have such protection. Some consideration should be made of the role and position of religion in a secular, liberal society.

Q15: In the UK, the age of minimum criminal responsibility is 10 but the age of sexual consent is 16. A 15 year old boy caught kissing a 14 year old girl on the mouth could thus be convicted of various sexual offences. Is this satisfactory?

This question mixes together two anomalies in British criminal law. England has one of the youngest minimum ages of criminal responsibility in the Western world (it is 12 in Canada, Scotland, France, Germany and Ireland), and the UN has recommended that all countries raise the age of minimum criminal responsibility to 12. Further, England has one of the highest minimum ages of consent for sex: it is typically 12 to 14 in Western Europe (but 18 in most of the US).

A **good candidate** must talk about whether or not the low age of criminal responsibility and high minimum age of sexual consent are justified. However, a strong candidate must interact with the question and be aware of the 'double whammy' effect these laws have.

One tension that must be identified is that the **law must be reasonable and realistic**. If the law were to criminalise activities which one is unlikely to be arrested for (which is inherent to the clandestine nature of underage mutually-consensual sex), it may bring the law into disrepute.

Candidates must have a balanced view, however, and acknowledge how a high minimum age for sexual consent can protect the vulnerable and how a low minimum age of criminal responsibility is politically popular separately, but the interaction between the two can be problematic. It may be helpful to talk about how law is influenced by culture and the 'traditional' British attitude towards law and order and openness about sex.

Ultimately, a successful candidate must interact with the question and come to a sensible, thoroughly-considered opinion. A range of conclusions are acceptable, namely that the law should **protect the young from harmful overly-early sexualisation** and because a 10 year old facing a charge will not go to an adult jail (the emphasis being on rehabilitation), or that the minimum age of criminal responsibility should be raised for the sake of compliance with international norms and the rights of the child, acknowledging their psychological immaturity and the sheer iniquity of charging children in an adult court, and that the age of sexual consent should be lowered so that the law should keep up with current societal norms, or some other combination of reform and consistency.

Q16: What are the fundamental differences between US and British Law? What are the implications of this?

It would be unfair to expect any technical knowledge from the candidate, so this need only be answered in general terms.

Primarily, we are concerned with the fact that the US has a **codified constitution**, and that there is therefore a clear separation of powers and the legislature, unlike in the UK, is not 'sovereign'. This means judges have the power to overturn unconstitutional legislation, and that in the US, the supreme source of authority is the constitution, not the will of Congress.

Another pertinent point is that the UK is a constitutional monarchy but the US has a President. Though the **monarch nominally has vast discretionary** powers but these are never exercised by the monarch per se. In contrast, the elected President can and does use his considerable powers. This can be linked to the earlier point about the UK's uncodified constitution and that constitutional conventions play an important role in the UK.

A further point that can be mentioned is that the US is a federal system with each state having equal and defined powers, whereas the UK uses a devolution system where full power nominally remains with Westminister, not, say, the Scottish Parliament.

All these points must be linked to basic ideas about the rule of law, legal certainty, the separation of powers and good governance. How exactly the implications of each of these differ is not essential. Rather, a strong candidate should demonstrate evidence of further reasoning, consider a number of perspectives, and show depth and clarity of thought. It would be helpful if they comment on whether or not the US or UK model is better, and whether or not the US model ought to be applied to countries with very different histories.

Q17: In France, if a person sees somebody drowning, they have a legal obligation to help them. Should this be the case in the UK?

This is about '**Good Samaritan Laws**'. The duty to rescue, however, is necessarily a limited one in practice. Candidates should consider this when analysing the actual legal effect of such laws.

Ideas about liberty and an understanding that it is fundamentally more restrictive to force someone to do something as opposed to prevent them from doing certain things (the basic premise of most law) are fundamental to this question.

It must be acknowledged that such laws are **morally attractive** to e.g., prevent repugnant events such as healthy adults ignoring a two year old drowning in a paddling pool.

In balancing the two, the role of the law in society and the influence of morality on law must be considered. The practical limits of such a law must be analysed too: it would be unreasonable to expect e.g. a man who cannot swim to try to save a drowning person. However, as the rescuers ability to rescue decreases and the danger involved in rescuing increases, the line to draw becomes blurred and a sensible legislature would generally give the benefit of the doubt to the rescuer, the one whose liberty is being restricted.

Ultimately, a nuanced, thoughtful response which weighs the two competing considerations is necessary. To be successful, links must be made to real-world implications, rather than just theoretical, philosophical considerations.

Q18: Is it fair to impose a height restriction on those wanting to become fire fighters?

This is a general question posed within a specific scenario. Ideas about **nondiscrimination and EU law** are relevant. However, it must be highlighted that functional job requirements do not constitute discrimination. Moving on from this, an intelligent candidate ought to question whether or not such a height requirement is a genuine job requirement or not as technology may be used to overcome this. Strong candidates may be aware that public bodies are required to act 'reasonably' (which they must define).

Though their entire response need not be legally-related, this question really tests a legal style of reasoning. This means that they must be able to weigh up and consider a number of factors and be aware of the context of the supposed 'discrimination'.

Q19: Your neighbor fixed your collapsing roof while you were away on holiday. Should you pay him for this?

This question links to ideas about contract: a good contract is one which predicates upon mutual consent. One cannot make a contract unilaterally -- is this assumption valid? Is it necessary? However, though some traction may be given to such a line of query, it should be accepted that the basic premise of contracts is one of agreement between free agents who should be at liberty to make decisions and negotiate according to their individual requirements.

With regards to this question, there is a **minor assumption** that must be challenged: did you ask your neighbour to perform this service and was any payment expected by either party when the agreement was made if this was the case?

However, given the fact that this question has arisen, it is likely that there was no agreement, or, at most, a casual request for a favour which may have been understood. In untangling these two possibilities, it must be acknowledged this is not a business context, and that the intention to create legal relations is improbable given that such arrangements are made informally and between (presumably) amicable neighbours who may even regard one another as friends.

Ultimately though, one may feel it appropriate to make some sort of contribution towards the cost of painting the fence, it must be acknowledged that this is not a business relationship. It would not be fair for the neighbour to do something unilaterally and expect payment had you not expressed a wish for him specifically to paint your fence. Even if I had simply wanted someone to paint the fence and casually mentioned this to my neighbour, it would be a pleasant surprise if my neighbour did this for free. It would not be appropriate, however, for my neighbour to demand payment unless previously stipulated or else it would be unfair to the householder who may have been able to get a cheaper price or more skilled painter if that was what he preferred.

The best answers should make some reference to the demands of **actual commercial transactions** and draw out appropriate principles that are necessary for the proper functioning of a capitalist society.

Q20: Why is the rule of law important?

This is a general question which invites the candidate to talk about a range of issues. A sound definition is required for the question to be answered successfully.

Strong candidates should be aware of the different conceptions of the rule of law. It goes beyond 'the law of rules' (that laws must be enacted by the appropriate authority) but is about a culture of fairness and fair-mindedness. The debate centres on to what extent values like human rights or democratic values can be 'read in' to legislation.

This should be linked to other constitutional values like the **separation of powers and parliamentary sovereignty** and how these sometimes competing demands need to be balanced against each other, and must be considered with reference to the values of British liberal democracy.

Strong candidates would have a wealth of examples e.g. the Belmarsh case.

Language Interviews

If you are applying for the French, German, Spanish or Italian version of the course and are invited to Oxford for an interview, you should expect to be given a short oral language test as part of the interview process. Such a test is important and you must show the necessary linguistic competence. However, it is important to emphasise that the decision as to whether to offer a place on the four year course is made first and foremost by reference to your potential as a law student, not by your performance in the oral language test.

The language test will be quite relaxed, normally with just yourself and a native speaker alone in a room. The **interview will likely be recorded**. You do not necessarily need to have a great deal of knowledge of the foreign legal system but you should be able to articulate what it is specifically that interests you about that legal system and why you want to spend an extra year of your degree studying it. Real passion for the language, culture, and country will get you a long way too, of course!

If you are applying for the four year Law with European Law course (to spend the year abroad in the Netherlands) you will not have this additional language interview, as the course in the Netherlands is taught entirely in English.

Q21: What is the difference between Course I and Course II (Law with Legal Studies in Europe) at Oxford?

Course II incorporates all of the elements of course I – you will study all of the same topics in years 1, 2 and will have the same choice of options open to you when you return form your year abroad in your 4th year. The difference between the two courses lies in the additional element of the study of the foreign legal system.

In your **first year**, you will take weekly language classes (French, Italian, Spanish, German or conversational Dutch). These classes will be around 2 hours per week. They are not obligatory but act as a really good way of allowing you to get to know the other students you will be going abroad within your 3rd year and keep up your language skills.

In your **second year**, you will take weekly introductory classes to your foreign legal system in the language of that legal system. These will be around 2 hours per week and there will rarely be additional work set. These are obligatory and provide a good basis on which you will build when you begin your studies on your year abroad.

In your **third year** you will study abroad at one of the selected universities. You will have exams in your 3rd year but these marks will not count towards your final degree grade, instead you must simply pass this year. You will likely be taking topics which first year law students in that jurisdiction take, but your work load will likely be much lighter than the average law student. This year is an Erasmus year and you will be supported by grants from the Erasmus program, furthermore, there are several Oxford-based grants which are available for students on Course II during their year abroad. You will be given the opportunity to completely immerse yourself in the local culture and custom, perfect your language, and get a real insight into how the law works in that country. You will also have much more spare time than you will have been used to in Oxford given the significantly lighter workload. This means you'll have more time for travel and recreation. This is a fantastic year.

In your **fourth year** you will be back in Oxford and your course of study will be exactly the same as that of someone on course I. You will not be examined on the foreign legal system in your finals.

Law Interview Questions

618. What do you understand by the rule of law?
619. Why is the rule of law important?
620. Is it fair to impose a height restriction on those wanting to become fire fighters?
621. If your neighbor fixed your collapsing roof while you were away on holiday, should you pay him for this?
622. What does it mean to 'take' another's car?
623. If the penalty for parking on a double yellow were death, and therefore nobody did it, would that be a just and effective law?
624. If we lived in a world of angels would there be any need to have the law?
625. Does a girl scout have a political agenda?
626. Why did you choose to study law?
627. Is someone guilty if they did not set out to commit a crime up they ended up doing so?
628. When does the state have the right to violate privacy?
629. Should the state have the right to violate our privacy?
630. Should the media be more regulated by the state?
631. Where does honesty fit into law?
632. Should the law exist to protect us from ourselves?
633. If a law limits or restricts our freedom to do something, is that an unjust law with regards to autonomy?
634. Should the law restrict our freedom of speech?
635. If a baby in shopping centre was strapped with a bomb, would you shoot the baby to save x number of people?
636. Should people have the right to die?
637. Should fat people have to pay extra on planes if they need to take two seats

638. Should airlines be allowed to charge people for using the toilet on a plane?

639. Would it be a good idea for there to be a minimum IQ for jurors in a trial?

640. What would it be like to live in a country with no laws?

641. In France, if a person sees somebody drowning, they have a legal obligation to help them. Should this be the case in the UK?

642. Should the law be black and white, or should it be flexible enough to look at each case on an individual basis?

643. Should the law be based on morality?

644. The Supreme Court has taken over the judicial functions of the House of Lords. What impact do you think this will have?

645. Should those who make the laws (i.e. politicians) and those who enforce the laws (i.e. judges) be kept separate?

646. Would it be wrong for judges to be elected?

647. What stops countries from invading each other on a daily basis?

648. A cyclist is injured following a road traffic accident in the day. He was cycling in a car lane rather than the cycle lane. Who is liable- the cyclist or the motorist? How about if the accident occurred at night and the cyclist had no lights?

649. What is the difference between the House of Lord and House of Commons? Who has more power?

650. Why are some professions exempt from Jury-duty?

651. If you were the prime minister, what laws would you change?

652. A manufacturing defect stops a parachute from deploying in a charity skydive leading to two people dying. Is this man-slaughter or murder?

653. A man is sentenced to seven years in prison after falsely being convicted of murder. It later transpires that the 'victim' is still alive. Can the 'convict' be sentenced again if he kills the 'victim' after he is released from prison?

654. Lots of legislation includes phrases like "beyond reasonable doubt"- what does this actually mean?

655. What are the legal implications of gay marriage?

656. To what extent should our data be available to the government? What about the data of foreign citizens?

657. What are the fundamental differences between US and British Law? What are the implications of this?
658. You've got a client who refuses to go to court despite being summoned for multiple charges. What advice would you give him?
659. A Field Marshall orders a soldier to kill his squad mate. Would this be murder?
660. A doctor is asked by a patient's family member to kill the patient as they are in a lot of pain. Would this be murder?
661. Which law is broken most frequently?
662. What is the point of having a judge when decisions are made by the jury?
663. It's raining and you forgot your umbrella, so you shelter in an unlocked car. Are you guilty of the offence of allowing yourself to be carried in a conveyance without the owner's consent?
664. I'm having trouble with the meaning of three words: Lie, Deceive, Mislead. They seem to mean something a bit similar, but not exactly the same. Help me to sort them out from each other.
665. What is the difference between manslaughter and murder? What is its significance?
666. Should we make stalking illegal?
667. What's the difference between a civil and criminal case?
668. What are the pros & cons about juries?
669. How do you know what you don't know?
670. What is the difference between a barrister and a solicitor?
671. What is a Queen's Counsel? How does one become it?
672. A parent slaps their child because they behaved badly. Is that abuse? What about if they caused a bruise?
673. Why is there no United States of Europe but there is a USA?
674. What were the consequences of 9/11 on western law?
675. Who has the power to write and change laws?
676. If you could change 3 laws which ones would they be?
677. To what extent did the NSA revelations impact on the British public?
678. What is the hierarchy of courts in the UK?
679. What law is broken every day by most people?
680. Are school uniforms a contravention of human rights?

681. A man holds a gun up to your head and says "shoot your father or I'll kil you both". You then shoot. Are you guilty of murder?

682. What about if he had said "shoot your father or I'll kill you".

683. Finally, what about it he had said "shoot your father or I'll kill him".

684. Are babies born with a moral code or is it learned?

685. Do we have an obligation to obey the law?

686. Why is Roman law relevant to our modern study of law?

687. What law is broken most frequently?

688. What's the point of a judge when laws are made by the jury?

689. What laws could we introduce to curb the obesity epidemic?

690. Why do we bother with environmental protection?

691. What is a country?

692. Define a miracle.

693. A new law is passed that makes parking on double yellow lines punishable by death. Thus, no one does it anymore. Is this a fair and effective law?

MODERN LANGUAGES

At the start of a subject interview for Modern Languages, an applicant may be asked to discuss a short text in the target language which will have been presented to them shortly before the interview.

During the preparation time, you will have been expected to read through the text thoroughly, and to **ready yourself for a short discussion** of its main ideas and features.

When reading through the text and preparing for discussion:

➢ If you don't understand every word in the passage you've been given then don't panic. It is probably supposed to be difficult, and applicants are not expected to have already achieved fluency in the language they wish to study.

➢ Apply the knowledge you have acquired at A-Level and from wider reading to unfamiliar scenarios. You may not recognise the text you have been asked to read, but that is probably deliberate.

➢ Think about the style of the text. You may not be told its source, so you will have to engage critically to decide what sort of text it might be. Does the style reflect that or an article or an extract from a novel? Does the type of language tell you anything about what time period the text might be from?

➢ Pick out parts of the text that you find interesting. The interviewers will be keen to see evidence of your personal response to the text. Is there an idiomatic phrase which you particularly like? Does a certain line remind you of another text you have already read? What effect does the passage and its use of language have on you as a reader?

➢ The interviewer will want to see that you've tried to read and comprehend the text as best you can, and also to have engaged critically with it.

> If there is a word or concept you don't understand, talk these harder aspects of the text through carefully and the interviewer will help you reach an answer. Be prepared to accept some help and assistance from the interviewer - that is no bad thing.

> Remember, making mistakes is normal. If you have misinterpreted a word or an idea, the important point is that you address the mistake head on and attempt to revise the statement, with the assistance of the tutors where necessary.

> Following a short discussion of the text, subsequent questions will reflect the various different elements of the Modern Languages course.

This interview will require you to demonstrate passion and a genuine desire to study your chosen subject, so be prepared to voice your personal interests, beyond those mentioned on your personal statement. Material mentioned on your personal statement can be used as a starting point for the conversation.

The tutors know what topics you have studied at A-Level within your chosen subjects. *They will **not** ask you for detailed knowledge about areas of your subject that you are unfamiliar with.* Nobody knows every aspect of their subject.

An applicant will most likely be asked about their reading/engagement with cultural material in their chosen language areas. It is worth emphasising that the Modern Languages courses at Oxbridge privilege the study of literature and that applicants will be expected to have pursued their personal interests beyond the remit of their A Level/IB/Pre U syllabus, even if they have not had the opportunity yet to study literature at school.

Learning a New Language

At both Oxford and Cambridge, there is the option to learn a new language *ab initio*. If one of the languages you have applied for is one which you have not previously studied, then you will be expected to demonstrate your curiosity and enthusiasm for learning it. You will not be expected to have developed knowledge of the language, but **you will be expected to have made a decent attempt at learning some of the basics**, and engaging with the culture of its speakers.

What Questions Might be Asked?

Most of the questions asked in the interview will be broad, allowing the candidate to use them as a springboard for discussing their personal interests.

Smaller sub-questions may be used by the interviewer to prompt and guide the candidate into an active discussion.

The main question may seem difficult, impossible or random at first, but take a breath and start discussing with your interviewer different ideas you have for breaking down the question into manageable pieces. Don't panic. **The questions are designed to be difficult** to give you the chance to show your full intellectual potential. They will help guide you to the right idea, if you provide ideas for them to guide. This is your chance to show your creativity, analytical skills, intellectual flexibility, problem-solving skills and your go-getter attitude. Don't waste it on nervousness or a fear of messing up or looking stupid.

As well as specific questions about a book, the course, or a topical issue in the language-speaking country, applicants may be asked questions of a more philosophical nature. These questions will not have one specific answer, rather they will serve as an opportunity for the applicant to consider an idea.

The interviewers will be looking for inquisitive minds that can engage creatively with new problems. Don't be afraid to present your trains of thought out loud- the interviewer will be just as interested in seeing *how* you tackle the question as to the response you give. Often the interview is most concerned with **how** you think and how you tackle difficult and challenging problems.

Worked Questions

Below are a few examples of how to start breaking down an interview question, complete with model answers.

Q1: Can we hear silence?

With a more abstract question such as this, it is best to try and talk through your thought process, engaging with the question and applying logic as best as you can to work through your ideas. If you are thrown by a question, start by linking it back to your subject. Think about the question in relation to the study of languages.

It is good idea to start by thinking about the subject of the question. A solid piece of advice for any humanities student: start by questioning the question:

What is silence? How do we define silence? How do we experience silence? What is the opposite of silence? Is silence a sound? Is silence a state independent of a listener? Does silence depend on an ear?

Asking these types of things out loud will demonstrate your active engagement with the original question.

Q2: What is language?

With broad questions such as these, it can be useful to **draw upon specific examples** to back up your argument. Try to analyse the role of language in day to day speech, and how that compares, for example, to the *language* as seen in a poem/text you have recently read. What are the common defining features of language? What are the differences seen in it usage according to context?

Think about what constitutes a language, the uses and limitations of language and the role and nature of communication structures.

Follow up questions may include: "Do you need more than one speaker for a language to exist?" And "Is a language only a language if it is spoken?"

Q3: What can we learn from a nation's literature?

This question provides an opportunity to demonstrate a real enthusiasm for critically engaging with literature - this is important as literature features heavily on the Oxbridge Modern Languages Courses.

With a question as broad as this, a strong response would **use a framework** in order to engage more incisively with the key issues at stake (the role of literature, the place of literature in the society, the relationship of literature to a given society). For example:

Nation and narration are inextricably linked. Literature creates a narrative for a society and its people. It can provide an aperture into new worlds: their cultural specificities, mindsets and histories.

From my initial engagements with literature from Latin America -namely readings of poems by Neruda- I have been struck by the ability of the writer to cast an eye onto the parallel worlds of his nation: in his verse, we find commentary on Chilean politics, embedded within a lyric which references the heritage of past civilisations.

I have read sections from the first and final parts of *Alturas de Machu Pichu* (1945). Here, in entering into a dialogue with his nation's ancestry, Neruda both celebrates the achievement of Machu Picchu, and condemns the exploitative slavery that made it possible. Furthermore, In *Canto XII of his Canto General,* -considered one of the greatest political poems of the last century- Neruda calls upon the dead to be born again and to speak through him. In doing so, he references the power of literature to connect us not only to the present, but to a nation's past.

Q4: What is the difference between language and linguistics?

This question encourages a **technical response**, demonstrating the candidate's understanding of the broad theoretical terminology that underpins their subject.

A well structured answer may begin by defining language and linguistics. The candidate will then draw the two definitions into dialogue in order to address the original question of 'difference'. The best responses may also reference eminent theorists of language.

Language is a system of signs which serves to enable the communication between beings. According to Noam Chomsky, language is a 'set of sentence, each finite in length, and constructed out of a finite set of elements.' And Aronoff states that 'it is impossible to separate language from literature, or politics, or most of our everyday human interactions. (2007)

Linguistics is the scientific study of language. The difference is that as a discipline of study, it applies itself to language. It is to explain language; it references and analyses the working mechanisms of these systems of signs. According to Aitchison, linguistics 'has a twofold aim: to uncover general principles underlying human language, and to provide reliable descriptions of individual languages' (1992)

Q5: Will software like "Google Translate" ever be able to replace human translators?

This question will allow a good candidate the opportunity to engage critically with pertinent questions in the current climate of language learning. It encourages the candidate to also consider its underlying question- what is the need for leaning languages today?

Thanks to the internet, we live in an increasingly interconnected world. Technology has been said to 'shrink' the world, bringing us closer together through instant means of communication. What's more, technology has been employed for the purposes of **transcending linguistic barriers** to communication, through innovations in computerised translation.

The availability of devices such as Google translate and other translations apps force us to consider whether machines will ever be able to fully replace human translators. However, because languages are complex and nuanced, **words often defined and understood according to a given context**, it seems unlikely that a machine alone could ever replicate the job of the human translator.

Through an article I read on Foreign Tongues, The Market Research Translation Agency, I was introduced to a program called Unbabel, which is a combination of technology and crowd-sourced human translation.

Unbabel first uses computers to translate a customer's inquiry, and then splits it into micro-tasks for its human translators to refine and check for errors. Unbabel then puts the text together and sends it back. Customers can send and receive their text through email, online, or through Unbabel's API.

So, when it comes to documents demanding accurate translation to the level of a native speaker, it seems unlikely that software as rudimentary as Google translate will ever be able to replace the human translator. Another way to engage with this question would be to implicate literature and the poetic voice.

Our use of language in accordance with aesthetic parameters (forms, rhyme, allegory, metaphor, simile, idiom) render literary language resistant to the face-value translations of the machine.

Q6: How are Latin American Spanish and European different?

This question encourages both a **historical contextualisation** and **technical understanding** of the Spanish language.

A good candidate will be able to demonstrate their understanding of this linguistic colonial legacy and its relation to the development of Latin American Spanish. They will also be able to cite some specific examples of difference between Latin American and European Spanish:

When Spanish colonisers travelled the world, they brought with them a language that was in the process of changing back at home. A linguist called Marckwardt came up with the term "colonial lag" to describe a situation where the language spoken in colonies does not keep up with innovations in the language in its country of origin. An example in English would be the use of fall in the USA and autumn in Britain; when British colonisers went to America, fall was more common than the Latin version in British English. The older, Germanic word fall later became obsolete in Britain but has remained in common use in the USA. This process happens with vocabulary but also with grammar. Later on, immigrant groups from different parts of Europe brought linguistic traditions with them to Latin America. In turn, these groups met different local linguistic traditions, creating variations in local dialects.

One of the clearest examples of that process is the **use of 'vos'**, primarily in Argentina, Paraguay and Uruguay. Originally a second-person plural, vos came to be used as a more polite second-person singular pronoun to be used among one's familiar friends. It was commonly used in Spanish when the language reached the southern cone of the Americas. It fell out of use in Spain but stayed in Rioplatense Spanish. Nowadays, just like 150 years ago, at a bustling Buenos Aires cafe, you are much more likely to be asked "de donde sos?" than "de donde eres?"

Then there is the question of pronunciation: in many parts of Central America, 's' isn't always pronounced and in Argentina, the 'double-l' that is usually pronounced like the 'y' in yellow is pronounced like the 's' in measure.

Q7: What was the most recent film you saw?

General questions such as these are often posed towards the start of modern languages interviews to help make the candidate feel at ease. They provide an opportunity to demonstrate your interest in your subject beyond the school syllabus.

It goes without saying that the question refers to a **foreign language film**, most likely one in the target language being tested in the interview.

A good answer to this sort of question (which could just as easily replace film with book, play, exhibition) will quickly progress from a direct response: "I watched *La Haine*, a French film directed by Mathieu Kassovitz" to some form of more interrogative analysis/expression of personal response to the film: "What I found particularly interesting about this film was its setting within such a brief timeframe- the film relays to its audience the 19 hours in the aftermath of a riot in the Parisian suburbs.

The pace at which we observe the aimless daily routine of the three young protagonists draws us into line with their perspective on events, as they struggle to entertain themselves, and frequently find themselves under police scrutiny. When Saïd and Hubert are racially humiliated and physically abused, resulting in their missing the last train home, having to spend a night on the streets, the cinematic frame, as employed by Kassovitz, serves with political agency to remind us of societal 'framing' and outcasting of these individuals. As such, this film has fed into my engagement with my A Level syllabus and our considerations of racism and integration in France, with respect to the riots in 2005 in Clichy-sous-Bois.

Q8: Tell me about what you have been doing in your A Level course.

This is another example of a question that may be used to put you at ease. Good responses to these questions will not simply list the various tasks and materials engaged with on the course; rather, they might draw upon one or possibly two areas which have been of particular interest, and talk about these in more detail.

This term we have studied a piece of literature for the first time. We are looking at Sartre's *Huis Clos*. I have particularly enjoyed engaging with the fundamentals of existentialist philosophy through the medium of theatre.

In fact, during the half term break, I went to see a production of the play in London in order to help conceive of the text more fully as a dramatic piece. I was interested to see in the performance the use of space and shape formation between the three characters to demonstrate the relational power-shifts within the trio.

I was also intrigued by the Valet, a character 'without-eyelids'. As the only character to move in and out of the closed room, entering with each of the characters, I thought we might read his unbreakable stare as a reflection of the unbreakable gaze within, of Estelle offering herself as mirror, and of the definition of self in relation to the other.

The interviewer may then pose further questions about the play, the eyelids, existentialism etc.

Q9: How has travel influenced your relationship with language?

Questions about travel are frequently asked in modern languages interviews- which is not to say that extensive travel is by any means expected of a candidate. Evidently, those who have partaken in excursions, school trips, exchanges or gap year travels will be able to reference these experiences. However, an absence of these opportunities will not put a candidate at a disadvantage.

A question such as this, above all, seeks to engage with the motivations for learning another language. When drawing from travel experience -or thinking ahead to future travel aspirations- what the candidate should consider is:

- What does it *mean* to communicate - in its broadest sense
- What does it mean to communicate with speakers of a different language
- How much of a nation's culture manifests itself in language
- Does does language provide an access point to that culture? How?

Q10: What is language?

Here, the greatest challenge lies in the **broadness of the question**. This is a subject which has been central to philosophical interrogation.

The important thing to keep in mind here is that sometimes the applicant's first response serves only as a discussion starter. There is no need to include everything you would want to talk about, the interviewers only want to hear a few points they can start from. They will then drive the discussion in the direction they want to.

It is perfectly reasonable for the application to ask for a minute to consider the question and organise their thoughts.

Candidates should try to move beyond the **'system of communication'** answer, perhaps by showing their awareness of theoretical problematisations of language:

- Estimates of the number of languages in the world: 5,000-7,000
- What constitutes a language? They can be spoken, signed, encoded.

Depending on their interests, the candidate may wish to reference the philosophy of languages, drawing upon the works of key thinkers of the 20th century: Wittgenstein, who argued that philosophy itself is really the study of language; or with regards linguistics, they could reference Saussure's distinction between sign and symbol, or the work of Chomsky.

Q11: Give me three reasons why reading is dangerous.

Antagonistic questions such as this are often unexpected, and as such, unprepared for. This is part of the exercise- to see how candidates respond and process a completely new stimulus. The interviewer will primarily be interested in the thought processes behind your response. With a question such as this, a stimulating response may manifest as a working through the various possible ways of interpreting the question:

Of course, we could on one level, consider this question in terms of pure practicality: we don't know how badly it can affect our **eyesight**...although I'm quite certain that's more to do with **Vitamin D and sunlight exposure**... so perhaps reading is at its most dangerous when done inside. Then there is the **environment**, and **increasing paper shortages**.

But its not just the act of reading, its also a question of the material being read. Propaganda is certainly dangerous. The disseminated written word, when imbued with malice or political agency, can become a potent form of contagion.

Q12: What was it about this book (mentioned in Personal Statement) that particularly caught your attention?

Questions framed in this manner are designed to elicit personal responses to cultural material. The interviewer will be interested to hear specifically about your reaction to the text in question. Giving opinions and backing them up with reference to parts of the text will be expected. The level of detail into which a candidate is able to go will demonstrate their level of preparation.

Cien Anos de Soledad was unlike any other book I have ever read. Through it, I have been introduced to magical realism and its distinctive form of narrative. To me, it felt a bit like lucid dreaming.

Despite having difficulty initially with keeping a firm grasp on the plot as it unfolded, due to the number of similarly named characters, I learnt to stop resisting such confusions, rather to embrace them as a crucial and intentional part of Garcia Marquez's cyclical narrative.

For me, it was striking to encounter a textual narrative which allowed for forms of linear progression, and other treatments of time which perhaps can be seen to allegorise the metaphor of history as a circular phenomenon, as seen through the recurrent characteristics in the six generations of Jose Arcadios and Aurelianos.

On a further note, Macondo's turn in the final chapter from a city of mirrors to a city of mirages can perhaps be read as a reflexive comment on the nature of literature itself.

It is likely that the interviewer will interrupt the candidate during this response, **commenting in reaction to the points** raised: "in what way did this compare to lucid dreaming?" or "what do you consider to be the effects of this cyclical narrative?" or "what do you mean by the nature of literature, how so?

Further Question Areas

If the applicant has mentioned linguistics as an area of interest, questions to do with the nature of language itself may also be posed. It may be worth looking at recent controversies/new schools of emergent thought in this field.

It has also become common for interviewers to ask about the changing status of language in the modern world, and the position/role/importance of multilingualism in an age of increasing globalisation. Consider crucial turning points in this narrative- the internet as a space for global communication etc. Think about why you still value the importance of learning new languages. What does it mean to study languages today?

MML Interview Questions

694. Why do some languages have so many tenses yet others manage fine with very little grammar?

695. Do you think the number of languages in the world will change in the next century?

696. Why can we infer from someone's accent?

697. How would you simplify English?

698. What are the difficulties in translating books like the bible?

699. Compare and contrast Spanish and Portuguese.

700. What determines how 'easy' a language is to learn?

701. Why do we desire fluency so badly when we can communicate adequately even as a beginner?

702. How is the German mindset different to the Russian mindset?

703. What was the most recent film you saw?

704. What was it about this book (mentioned in Personal Statement) that particularly caught your attention?

705. What does language mean to you?

706. How has travel influenced your relationship with language?

707. What is a language?

708. Translation is reproduction. How would you respond?

709. Why learn a language in a globalising world?

710. How would you describe the relationship between speech and writing, in relation to language?

711. In your personal statement you describe music as a language. Would you care to expand?

712. What attracts you to French/Spanish/Italian culture?

713. What is it that interests you about Latin American culture in particular?

714. Does language define our identity?

715. What French poetry have you read?

716. Is poetry a different language to a novel or a short story?

717. In your A Level course you have looked at social tensions in France. Tell me about what you have learned?

718. Is literature a different language to speech?

719. What is your opinion on ambiguity?

720. What is your favourite word?

721. If you could make up a word, what would it be?

722. What is the difference between Chinese whispers and translation?

723. How would you describe a cucumber to an alien? How would you do it in Spanish?

724. How malleable are our thoughts?

725. Is there any point studying languages with the advent of modern electronic translators?

726. Britain declares war on Europe. What advice would you give to the ministry of defence if they asked you what level of French/German/Spanish each of their personnel should have?

727. Why causes a language to evolve? Can this be stopped? How?

728. What is an accent? How do they arise?

729. To what extent does a countries culture dictate a language's vocabulary?

730. How do babies learn a language?

731. What is the quickest way to learn a language?

732. How many languages could someone learn?

733. What difficulties arise if you study two languages at the same time?

734. How can you tell if a noun is masculine, feminine or neutral in German?

735. What difficulties do Europeans have with English? What about Asians?

736. How would you improve Google translate?

737. Who is your favourite author? What other works of theirs have you read?

738. Can a language ever truly die?

739. Does a language need to have letters? Can it be made just of numbers? Is grammar therefore necessary?

740. What makes a language 'modern'?

READING LISTS

The obvious way to prepare for any Oxbridge interview is to **read widely**. This is important so that you can mention books and interests in your personal statement. It is also important because it means that you will be able to draw upon a greater number and variety of ideas for your interview.

➤ **Make a record** of the book, who wrote it, when they wrote it and summarise the argument. This means that you have some details about your research in the days before the interview.

➤ Reading is a passive exercise. To make it genuinely meaningful, you should **engage with the text**. Summarise the argument. Ask yourself questions like how is the writer arguing? Is it a compelling viewpoint?

➤ **Quality over quantity**. This is not a race as to how many books you can read in a short period of time. It is instead a test of your ability to critically analyse and synthesise information from a text – something you'll be doing on a daily basis at university.

Biology & Medicine

➤ *Bad Pharma*: Ben Goldacre
➤ *Trust me I'm a Junior Doctor*: Max Pemberton
➤ *The Selfish Gene*: Richard Dawkins
➤ *Genome*: Matt Ridley
➤ *The Single Helix*: Steve Jones
➤ Nature via Nurture: Matt Ridley
➤ *Bully for Brontosaurus*: Stephen Jay Gould
➤ *The Extended Phenotype*: Richard Dawkins

Psychology

- *The Man who Mistook his Wife for a Hat: Oliver Sacks*
- How the mind works: Steven Pinke
- *Predicatbly Irrationl:* Dan Ariely
- *Thinking, Fast and Slow:* Daniel Kahneman

Chemistry

- *The Disappearing Spoon*: Sam Kean
- *Uncle Tungsten*: Oliver Sacks
- *A Short history of nearly everything*: Bill Bryson
- *Reactions- The private life of atoms*: Peter Atkins

Physics

- *A Brief History of Time:* Stephen Hawking
- *The Feynman Lectures on Physics:* Richard Feynman
- *Three Roads to Quantum Gravity:* Lee Smolin
- *Death by Black Hold:* Neil deGrasse Tyson

Engineering

- *How do wings work?* Holger Babinsky
- *Structures- or why things don't fall down*: JE Gordon
- *Remaking the World*: Henry Petroski
- *Sustainable Energy*: David MacKay
- *Success through Failure*: Henry Petroski

Material Sciences

- *Stuff Matters*: Mark Miodwnik
- *Bright Earth*: The invention of colour: Phillip Ball
- *Where stuff comes from*: H Molotch
- *Materials for Engineering*: JW Martin

Maths

- *The Man Who Knew Infinity*: Robert Kanigel
- *A Mathematician's Apology*: GH Hardy
- *Fermat's Last Theorem*: Simon Singh
- *Game, Set and Math:* Ian Stewart

Law

- Glanville Williams: *Learning the Law*
- Richard Susskind Tomorrow's Lawyers: *An Introduction to Your Future*
- Tom Bingham: *The Rule of Law*
- Anthony King: *The British Constitution*
- Nicolas J McBride: *Letters to a Law Student: A Guide to Studying Law at University*
- Helena Kennedy: *Just Law*

MML

French:
- Margaret Jubb and Annie Rouxeville, *French Grammar in Context*
- Glanville Price, *A Comprehensive French Grammar* (Blackwell)
- Roger Hawkins and Richard Towell, *French Grammar and Usage*

Spanish:
- *A Spanish Learning Grammar*, Pilar Muñoz & Mike Thacker (London: Arnold, latest edition)
- Grammar Practice: *Uso de la gramática española - nivel elemental, Francisca Castro* (Edelsa, Spain, latest edition).

German:
- *German Grammar in Context*
- S. Fagan, *Using German Vocabulary*, (2004)

Classics

Texts in Translation:
➢ *The Iliad*, Homer
➢ *The Odyssey*, Homer
➢ *The Aeneid*, Virgil

Secondary Works:
➢ The Oxford Classical Dictionary, Oxford University Press
➢ *Classics: A Very Short Introduction* (Beard/Henderson), Oxford University Press
➢ Any scholarly works that take your interest, especially if relevant to texts you have read. E.g. Those interested in Roman History should consider reading Andrew Wallace-Hadrill.

Geography

➢ Sassen. S: *The Global City: New York, London, Tokyo*
➢ Fanon. F: *The Wretched of the Earth*
➢ Brockington, Duffy and Igoe: *Nature unbound: conservation, capitalism and the future of protected areas*
➢ Gray, L.C. and Moseley, W.G.: *A geographical perspective on poverty-environment interactions. The Geographical Journal*

Earth Sciences

➢ Davidson, J et al: Exploring Earth: *Introduction to Physical Geology*
➢ MacDougall, JD,:*A Short History of Planet Earth: Mountains, Mammals, Fire and Ice (Wiley Popular Science)*
➢ Nield, T: Supercontinent: *Ten Billion Years in the Life of Our Planet*
➢ Zalasiewicz, J.A. & Williams, M.: *The Goldilocks planet: the four billion year story of Earth's climate*

History

➤ E.H. Carr: *What is History?*
➤ Richard J. Evans: *In Defence of History*
➤ Marc Bloch: *The Historians Craft*
➤ Josh Tosh: *The Pursuit of History*
➤ Geoffrey Elton: *The Practice of History*
➤ Marc Bloch: *The Historians Craft*
➤ Josh Tosh: *The Pursuit of History*
➤ Geoffry Elton: *The Practice of History*
➤ Richard J. Evans: *In defence of History*
➤ Andrew Marr: *A History of Modern Britain*

Economics:

➤ The Economist / The Financial Times
➤ Steven Levitt: *Freakonomics*
➤ Partha Dasgupta Economics: *A Very Short Introduction*
➤ Paul Krugman: *End this Depression Now!*
➤ Robert L Heilbroner: *The Worldly Philosophers*
➤ Dan Ariely: *Predictably Irrational*

PPE:

➤ J.S. Mill: *On Liberty*
➤ Jeremy Bentham: *Defence of Usury*
➤ Niall Ferguson: *The Ascent of Money*

English

Think about how your other subjects might illuminate your study of English. For instance, perhaps you study Psychology, and can use this framework to criticise Freud's theory of the Oedipus Complex in relation to Hamlet. You might study History and find this invaluable when analysing Shakespeare's history plays, informing your arguments about the importance of myths and legends, the theme of nationality, or tropes of traditional kingship, and so on. Even more interestingly, you might have studied Physics, Music, or Maths: did these otherwise distinct subjects enhance your study of English in a more oblique way?

There are infinite guides out there for English reading, but the main thing is to follow your interests like a cultural sniffer-dog. A few useful guidelines are given below for general reading around the subject.

There are many anthologies which can give you an excellent overview of chronological literary periods and 'traditions'. **Margaret Drabble's** *Oxford Companion to English Literature* will provide a wide-ranging scope, while **Andrew Sanders'** *Short Oxford History of English Literature* is very useful too. For poetry in particular, *The Norton Anthology of Poetry*, **ed. by Ferguson, Salter and Stallworthy** is good, while **Christopher Ricks's** *Oxford Book of English Verse* is a detailed spectrum of styles of poetry, with a fantastic introduction, which he expands upon in his *The Force of Poetry* or *Essays in Appreciation*. Pair this with oft-studied essayistic collections like **T.S.Eliot's** *Selected Prose of T.S. Eliot*, or **William Empson's** *Seven Types of Ambiguity*, which will make you think deeper about the art of studying poetry and the difficulties of being a good critic.

It is worth investing in a meaty critical anthology like **Bennett and Royle's** *An Introduction to Literature, Criticism, and Theory* which will give you a rough but valuable guide to a chronological overview of critical history, which you can dip in and out of easily for reference. **The** *Norton Anthology of Theory and Criticism*, is another valuable guide. However, use these as rough outlines, and broaden your thinking with **Terry Eagleton's** *Literary Theory*, which will provocatively debate many of these terms and ideas. A more readable guide is **James Wood's** *How Fiction Works*, which is a broad but detailed examination of the novel as a genre.

It can also be useful to have a dictionary like **Chris Baldick's** *The Oxford Dictionary of Literary Terms*, which will have bite-size snippets of information in the form of comprehensive definitions.

Pair this with **Raymond Williams' *Keywords***, which is in effect a radical literary dictionary designed to make you question and expand these straight-forward definitions. Brush up on your practical criticism and close reading skills with **John Lennard's *The Poetry Handbook: A Guide to Reading Poetry for Pleasure and Practical Criticism*** – a true classic, and very readable. Pair this with giving yourself exercises in close reading, setting yourself extracts and thinking about what you might discuss or point out.

If you read any classics, read **Homer's *Iliad*** and ***Odyssey*, Ovid's *Metamorphoses*** and **Virgil's *Aeneid*** in any reputable translation if you have the time, preferably in the Penguin or Oxford World Classics editions: these are foundational, and genuinely will prove incredibly useful in deciphering allusions. The same applies to the **Bible**, or at least a selection of the most pivotal sections: Genesis, Exodus, The Song of Songs, the gospels of Matthew, Mark, Luke, and John, Revelation, the Book of Job, the Song of Solomon, etc. If you find this theological approach interesting, go on to read **John Milton's *Paradise Lost***, which is surprisingly absorbing in its poetic dramatisation of Adam and Eve; Alastair Fowler has edited an excellent critical edition.

It may sound obvious, but read or watch as many of **Shakespeare's** plays and poems as you can; they really are foundational, and will stand you in good stead throughout your course; a guide like *Reading Shakespeare's Dramatic Language: A Guide* by **Hunter, Magnusson, and Adamson** will provide a readable introduction to the specifics of Shakespearean verse. Think more about the practical aspects of staging plays and theatrical history, from stage building to props, aspects which are often neglected at A-Level: **Tiffany Stern and Farah Karim-Cooper's *Shakespeare's Theatre and the Effects of Performance*** is fantastic, as is **Stern's *Making Shakespeare: From Stage to Page*** and **Andrew Gurr's *The Shakespearean Stage***. In general, Cambridge and Oxford/Blackwell Companions are always very good and provide strong leads for further reading, such as **Hodgdon and Worthen's *A Companion to Shakespeare and Performance***, but feel free to use modern dramatic criticism like **Peter Brook's *The Empty Space*** to deepen your ideas.

Archaeology

- Timothy Darvill. 2010. Prehistoric Britain. 2nd Edition. London: Routledge.
- Clive GAMBLE. 2000. Archaeology: The Basics. London: Routledge.
- Ian Hodder. 2012. Archaeological Theory Today. 2nd Edition. Cambridge: Polity.
- Barry Kemp. 2005. Ancient Egypt: Anatomy of a Civilization. 2nd Edition. London: Routledge.
- Colin Renfrew and Paul Bahn. 2012. Archaeology: Theory, Methods, and Practice. 6th Edition. London: Thames & Hudson.
- Chris Scarre. 1998. Exploring Prehistoric Europe. Oxford: Oxford University Press.
- Chris Scarre. 2009. The Human Past: World Prehistory and Development of Human Society. 2nd Edition. London: Thames & Hudson.

Biological Anthropology

- Robert Boyd and Joan Silk. 2012. *How Humans Evolved*. New York: Norton.
- Robert Foley & Roger Lewin. 2003. *The Principles of Human Evolution*. 2nd Edition. Oxford: Wiley-Blackwell.
- Peter Gluckman and Mark Hanson. 2004. *The Fetal Matrix*. Cambridge: Cambridge University Press.
- Matt Ridley. 2004. *Nature via Nurture*. New York: Harper Collins.
- Chris Stringer. 2012. *The Origin of our Species*. London: Penguin.
- Jared Diamond: *Guns, Germs and Steel*

Politics

- Benedict Anderson. 1983. Imagined Communities: Reflections on the origins and Spread of Nationalism. London: Macmillan.
- Headley Bull. 1977. The Anarchical Society. London: Macmillan.

- John Dunn. 2005. Setting the People Free: The Story of Democracy. London: Atlantic.
- Niccolo Machiaveilli. 2003 (1532). The Prince. London: Penguin.
- James Mayall. 2000. World Politics: Progress and its Limits. Cambridge: Polity.
- David Runciman. 2006. Politics of Good Intentions: History, Fear, and Hypocrisy in the New World Order. Princeton: Princeton University Press.
- James C Scott. 1998. Seeing Like a State: How Certain Schemes to Improve the Human Condition have Failed. New Haven: Yale University Press.
- Adam Watson. 1992. The Evolution of International Society. London: Routledge.

Social Anthropology

- Lila Abu-Lughod. 1986. Veiled Sentiments: Honor and Poetry in a Bedoin Society. Berkeley: University of California Press.
- Adam Ashforth. 2005. Madumo: A Man Bewitched. Chicago: University of Chicago Press.
- Rita Astuti, Jonathan Parry, and Charles Stafford. 2007. Questions of Anthropology. Berg: Oxford.
- Thomas Boellstorff. 2008. Coming of Age in Second Life. Princeton: Princeton University Press.
- John R. Bowen. 2007. Why the French Don't Like Headscarves: Islam, the State, and Public Space. Princeton: Princeton University Press.
- Michael Carrithers. 1993. Why Humans Have Cultures. Oxford: Oxford University Press.
- Sharon E. Hutchinson. 1996. Nuer Dilemmas: Coping with Money, War, and the State. Berkeley: University of California Press.
- Jean La Fontaine. Speak of the Devil: Tales of Satanic Abuse in Contemporary England. Cambridge: Cambridge University Press.
- Joel Robbins. 2004. Becoming Sinners: Christianity and Moral Torment in a Papua New Guinea Society. Berkeley: University of California Press.

➤ Michael Stewart.1997. The Time of the Gypsies. Colorado: Westville Press.
➤ Yunxiang Yan. 2009. The Individualization of Chinese Society. Berg: Oxford.

Sociology

➤ Nicholas Abercrombie. 2004. Sociology. Cambridge: Polity.
➤ Anthony Giddens. 2006. Sociology (5th edition). Cambridge: Polity.
➤ Anthony Giddens. 1973. Capitalism and Modern Social Theory. Cambridge: Cambridge University Press.
➤ J.A. Hughes, W.W. Sharrock, and P.J. Martin. 2003. Understanding Classical Sociology. London: Sage.
➤ K.J. Neubeck and D.S. Glasberg. 2005. Sociology: Diversity, Conflict, and Change. Boston: McGraw Hill.
➤ W. Outhwaite (ed). 2003. The Blackwell Dictionary of Modern Social Thought. Oxford: Blackwell.
➤ Richard Sennett. 2006. The New Culture of Capitalism. New Haven: Yale University Press.

HSPS

➤ Karl Marx: Communist Manifesto
➤ Hogg & Vaughn: *Social Psychology*
➤ Schaffer: *Introducing Child Psychology*
➤ Durkin Blackwell: *Introducing Child Psychology*
➤ Schaffer: *Making Decisions About Children*
➤ Manfred Steger Globalisation: *A Very Short Introduction*
➤ Jan Art Scholte Globalization: *A Critical Introduction*
➤ Colin Hay: *Why we Hate Politics*
➤ Andrew Gamble: *Politics and Fate*
➤ Bernard Crick Democracy: *A Very Short Introduction*
➤ Joy Hendry: *An Introduction to Social Anthropology*
➤ Chris Browne & Kirsten Ainley *Understanding International Relations*
➤ Nicholas Abercrombie: Sociology: *A Short Introduction*

FINAL ADVICE

Before Your Interview

➢ Make sure you understand your curriculum, your interview will most likely use material from your school courses as a starting point.

➢ Remind yourself of the selection criteria for your subject.

➢ Read around your subject in scientific articles and books, visit museums, watch documentaries, anything which broadens your knowledge of your favourite topics, while demonstrating your passion for your subject – they may ask you at interview which articles you've read recently to check you are engaged with the subject. Scientists should try New Scientist's online articles to start you off; TED talks are also a great way to be quickly briefed on cutting-edge research, and it's more likely you will remember the name of the researcher, etc.

➢ Practice common questions or sample questions – this is better done with a teacher or someone you are less familiar with or who is an experienced interviewer.

➢ Make up your own questions throughout your day: Why is that flower shaped like that? Why is that bird red-breasted? Why does my dog like to fetch sticks? What did I mean when I said that man wasn't 'normal', and are those the criteria everyone uses? How do I know I see the same colours as others?

➢ Re-read your personal statement and any course-work you are providing. Anticipate questions that may arise from these and prepare them in advance.

➢ Read and do anything you've said you've done in your application – they may ask you about it at interview!

➢ Check your interview specifications – which types of interview you will have for which subjects, how many there will be, where, when and with whom they will be so there are no surprises.

On the Day of Your Interview

➤ Get a good night's sleep before the big day.

➤ If you are travelling from far away, try to arrive the night before so that you're fresh in the morning. Getting up early in the morning and travelling far could tire you out and you might be less focussed whilst being interviewed. Many colleges will provide you accommodation if you're travelling from a certain distance away.

➤ Take a shower in the morning and dress to your comfort, though you don't want to give a sloppy first impression – most opt for smart/casual

➤ Get there early so you aren't late or stressed out before it even starts.

➤ Smile at everyone and be polite.

➤ Don't worry about other candidates; be nice of course, but you are there for you, and their impressions of how their interviews went have nothing to do with what the interviewers thought or how yours will go.

➤ It's OK to be nervous – they know you're nervous and understand, but try to move past it and be in the moment to get the most out of the experience.

➤ Don't be discouraged if it feels like one interview didn't go well — you may have shown the interviewers exactly what they wanted to see even if it wasn't what you wanted to see.

➤ Have a cuppa and relax, there's nothing you can do now but be yourself.

The Most Important Advice...

❖ Explain your thought processes as much as possible – it doesn't matter if you're wrong. *It really is the journey; not the destination that matters.*

❖ Interviewers aren't interested in *what you know*. Instead, they are more interested in *what you can do* with what you already know.

✗ **DON'T** be quiet – even if you can't answer a question, how you approach the question could show the interviewer what they want to see.

✗ **DON'T** rely on the interviewer to guide you every step of the way.

✗ **DON'T** ever, ever, ever give up.

✗ **DON'T** be arrogant or rigid –you are bound to get things wrong, just accept them and move on.

✗ **DON'T** expect to know all the answers; this is different than school, you aren't expected to know the answer to everything – you are using your knowledge as a foundation for original thoughts and applications under the guidance of your interviewer.

✗ **DON'T** think you will remember everything you did/wrote without revising.

✗ **DON'T** be afraid to point out flaws in your own ideas – scientists need to be self-critical, and the interviewer has already noticed your mistakes!

✗ **DON'T** be defensive, especially if the interviewer is hinting that your idea may be on the wrong path – the interviewer is the expert!

✗ **DON'T** get hung up on a question for too long.

✗ **DON'T** rehearse scripted answers to be regurgitated.

✗ **DON'T** answer the question you wanted them to ask.

✗ **DON'T** lie about things you have read/done (And if you already lied in your personal statement, then read/do them before interview!)

✓ **DO** speak freely about what you are thinking and ask for clarifications.

✓ **DO** take suggestions and listen for pointers from your interviewer.

✓ **DO** try your best to get to the answer.

✓ **DO** have confidence in yourself and the abilities that got you this far

✓ **DO** be prepared to discuss the ideas and problems in your work.

✓ **DO** make many suggestions and have many ideas.

✓ **DO** show intellectual flexibility by taking suggestions from the interviewer.

✓ **DO** take your time in answering to ensure your words come out right.

✓ **DO** research your interviewers so that you know their basic research interests. Then ensure you understand the basics of their work (no need to go into detail with this).

✓ **DO** prepare your answers to common questions.

✓ **DO** answer the question that the interviewer has asked – not the one you want them to!

✓ **DO** practice interviews with family or teachers – even easy questions may be harder to articulate out loud and on the spot to a stranger.

✓ **DO** think about strengths/experiences you may wish to highlight.

✓ **DO** visit www.uniadmissions.co.uk/example-interviews to see mock interviews in your subject. This will allow you to understand the differences between good and bad candidates.

Afterword

Remember that the route to a high score is your approach and practice. Don't fall into the trap that *"you can't prepare for oxbridge interviews"*– this could not be further from the truth. With targeted preparation and focussed reading, you can dramatically boost your chances of getting that dream offer.

Work hard, never give up, and do yourself justice.

Good luck!

This book is dedicated to my grandparents – thank you for your wisdom, kindness, and endless amounts of love.

Acknowledgements

I would like to express my gratitude to the many people who helped make this book possible. I would like to thank *Dr. Ranjna Garg* for suggesting that I take on this mammoth task and providing invaluable feedback. I am also grateful for the 30 Oxbridge tutors for their specialist input and advice. Last but by no means least; I am thankful to *David Salt* for his practical advice and willingness to discuss my ideas- regardless of whether it was 4 AM or PM.

About UniAdmissions

UniAdmissions is an educational consultancy that specialises in supporting **applications to Medical School and to Oxbridge.**

Every year, we work with hundreds of applicants and schools across the UK. From free resources to our *Ultimate Guide Books* and from intensive courses to bespoke individual tuition – with a team of **300 Expert Tutors** and a proven track record, it's easy to see why UniAdmissions is the **UK's number one admissions company**.

To find out more about our support like **Oxbridge courses** and **tuition**, check out www.uniadmissions.co.uk

THE ULTIMATE
PERSONAL
STATEMENT GUIDE

✓ All Major Subjects   ✓ Expert Advice
✓ Every Statement Analysed   ✓ 100 Successful Statements

**Rohan Agarwal
David Salt**

UniAdmissions

www.uniadmissions.co.uk/our-books

THE ULTIMATE TSA GUIDE

300

PRACTICE QUESTIONS

- ✓ Fully Worked Solutions
- ✓ Time Saving Techniques
- ✓ Annotated Essays
- ✓ Score Boosting Strategies

2017 ENTRY

Rohan Agarwal
Jonathan Madigan

UniAdmissions

www.uniadmissions.co.uk/tsa-book

THE ULTIMATE
BMAT GUIDE
600
PRACTICE QUESTIONS

- ✓ Fully Worked Solutions
- ✓ Time Saving Techniques
- ✓ 10 Annotated Essays
- ✓ Score Boosting Strategies

2017 Edition

Rohan Agarwal

UniAdmissions

www.uniadmissions.co.uk/bmat-book

TSA INTENSIVE COURSE

If you're looking to improve your TSA score in a short space of time, our **TSA intensive course** is perfect for you. It's a fully interactive seminar that guides you through sections 1 and 2 the TSA.

You are taught by our experienced TSA experts, who are Oxbridge graduates that excelled in the TSA. The aim is to teach you powerful time-saving techniques and strategies to help you succeed for test day.

- ➢ Full Day intensive Course
- ➢ Copy of our acclaimed book "The Ultimate TSA Guide"
- ➢ Full access to extensive TSA online resources including:
- ➢ 4 complete mock papers
- ➢ 300 practice questions
- ➢ Fully worked solutions for all TSA past papers since 2008
- ➢ Online on-demand lecture series
- ➢ Ongoing Tutor Support until Test date – never be alone again.

Timetable:
- ➢ **1030 - 1300:** Problem Solving
- ➢ **1300 - 1330:** Lunch
- ➢ **1330 - 1530:** Critical Thinking
- ➢ **1530 - 1700:** Writing Task
- ➢ **1700 - 1730:** Debrief
- ➢ **1730 - 1800:** Questions

The course is normally £115 but you can get **£ 10** off by using the code "*BKTEN*" at checkout.

www.uniadmissions.co.uk/tsa-courses

£10 VOUCHER: BKTEN

BMAT INTENSIVE COURSE

If you're looking to improve your BMAT score in a short space of time, our **BMAT intensive course** is perfect for you. It's a fully interactive seminar that guides you through sections 1, 2 and 3 of the BMAT.

You are taught by our experienced BMAT experts, who are Doctors or senior Oxbridge medical tutors who excelled in the BMAT. The aim is to teach you powerful time-saving techniques and strategies to help you succeed for test day.

- ➤ Full Day intensive Course
- ➤ Copy of our acclaimed book "The Ultimate BMAT Guide"
- ➤ Full access to extensive BMAT online resources including:
- ➤ 4 complete mock papers
- ➤ 600 practice questions
- ➤ Fully worked solutions for all BMAT past papers since 2003
- ➤ Online on-demand lecture series
- ➤ Ongoing Tutor Support until Test date – never be alone again.

Timetable:

- ➤ **1000 – 1030:** Registration
- ➤ **1030 – 1100:** Introduction
- ➤ **1100 – 1300:** Section 1
- ➤ **1300 – 1330:** Lunch
- ➤ **1330 – 1600:** Section 2
- ➤ **1600 – 1700:** Section 3
- ➤ **1700 – 1730:** Summary
- ➤ **1730 – 1800:** Questions

The course is normally £115 but you can get **£ 10** off by using the code *"BKTEN"* at checkout.

www.uniadmissions.co.uk/bmat-course

£10 VOUCHER:
BKTEN

OXBRIDGE INTERVIEW COURSE

If you've got an upcoming interview for Oxford or Cambridge school – this is the perfect course for you. You get individual attention throughout the day and are taught by specialist Oxbridge graduates on how to approach these tricky interviews.

- Full Day intensive Course
- Guaranteed Small Groups
- 4 Hours of Small group teaching
- 4 x 30 minute individual Mock Interviews +
- Full written feedback so you can see how to improve
- Ongoing Tutor Support until your interview – never be alone again

Timetable:

- **1000 - 1015:** Registration
- **1015 - 1030:** Talk: Key to interview Success
- **1030 - 1130:** Tutorial: Dealing with Unknown Material
- **1145 - 1245:** 2 x Individual Mock Interviews
- **1245 - 1330:** Lunch
- **1330 - 1430:** Subject Specific Tutorial
- **1445 - 1545:** 2 x Individual Mock Interviews
- **1600 - 1645:** Subject Specific Tutorial
- **1645 - 1730:** Debrief and Finish

The course is normally £295 but you can get **£ 35** off by using the code "*BRK35*" at checkout.

www.uniadmissions.co.uk/oxbridge-interview-course

£35 VOUCHER:
BRK35

NOTES

NOTES

CPSIA information can be obtained at www.ICGtesting.com
Printed in the USA
LVOW10s2027190416

484338LV00029B/524/P